God Bless Our Cubicles

God Bless Our Cubicles

Sustaining Spirituality in the Workplace

MEG GORZYCKI

RESOURCE *Publications* · Eugene, Oregon

GOD BLESS OUR CUBICLES
Sustaining Spirituality in the Workplace

Copyright © 2019 Meg Gorzycki. All rights reserved. Except for brief quotations in critical publications or reviews, no part of this book may be reproduced in any manner without prior written permission from the publisher. Write: Permissions, Wipf and Stock Publishers, 199 W. 8th Ave., Suite 3, Eugene, OR 97401.

Resource Publications
An Imprint of Wipf and Stock Publishers
199 W. 8th Ave., Suite 3
Eugene, OR 97401

www.wipfandstock.com

PAPERBACK ISBN: 978-1-5326-7563-8
HARDCOVER ISBN: 978-1-5326-7564-5
EBOOK ISBN: 978-1-5326-7565-2

Manufactured in the U.S.A.　　　　　　　　　　　　　　JANUARY 21, 2019

This book is dedicated to Judie, my mother, and Tom, my father. They taught me that although work could be exhausting and strenuous, it was a joy to see the fruits of responsibility, creativity, effort, and persistence. They also demonstrated that it is a blessing to donate labor to those with great needs and few resources. This book is also dedicated to my siblings: Terri, whose wit and intuition amazes and humbles me; Louise, whose integrity and faith shines a light for me; Martha, whose wisdom and sense of aesthetics bring me peace; Joe, whose heart and mind have led me to vital insights and good thoughts, and Tony whose resilience and creativity inspire me.

Contents

Preface | ix
Acknowledgements | xiii

1   Introduction | 1
2   God and Prosperity | 18
3   Dragging God into the Workplace | 36
4   Song of the Whistle Blowers | 46
5   Get Off Your Cross | 63
6   Spiritual Rubber on the Material Road | 71
7   Quit the Weasel | 84
8   Geezers and Goslings | 94
9   Leading for Loot | 106
10 All Hail the Grand Poobah | 123
11 Higher Education and Hire Education | 140
12 The Great Crossing | 153

Bibliography | 165

Preface

I HAVE A CONFESSION to make. During the composition of this text, I was needled by voices inside my head: "Who are you to talk about God and spirituality in the workplace? Nobody wants to get all sanctimonious about work—that doesn't put bread on the table! God belongs in church, not a cubicle!" I mentally argued back: "Yes, we need to eat, but we are having a collective nervous breakdown here! Our workplaces are toxic, corporate greed is devouring corporate integrity, and law-makers don't seem to give a hoot—and, I do not believe that the Good Lord put us on this planet to crucify each other and our own humanity for the sake of a paycheck!" I thought about individuals who gnawed and clawed their way through careers, and then suddenly turned to the Almighty for mercy as their mortality came into view. I reasoned: "Spirituality must be relevant to our material lives, right here, right now, and if it is not, then it is little more than superstition activated at the hour of our death, with hopes that our sudden piety will magically open heaven's gate."

I have thought about how tough this text is on capitalism as we know it. The negative voice hissed, "You just want to bash the wealthy and rebuke capitalism." Another part of my brain thundered: "That's a load of balderdash!" Capitalism, like all economic systems, is morally neutral by nature and can be corrupted at any time by policies that shower great favor and fortune on some while dispossessing others. I am not writing to resurrect Karl Marx and Vladimir Lenin. I am writing to address the pain and despair that we face in the workplace, the resentment we have toward leaders who have not been good shepherds, and to offer some thoughts about how we might use our spirituality to maintain hope, good will, integrity, and courage to fight for just causes in workplaces that are broken.

Everyone needs a wake-up call. All of us, rich and poor alike, have contributed to our society's economic woes, as the following list reveals.

1. The wealthy often use wealth to create advantages for themselves, such as tax reductions, zoning laws, corporate subsidies, deregulation of oversight, and bailouts in the wake of financial mismanagement; and, these advantages often come at the expense of the working class, poor, and vulnerable.

2. Workers often abuse employers and customers by being mean, indifferent to the quality of their work, or by demanding tenure for incompetent employees.

3. The general public suffers when individuals fake injuries to collect disability and gain access to public resources and benefits by way of fraud.

4. We hurt ourselves and others by accruing debt we cannot pay, by having children that we cannot support, or by failing to raise children who are motivated to learn, willing to work hard, and interested in being responsible citizens.

Some economic troubles are the result of honest mistakes. Others are due to the willingness of some people to make messes and expect others to clean them up. This book looks at our economic system because it impacts our material well-being, and influences the way we think about work and wealth. Our form of capitalism, for example, created conditions wherein many elders who expected to retire at age 65 cannot afford to do so, and wherein government employees have been forced into furloughs and wage freezes as public revenue is redirected to pay for corporate bailouts. Our form of capitalism has created something besides shifts in how long people work or how many members of one family need to work in order to survive. It has created uncertainty and antagonism between people who should get along and help each other. The spiritual and psychological consequences of selfishness and exploitation do not always show up on financial spreadsheets. The consequences are often the feelings we have about entitlement and what we owe others, or the attitudes we have towards co-workers and neighbors. The consequences might include a lost sense of hope that is transferred into our personal relationships, or a diminished willingness to serve the common good.

As sentences found their way to the pages, it was impossible for me to forget that for most of our waking lives, we are surrounded by the voice of eternal want. Ads are echo chambers of our own vanity and materialism. We have normed our want, and frequently cannot tell the difference

Preface

between necessities and luxuries. We see our entitlement in high definition, but the view of those made poor, homeless, sick, and despondent by our entitlement live in the cloudy fuzz of our peripheral vision.

As I penned this text, I thought about what it means to be a "Christian nation." It seems that while many of us are concerned about the soul's salvation, we resent Christianity's call to put people before things, and to protect and love the vulnerable, poor, and outcast. Inside most of us, there will always be a little kid who is tempted to steal from the cookie jar when nobody is looking, and then blame someone else when we get caught with crumbs on our faces. However, I do not believe that we are manifestly destined to steal, cheat, and lie. With that in mind, I write about the blessings of awareness, conscience, knowledge, courage, humility, charity, and the spiritual gifts that allow us to be in the material world without being morally putrefied by it.

This book is not so much about revolutionizing our workplaces, industries, and institutions—although some might be much improved by such revolution—it is about revolutionizing ourselves. It is about taking a second look at what troubles us about our jobs and co-workers, and discovering the ways we have created our own hell. It is about potential pathways out of the inferno. Readers will meet individuals who did not like what was happening on the job and furiously demanded institutional reforms, people who selflessly and patiently worked with others to improve their professions, and others who quietly packed up their cubicles and quit. Each who has grievance must determine which response is right for him or her. Whether we believe in God or not, every encounter we have with others in the workplace is an opportunity to do something good for others, do something dastardly, or to be wholly indifferent. Every encounter is also an opportunity for personal spiritual growth and maturation.

I expect that many readers have their own internal voices that ridicule the idea that spirituality has much to do with the workplace. While one voice snarls, "Business is not about warm and fuzzy, it is about making money," the other screams, "I don't want anybody pushing a personal savior down my throat!" I hear these voices and my response is simple. First, I believe compassion and integrity can generate as much profit as we actually need to sustain ourselves; and second, the conversation about spirituality in this book is not a Trojan horse sent to convert readers to a particular creed or institutional orthodoxy, but a conversation about improving self-awareness and making healthy and charitable choices in our lives.

Preface

I trust that readers have their own internal voices. I hope those voices rebel against raging materialism, and ask, "What does prosperity mean if we are made miserable and transformed into savage beasts in its pursuit?" In a world where we are urged to treat people like things, I pray we amplify the spiritual voice urging us to love and respect human dignity.

Lastly, I wanted to compose text that satisfies the requirements of scholarly work while at the same time creating a narrative that is accessible and interesting to a variety of readers, including workers across all classes. This was a challenging task. I trust that readers can relate to the stories and commentary in this book, and hope that they offer some insights to their own spiritual journey.

Acknowledgements

Nearly everyone in this book who told their story did so anonymously. Sadly, more times than not, that was because they feared unpleasant consequences for speaking out. I am sincerely grateful not only for the willingness of family and friends to speak to me about our work experiences, but about their private thoughts and feelings about life and its meaning. I am also thankful to friends and family who listen to me yammer and yowl—at times like a wounded moose stuck in a burning peat bog—and who still extend their care and support. Special thanks to Pam Howard, Geoffrey Desa, Diane Allen, and Barb Haber for helping me improve my thinking as I write, and my writing as I think.

1

Introduction

CHOPPED LIVER

"It ain't pretty being in your fifties," Betty growled. The veteran accountant twisted the cinders at the end of her cigarette against an antique ashtray from a Las Vegas casino and complained:

> You are at peak performance; you got your credentials; you have demonstrated your expertise, your leadership, and your willingness to make personal sacrifices for the good of the team, and what' ya get? You get a supervisor fresh out'a college who got the position by virtue of being a cheap hire who would be a yes man, and you got nowhere to run. I got twice as much energy as Mr. Twenty-Year-Old and I would like to find a job in another company at the level I have earned, and paid what I deserve. But, when you are in your fifties, nobody wants you. They think you are gonna need a respirator in the interview or retire in a week. They see you as a creature from the generation that wouldn't die! And God forbid you should know more than the boss— cuz boy oh boy, people at the top get pissed off when people at the bottom know more than they do. I just wanna scream, "I was an expert at this when you were still learning how to add and subtract—what am I—chopped liver?"

Alex chimed in, "I hear ya, but ya don't have to be over fifty to get treated like that. He continued:

My cousin, Jeff, who was in his thirties was run out of a job because one administrator, Scott, decided that his unit was unnecessary. He wanted to impress the suits and came up with a money-saving plan. He convinced them to cut the unit's budget and redistribute assignments. Everyone in the unit tried to get reclassified or assigned to another unit, but that one administrator just took dug in his heals. Scott did not approve *even one* of those petitions. He blocked efforts to fund projects and blocked every other unit's effort to collaborate with my cousin's unit. Then things got personal . . . Scott started assigning work outside people's job descriptions, and when they pushed back, he accused them of being insubordinate. Jeff finally quit. Seven months later, they got a new unit to do exactly what Jeff's unit was doing all along.

Francine, another acquaintance, stated that her biggest problem on the job was "the fact that you can't talk about improvement—even if you're talking about really dangerous stuff that goes on— without somebody accusing you of being America's biggest bigot." She said:

> There's this supervisor we have at work, and some of the staff call her "Rosie Rainbow" because she is always talking about how we respect diversity and equality. So, after a few months of when she hired Benji—he's one of the guys who gives you your actual driving test—I noticed that he routinely passed drivers who were driving really badly. One drove over the curb to get out of the parking lot, another failed to signal his turns, another barreled through the stop sign at the corner, and this old lady had a hard time accelerating and breaking without giving everyone in the car whiplash. I mentioned it to another staffer, and she said that everybody knows that when you fail your behind-the-wheel, you try and get Benji for your next test, especially if you are 'anything but white.' I know that Rosie is being pressured to hire more minorities. I know that she is sensitive about accusations that people of color flunk their driving test more than white people flunk, and I got no problem with people of all nations driving. But, I expect our staff—no matter what color they are— to hold high standards of safety, and not give bad drivers a license. A license is not a birthright! If people show you that they can handle a 2,000 pound box of metal on wheels at 65 miles an hour and obey the rules of the road— great, give 'em a license. But this guy passes people who clearly don't have good driving skills and everyone is afraid to say so. Nobody wants to say anything cuz when you do, Rosie assumes that you

INTRODUCTION

got personal problems and you're using the safety thing as a smoke screen for your own racism.

An old high school chum, Brenda, cautioned me that anyone looking for a teaching position in the organization in which she worked would do well to forget about the entire district. She quizzed, "Do you know why the turnover rate is so high here?" I took some guesses. She replied, "You got half of it right—we are understaffed and underpaid, but here, when the kids hit the teachers, or act out in the classroom, or come to class on drugs, the parents support the kids and accuse the teachers of being idiots." I inquired, "What about alternative schools?" Brenda laughed, "We *are* the alternative school." I asked about district leadership. "The district has only so much money, and that is one part of the problem; but, the other part of the problem is that the administration is mostly made up of politicians who have never taught and have no pedagogical expertise." I prodded my friend about what kept her in her teaching position. Sadly, it was not faith in education or the love of mentoring young people. It was the paycheck.

Many Americans are miffed about how they are treated on the job and disillusioned about professions they once thought were noble. Some are discouraged and disgusted by sexual harassment.[1] Many are angry because they feel like they played by the rules, earned their degrees, got to be very good at what they did, and were not properly rewarded or respected. Some are upset because the rules of the game changed in the middle of their career, and, rather than find a way to value their service and skills, organizations rolled over them to pave the way for "progress." Many are flabbergasted and dismayed that the wisdom of elders and veteran employees is reflexively scuttled for the latest trend. Others are upset by the gap between what the organization says it stands for and what it actually does. Many are frustrated and irritated by how the pressure to be "politically correct" has sabotaged conversations about legitimate concerns of safety, sustainability, competence, and quality in the workplace.

NOT A HAPPY PICTURE

For millions of Americans, facing another day on the job is like a Dickensian scene wherein men and women slavishly grind away at tedious tasks,

---

1. Graff's, "Sexual Harassment" states that 59 percent of women and 27 percent of men report that they have been sexually harassed on the job; see para. 6.

while pompous and belligerent managers heap abuses upon them and pay them poor wages. For some, going to work is a daily reminder that they are little more than replaceable cogs in a machine, and that their well-being will never be as important as "the bottom line." There are plenty of numbers to back the assertion that Americans are fed up with work, not only because the workplace is often an unpleasant and dysfunctional place, but fed up because the economy itself seems to be hostile to the working classes.

Millions of Americans work hard and receive little for their effort, loyalty, and skill. In 2016, about 80 million workers age sixteen and older were paid at hourly rates, and among these workers, roughly 701,000 took home the federal minimum of $7.25 per hour, while 1.5 million earned less than the federal minimum wage.[2] The federal poverty threshold for a single person in 2016 was $13,920.00,[3] and in San Francisco that year, one-bedroom apartments averaged $3,330.00—about three times that of the monthly income for someone earning minimum wage.[4] Minimum wage earners would have done better in Topeka, Kansas that year, as they could have found a one-bedroom apartment for around $800.00 per month and thus spent "only" 69 percent of their monthly income for housing.[5]

Experts chortle that the normal ups and down of supply and demand determine the distribution of compensation, as if real human beings made no real decisions about minimum wage, corporate subsidies, outsourcing, rent control, or pensions and health care. Some tell us that increases in minimum wages will throw millions out of work,[6] while others insist that unemployment due to increases in minimum wages are too small to be statistically significant.[7] Unemployment is caused by factors other than wage regulation, such as the relocation of American industries to foreign countries, the mechanization of labor, and the amount of profit that is reserved for executive bonuses and stockholders. All of these factors involve choices.[8]

---

2. United States Department of Labor, "Characteristics of Minimum Wage Workers," lines 1–5.

3. United States Department of Health and Human Services, "Computation," see table.

4. Brinklow, "SF Rents Close," lines 3–8.

5. Department of Numbers, "Topeka Kansas," Table *Real Gross Rent*.

6. Ryan, "The Truth about Minimum Wage," para. 11–12.

7. Belman & Wolfson, *What Does the Minimum Wage Do?* Pp. 2, 16, 70.

8. See Janoski, et al. *The Causes of Structural Unemployment*.

INTRODUCTION

Despite our distance from Victorian London, many workers in America are in a dismal state. In 2012, roughly one half million children worked in the agricultural industry across the United States. As young as six years old, they harvested 25 percent of crops grown in the country— including grapes in California, onions in Texas, and sugar beets in Minnesota—each earning about $1,000.00 a year for their backbreaking efforts.[9] Child laborers work in meat packing industries and on construction sites. The Federal Occupational Health and Safety Administration complains it does not have the resources to inspect every company or follow up on all reports of foul play, and so children remain on the job despite the laws against it.[10]

In 2015, the U.S. Bureau of Labor Statistics revealed that 4,836 workers died on the job that year, while the Center for Disease Control and Prevention noted that about 50,000 deaths each year occur due to work-related illnesses.[11] In his book, *Dying for a Paycheck*, Stanford Professor of Business and Organizational Behavior, Jeffrey Pfeffer, reported that over half of all employees say they have been made sick from stress related to work, and that many of the distressed psychologically break down and commit acts of violence against others or themselves.[12] He asserts that various schemes and strategies to increase profits are, in many cases, sabotaging profit because they result in losses due to lower productivity and sick pay. The professor also argues that unbridled capitalism and resistance to regulation are sources of unnecessary suffering, and suggests that only a whopper of a lawsuit might reign in greedy Goliaths who seem indifferent to new models of sustainability.

Hard physical labor strains our bodies on the job, while incompetence, bullying, poor compensation, harassment, and disrespect in the workplace diminish our morale and wound us spiritually. In the United States, only 32 percent of workers report that they are engaged in their jobs, and feel both passion for their work and a deep connection to their companies.[13] A study of technology workers who left their jobs revealed that 37 percent of those who quit did so because of mistreatment on the job and discrimination, and/or sexual harassment.[14] In 2016, the U. S. Equal Employment Oppor-

---

9. York, "Do Children Harvest Your Food?" See full story.
10. Semuels, "How Common is Child Labor in the U.S." para. 1–12.
11. Kamel, *Dying to Work*, p. 4.
12. Pfeffer, *Dying for a Paycheck*, pp. 9–17.
13. Mann and Harter, "The Worldwide Employee," lines 3–11.
14. Kurtz, "Here's the Single Biggest Reason," lines 1–7.

tunity Commission (EEOC) reported that of the 91,503 complaints about workplace harassment, 45 percent were based on sex and the remainder were based on race, ethnicity, age, and disability.[15] These complaints do not include those filed under state or local agencies. A 2016 EEOC investigation noted that about 75 percent of those who experienced harassment on the job never reported their experiences to supervisors or union representatives, and that administrative accountability for abuse was lacking.[16]

Recently, a study of 17,000 workers found that 71 percent were looking for new jobs, and that workers are restless because they are dissatisfied with low pay and poor recognition.[17] In the study, 64 percent said that their employers did not support them, and that a majority of workers resent their co-workers. It also noted that, because of unhappiness on the job, over half of employees engaged in unhealthy behaviors, such as substance abuse.

Job dissatisfaction and low morale in the workplace impact employees across all skills levels. In a recent study, 22 percent of physicians and 35 percent of nurses reported that they had left jobs in the past and were considering another job move because they had experienced moral distress in their work.[18] Moral distress refers to the conflict and anxiety one experiences when institutional norms and policies prevent workers from taking ethically appropriate action when they believe it is imperative to do so.[19] In this instance, moral conflicts arose over directives for unnecessary tests, pressure to decrease care in order to save money, assigning under-skilled staff to care for patients, and communications that deliberately misled patients and their families.

Our health care industry is not so healthy. A Physicians Foundation study of 20,000 doctors found that 80 percent indicated that they were over-extended in their duties or working to full capacity, and that they were frustrated by federal regulations that reduce their autonomy and compensation.[20] A study of 600 nurses found that 43 percent believed their work environment was not healthy, as: 45% reported being harassed or bullied by other nurses; 41 percent reported being harassed or bullied

---

15. U.S. Equal Employment Opportunity Commission, "EEOC Releases," Section B.
16. U.S. Equal Employment Opportunities Commission, "Select Task Force," p. 2.
17. Marks, "Study: 71 Percent," para 1–3.
18. Austin, Saylor, and Finley. "Moral Distress."
19. Jameton's, *Nursing Practice* comprehensively addresses ethical crises in nursing.
20. Physicians Foundation. *2014 Survey of America's Physicians*, p. 8.

Introduction

by administration; and, 38 percent reported being bullied by physicians.[21] About 17 percent of nurses leave their jobs after one year, and to replace and train just one costs tens of thousands.[22] Nationally, the cost of nurse turnovers for large hospitals is roughly $6 billion annually.[23] Patients often suffer adverse outcomes because of turnover rates. Patient falls and pressure ulcer rates tend to increase when being tended by a novice nurse rather than one with many years of practice.[24] Turnover trends like these appear in other workplaces.

In K-12 education, about 8 percent of teachers leave the profession annually to find work in other careers, citing discontent with pressure to meet standardized testing goals, lack of advancement opportunities, and poor administrative support.[25] Teacher turnover rates are higher in urban schools heavily populated by ethnic minorities and children from poor families.[26]

Annually, the turnover rate for police officers is nearly 11 percent, owing to stress on the job, lack of supervisor support, low wages, and role ambiguity.[27] In Chicago, it costs roughly $140,000.00 to train a new police officer, and in many Chicago suburbs, where some officers earn less than $12.00 an hour, insufficient funding for training and supervision has led to the retention of officers who have questionable patterns of shooting suspects.[28]

Many who leave their jobs do so because leaders do not lead well.[29] Low morale is an expensive disaster that costs the U.S. about $500 *billion* dollars annually in productivity.[30] As workers increasingly suffer from stress and illness caused by conditions in their work environments, the cost of health care increases.[31] In addition, the fraud and theft committed by

---

21. Buttaccio. "3 Reasons Why Nurses are Leaving the Profession," lines 13–21.
22. Li and Jones. "A Literature Review of Nursing Turnover Costs."
23. Jones, "Revisiting Nurse Turnover Costs: Adjusting for Inflation."
24. Mark, Sayler and Wan, "Impact on Organization" and Warshawsky, et al., "The Effect."
25. Carver-Thomas and Darling-Hammond, *Teacher Turnover*, pp. 24–29.
26. Ibid.
27. Wareham, Smith, and Lambert. "Rates and Patterns."
28. Smith, "What Happens," lines 15–20.
29. Hedges, "8 Common Causes of Workplace Demotivation," para. 12.
30. Clifford, "Unhappy Workers Cost the U.S," lines 1–6.
31. Azagba and Sharaf. "Psychosocial Working Conditions."

disgruntled workers may account for as much as 20 percent of all business failures.[32]

Admittedly, making comparisons between the grinding filth and want of the nineteenth century and the relative comfort of working class prosperity of the twenty-first century seems ridiculous. Indeed, even the less affluent among Americans can spend their pennies in a consumer paradise. Living in a consumer paradise, however, does not mean that we are happy, fulfilled, or secure in our lives. It does not mean that we are doing a good job of creating a sustainable economic paradigm. Living in a consumer paradise does not mean we are tightly bound to spiritual moorings and values, or enabling others to do the same.

IT'S A SPIRITUAL THING

Beyond the fiscal, physiological, and psychological consequences of workers' stress and unhappiness, lies the spiritual consequences. These wounds are not always apparent even to those who suffer from them. We often attribute our suffering to fatigue, depression, or frustration to physical or psychological things rather than recognize that our spirits are in great distress. In addition, we often point to external factors for our misery without examining our own personal contributions to distress and dysfunction in the workplace.

Spiritual injuries are similar to psychological wounds, and are caused by the same things, such as discrimination, rejection, public humiliation, marginalization, predatory sexual behavior and economic insecurity.[33] What makes an injury spiritual in nature is that it tends to extinguish our sense of humanity and replace it with the notion that we are just an interchangeable cogs in the great machinery of life. Spiritual injuries may also diminish the belief that we have the right to dignity and respect. The spiritual injury often causes us to mock the idea that we are created for a scared purpose, and that this sacred purpose extends into our work lives. The spiritually wounded sometimes abandon high moral standards because they are ridiculed for having such standards. In the extreme, spiritual injuries sometimes cause people to curse God, or reject the notion that there is such a thing a benevolent higher power or divine Creator.

---

32. Coffin, "Breaking the Silence."
33. Scott, Sr., *Healing the Broken Spirit*, pp. 12–13.

Introduction

Spiritual injuries might be the result of experiencing prejudice in the workplace, or enduring administrative indifference to employees' basic needs. It might be the result of having to stand behind false claims that the company routinely makes for the purpose of winning the consumer's trust or securing private investment. They might occur because people who openly advocate for fairness or compassion in the workplace are themselves openly scorned and victims of gossip that injures their reputation and promotion.

Spiritual injuries have serious consequences. They rupture associations with good friends and family. They frequently cause people to walk in fear and defensiveness rather than faith and trust. Spiritual injuries often afflict the believer's sense of cosmic order, causing a sense of disorientation in one's philosophical, theological, and moral outlooks.[34] Liu, an acquaintance who works for a postal service told me how he lost his morale:

> I can't wait to retire. Things have really changed over the years. It used to be when somebody retired, they got a party and a nice gift, and everyone had a chance to say thank you for your 30 years of service. Now, there is no party. I go to work and ask where is so-and-so, and somebody says, 'oh, he retired last week—there was a sign on the wall—didn't you see it?' The supervisors monitor us now with cameras, and we are only supposed to take so much time with each customer. If we take more time, we get in trouble. If we are short-staffed, it doesn't matter—that just means we have to be faster. They will sit in front of their screens and watch the staff get overrun with customers, but will not leave their office to open another service window to help us. It used to be that supervisors helped out when things got crazy . . . They respected loyalty and wanted you to be friendly with the customers and not make them feel like they were taking too much time. Now, loyalty and courtesy do not matter—your name doesn't even matter. What matters is that your hands are always moving and you never complain. I wasn't raised to think of work the way that my boss sees it, but that's the way it is.

The woes that afflict the workplace are not caused only by impersonal market fluctuations, they are caused by how individuals relate to each other. They are about the unspoken agreements that concern society's wellness, and in particular, the social contract whereby workers are given a secure

---

34. Pasquale's *Sacred Wounds* explores the trauma generated by religious fundamentalism and bigotry.

job and living wage in exchange for their fidelity and honest labor. As employers pursue new strategies for profit-making, the unspoken social agreement has changed. A cashier at a large grocery outlet made the point as she chatted with me at the checkout. A cheerful woman in her sixties, she said that she was tired, but always opted for faith in God and kindness. When I asked about what it was like to work for the company, she replied, "You know, we are very busy here, and we always need more workers, but our hours are always being cut." I said, "That sounds odd—you always have a hiring sign on the doors." She said that the company would rather hire part-time workers who are not entitled to benefits than to hire full-time employees who are entitled to benefits. "That is why the turnover is so high here . . . its bad enough that ya can't earn a living here on part-time pay, but what really kills ya is the manager who wants you to do in four hours what it takes a normal person to do in a full shift."

From a spiritual perspective, it is almost impossible to calculate the losses incurred when workers are disgruntled, demoralized, and disengaged. How does one measure the damage done to our identities, our sense of self-worth, our hopes, dreams, and our will to give our best to the world? The wounds to our sense of self tempt us to abandon love of neighbor, put on our canine suits, and get gruff in a dog-eat-dog world. The suffering employee frequently lives with despair that is translated into anger towards loved ones, alienation from family and friends, and a cynical disposition towards society and its well-being. It common for disillusioned and demoralized workers, who were once passionate about their occupation and helping others, become bitter and denounce what they once thought of as a sacred vocation as "corrupt" or a "a waste of time and money." They often feel like chumps for believing disingenuous promises of the employer, or for working so hard when others were careless and lazy, yet fully compensated.

BARGAIN BASEMENT

What is this spirituality that is supposed to sustain and guide us in the material world? It is not the same as religion, it is bigger. Religion pertains to institutional doctrines, creeds, rituals, and corporate preservation, and it might facilitate spiritual development, but it is not spirituality itself. Religion does not always get us to the deepest depths of our spirituality. Spirituality is the meditative, intuitive, aesthetic, and transcendental encounter with the sacred within. It is about awareness of how we might create a self

Introduction

that broadens and deepens possibilities for love and compassion. It nudges us to confront the ways we indulge our egos, and sabotage the well-being of others and ourselves with our own fears, insecurities, greed, and vanity. Spirituality focuses our attention on causes greater than ourselves which may seem abstract and other worldly.[35]

Some say spirituality is a quest for the scared within and without.[36] Others say spirituality is a way of seeing that helps us become objective about ourselves, and coaxes us face our own denial of how attachments to material wealth, power, and popularity have affected our morals.[37] Whereas religion provides us with moral instruction and institutional rituals for forgiveness and reconciliation, spirituality is thing that keeps us from mistreating others in the first place.

Wounded and dissatisfied workers often put their spirituality on hold during working hours, and tell themselves they must endure inhumanity on the job for the sake of paycheck. When the going gets tough, spirituality and other cherished ideals often gets dumped in the bargain basement with all the broken toys and mismatched shoes. Some barter with God: "Lord, just let me get my benefits and pension all lined up, and once I retire, I will renew my spirituality and be human again." In the material world, we typically believe that everything, even our own connection to God, can be negotiated.

In Western culture, reciprocity is often at the center of our morality and is the cornerstone of the conditions we impose on our love for others. Strict reciprocity requires an eye for an eye. It lives in the covenants between tribes and gods, whereby god will shower the faithful with protection and prosperity in exchange for obedience and worship. Spirituality is bigger than the bargain, however, it is a way activating love even when it is not reciprocated. It is a way of loving our neighbors so thoroughly that bargaining with God for favor is not only offensive, it is unnecessary. Jesus seemed to be getting to this point when he advised his followers to turn the other cheek when struck, and to offer up one's cloak when sued for one's shirt (Matt. 5:38–40). Bargaining with God or our Higher Power about when

---

35. Benner, "Toward a Psychology of Spirituality."
36. Hill, et. al., "Conceptualizing Religion and Spirituality."
37. Ruiz's *Four Agreements*, De Mello's books, *Awareness* and *The Way to Love*, and R. King's *Thomas Merton and Thich Nhat Hanh* see spirituality as a means of moving beyond the illusions that dominate our lives.

we will and will not activate our spirituality is another way of not seeing ourselves in our brothers and sisters.

Why talk about our spirituality in the workplace? What is the big deal here? As an acquaintance barked, "I don't have the luxury to get all philosophical about my job or whether the government gives a damn about the working class . . . I gotta' pay the bills and I just thank God I have a job!"

THE BIG DEAL

So what is the big deal? The big deal is that, on average, we spend between 25 and 35 percent of our time on Earth in gainful employment. The big deal is that we spend a significant part of our lives in environments that often encourage us to sidestep our spiritual teachings for the sake of our financial security and material ambitions. The big deal is, that if we ignore the way we behave on the job and in market place, we may suffer, cause suffering, and become people we do not want to be. The big deal is that if we do not improve our awareness of how our own attitudes and actions impact others, we may pass through life never having reached our own potential to leaven God's love into corners of our world that needed it most.

Each decision in our lives affects our spiritual growth and well-being. Imagine, for example, that one third of our diet consisted of sugar. Dutifully eating three times the recommended amount of sugar every day would eventually cause health problems that would affect us every day, every hour, not just for 33 percent of our time. Everything we ingest physically and psychologically ultimately affects our spirituality in the same way. As Rabbi David Cooper observed, "Things are more important that we think they are . . . Each event that we experience has a deeper message if we have the eyes to see and the ears to hear."[38] It stands to reason that the fears, anxieties, anger, and frustration we feel at work often spills into our social and family lives.

How many of us go to work with the idea we might discover something of mystical significance, or something about our lives that forever changes the way we see things? Since we live in a culture that compartmentalizes our lives, most of us are probably living in a state of dis-integration: our spirituality is in one box, and our social lives are in another box. As I became aware of my own dis-integration, I often wondered whether my spiritual self would recognize my social self, as the two sometimes seem

---

38. Cooper, *God is a Verb*, p. 6.

Introduction

so ridiculously opposed. God does not call a "time-out" on our spiritual development just because we are on the employer's clock. In the most radical sense, employers have no clock: for the faithful, all time belongs to God.

What is the point of talking about the woes of the workplace in a society in which the working and middle classes have so much more comfort and access to resources than does half of the planet's population?[39] Is it not a little bit self-indulgent or perhaps even obscene to talk about abusive co-workers, or unfair labor practices and management practices, when millions of people around the world lack food, health care, sanitation, shelter, clean water, and civil rights?

If the point of this book were about using spirituality to get all the material advantages and rewards we want in the workplace, then, yes, this discussion would be like the tantrum of a spoiled child. This book, however, is not about strategies to enrich ourselves, techniques for moving up the corporate ladder, or methods for winning the praise and approval of others; it is about sustaining spirituality in the workplace, and leveraging it to help us when we need help. This book is not about how to make the workplace over in our own image, or creating utopias. It is about improving one's own awareness of and sensitivity to how our own values, attitudes, and behaviors might be more closely aligned with spirituality grounded in love of neighbor. If improvements in our awareness results in workplace reforms, that would be a terrific bonus.

The discussion of our own values, attitudes, and behaviors does not excuse the bad behavior of business leaders and elected officials. One could argue that the world would be a better place without some organizations and some leaders, and one might be correct; but, those claims are topics for another discussion. This text recognizes the complexity of suffering and abuse in the workplace and holds that both employers and employees bear some responsibility for the state of economic affairs.

Human nature makes it inevitable we will always have employers who treat workers poorly, and inflict serious harm to the environment and unsuspecting populations. Years after the mortgage meltdown of 2008, the banking titan, Wells Fargo, which employs about 263,000 people, proved that not even a great recession can hold back the tide of greed. It set up 3.5 *million* fake bank and credit card accounts and fraudulently collected fees from their victims for doing so.[40] The retail behemoth, Walmart employs

---

39. World Bank, *Poverty and Shared Prosperity*, pp. 35–50.
40. Egan, "Wells Fargo." Also see White, "One Year After," lines 1–7.

about 2.1 million people, was very creative in its lust for loot. It was sued for taking out "dead peasant" life insurance policies on their employees, and then collecting on the policies when the employee died, while the employee's family knew nothing about the policies.[41] Duke energy Corporation, which employs about 28,700, led corporate air pollution in 2011 by dumping 126.8 million tons of carbon dioxide into the atmosphere.[42] Rather than decrease its carbon emissions in the face of climate change, Duke increased its discharge in 2012 to nearly 134.3 million tons.[43] The moral of the story is that we are willing to hurt each other, not just incidentally or a little bit, but systematically on a grand scale, for profit and for convenience.

The paradox of affluence is that it exacts collateral damage. We thrive because we kill plants and animals to eat them. We can fly from coast to coast in just a few hours because we are willing to disperse particulates from spent fossil fuels into the air. We can buy a new shirt or toaster for low prices because we support low wages with zero benefits for factory and farm workers. Capitalism's cheerleaders assure us that in the end, the greater good is always served.

We are forced to live with paradox and the constant need to discern our moral way amidst a bevy of choices. This book offers no way out of the paradox. I believe our spirituality has not been given to us to dispel paradox, but to humble us and help us with damage control. Paradox teaches us to pay attention to the consequences of our behavior. Spirituality urges us to act like consequences matter, and to sharpen the edges of our discernment with truth and compassion.

In order to understand the big picture of woes in the workplace, it is necessary to recognize that real people make real choices to cause or allow these woes to exist and fester. We choose to see injustice or ignore it; we choose to participate in unhealthy dynamics or we do not; and, we choose to rationalize hurtful behavior or we stand on principle that there is no justification. Spirituality begins with the individual's response to intuitive empathy, or what some call "God's invitation to love." Spirituality does not begin with the organization's manual of employee conduct or federal and state laws.

---

41. Schultz and Francis, "Companies Profit, 37–40." Also see Spurgin, "The Problem with Dead Peasants."

42. Forbes, "America's Worst," slides.

43. McMahon, "And the Biggest Power Polluter," lines 7–8.

Introduction
WHY THIS BOOK?

This book was motivated by the realization that I know very few people who are truly, 100 percent happy, fully engaged, and fulfilled on the job. Dozens of friends, family members, and acquaintances who all worked in different professions all seemed to be telling me the same story. They say, "Things have changed." They say "Employers care way more about money than they care about people," and "There is no security like there used to be." They complain, "Incompetent people get promoted, and people who object are reprimanded."

The sincerity of the people who told me their stories is compelling. People generally want to feel good about what they do for a living, and they want to be good at what they do. They want to work in healthy environments that respect their humanity. They also want to know how to approach people who hurt them and to know when to walk away from environments that are too toxic for them to fight.

The purpose of this essay is to explore how our attitudes and actions affect the workplace, and how to activate our spirituality when our jobs are a source of pain, conflict, and unhappiness. This text will address what organizational policies can do to foster respect and human dignity in the workplace, and focuses on what we as individuals can do to be a source of goodness and wellness. This essay will examine how we might leverage our spirituality to transform our expectations about the workplace, and to welcome the workplace as a place rich with opportunities for spiritual development.

A key premise of this book is that, for all who take their spirituality seriously, all jobs are ministries. They are ministries not only because they give us the opportunity to serve and support our colleagues and communities, but because they are venues in which individuals may, knowingly or not, also minister to us with caring guidance and support. As the spiritual aspect of our humanity places us in the presence of God, we always occupy sacred space. Thus, our factories, offices, executive suites, clinics, classrooms, stock rooms, check-out stands, delivery trucks, farms, labs, stations, and cubicles are all sacred spaces.

This book is intended for people who struggle in their work environments. It is also written to spark discussions in classrooms and religious retreats where people analyze human relations, and undertake introspection and discussion about their relationship to the material world. This book holds that human beings are spiritual beings who are influenced by secular ideas that compete with theological and spiritual teachings. It is important to understand those secular ideas, their appeal, and their implications for spirituality, because without such understanding, we are vulnerable to irresponsible and cruel propaganda.

ORGANIZATION OF TEXT

This book is organized by topics. The second chapter explores how religious and secular ideologies have influenced American ideas about wealth and work. Chapter three addresses the evangelism and political correctness on the job. Chapter four examines what whistle blowers teach us about the power of integrity. Chapter five explores the ways we use spirituality as an excuse to be passive in the face of suffering and abuse, while chapters six and seven explore some strategies for overcoming our own fear and inertia. Chapter eight addresses the importance of intergenerational understanding and cooperation. Chapter nine explores the dark side of corporate culture and its consequences, while chapter ten considers the meaning of leadership. In chapter eleven, readers will examine formal education's role in fostering business ethics. The last chapter summarizes thoughts about how to overcome resistance to activating spirituality in the workplace.

Each chapter provides a list of questions that readers, instructors, and retreat facilitators may find helpful in starting conversations about our experiences and needs. Readers should note that all references to biblical scripture, unless otherwise indicated, are taken from the *New Oxford Annotate Bible with the Apocrypha* (RSV).

REFLECTIONS

1. Define spirituality. What are the principle characteristics of your spirituality and where did you learn them?

2. Do you consciously integrate spirituality into your role as a worker, a student, or a consumer? What might be the benefits of doing so? Explain.

3. Describe your own experiences in the workplace and how they affect your sense of self and regard for others.

4. What thoughts and feelings do you experience when you see homeless or unemployed people? What are your thoughts and feelings

INTRODUCTION

about people who collect public assistance to survive? Have you ever lied about these feelings or thoughts in order to make yourself look good? What do your thoughts and feelings tell you about your love for others?

5. Recall a time when you felt abused, or harassed on the job, and describe how you reacted. In hindsight, does the experience have any spiritual implications for you?

6. What do you hope to learn as a result of exploring the stories and comments in this book?

7. Instructors: To what extent do you facilitate student inquiries into the nature of wellness, integrity, and compassion in the workplace and economy as a whole, and why these things matter? Do you believe you have an obligation to guide students' reflection on these matters? Why?

2

God and Prosperity

WE GOT STORIES

MANY PEOPLE HAVE IDEAS about work and wealth that blend notions about God and human nature. We are not always aware of these notions, and sometimes we think about these things only when confronted with a great controversy or personal crisis. The tales and myths we treasure house ideologies that have long lives. Like radioactivity, ideologies linger in the environment and are absorbed into our DNA without notice. Spirituality is often shaped by what we believe and assume about the material world and human nature. An understanding of secular ideologies about work and wealth helps us to clarify the ideas that compete with spiritual teachings. A stroll down "history lane" shines a light on some of our cherished beliefs, and reveals how technological, economic, and cultural phenomena have influenced, our spiritual outlook.

God has always been part of the American conversation about work and wealth. Traditional American grade school history told the story of how God blessed the pioneers, farmers, and industrialists with prosperity as a reward for their hard work. High school introductions to economics left us with the impression that American capitalism is an especially enlightened system, and that questioning this is a sign of stupidity. Many Americans were raised to believe that poverty pointed to deficits of character, and that the individual's destitution had little to do with institutional behavior or social prejudices.[1] Statistically, 46 percent of Christians and 29 percent of non-Christians in the U.S. believe that poverty is a self-inflicted condition.[2] Further, many believe that tampering with the distribution of wealth might have an adverse effect on their chances of becoming rich.[3]

We are economic creatures who want social norms and legal traditions to give us advantages on the road to prosperity. We are story-telling creatures too, and that means we can invent rationalizations for creating advantages for some and not for others. Our stories might contain esoteric theories, or myths disguised as science, or be touted as God's revelation. We like to situate God into our rationales because it gives us a sense of divine vindication. Our stories reveal the ways we have defined "love of neighbor" in ways that have often appeased our consciences, even when our activities have injured others.

TRICKLE-DOWN REDEMPTION

Scientific economic theory did not exist before the 1400s. The Catholic Church, the dominant institution in European life after Rome fell, saw matters of labor, wealth, and commerce as moral matters rather than a subject of social science.[4] The Church's teachings on moral matters was rooted in its concept of original sin, Adam's and Eve's disobedience in Eden (Genesis 3:17–19). The moral of the story was clear: Adam and Eve ate the forbidden fruit, God booted us off the gravy train, and from then on, the price of bread was toil and sweat.

Throughout the middle ages, Western theologians and lawmakers viewed work and social organization primarily through the lens of Paul's letters and Augustine's essays. These men had no objection to the fact that society was organized by class, and that some had more property, wealth, and power than others had.[5] Our medieval ancestors grew up confident

---

1. In 2013, 8.9 million Americans who worked full time were still in poverty; see Steenland, "Working Full Time." Steenland notes that Congressional members made 12 times more than minimum wage, para. 3, 12.

2. Zauzmer, "Christians," para. 1–3.

3. Rapoza, "Despite Crisis," para. 1–8.

4. Wood, *Medieval Economic Thought*, pp. 1–4.

5. See Rom. 13:1–7 and Eph. 6:5. Both Paul and Augustine believed that Christianity would leaven civil society with love, mercy and justice, and that neither the presence of slavery nor an aristocracy neutralized this potential. See Markus, *Saeculum*.

that class hierarchy, slavery, and the privileges of the elite were divinely ordained.[6] Medieval Christians believed that God's distribution of power and wealth was part of a plan for salvation.[7] Obedience to one's superiors offered a type of trickle-down redemption. Therefore: peasants had to be subservient to landlords; landlords owed obedience to kings; kings had to obey popes, and popes had to be subservient to God. Though challenged and modified, this perspective of cosmic order never completely disappeared.

In the 13th century, Thomas Aquinas "reconciled" Christianity and Aristotelian philosophy, and opened a path for Christian scholarship in the sciences.[8] [9] His approach to the matter of property parted ways with early Christians, who championed communal property.[10] Aquinas held that, by natural law, all things should be owned in common, but because sin had corrupted human beings, reason dictated that private ownership would result in the best care and use of property.[11] He taught that property provides a means for humanity to be co-creators with God.[12] He believed that private ownership was immoral only when people hoarded it and deprived the community of needed resources.[13] He held that the marketplace was immoral only when fraud and deception deprived buyers of a fair price.[14]

The Church taught that the seven deadly sins, which included sloth and greed, were mortal threats to the soul. It taught that acedia, a particular form of sloth characterized by indifference to God and rejection of one's calling to serve God, was especially offensive.[15] [16] Christianity did not expunge greed and sloth from society, and it may have contributed to these behaviors by preaching that the sins of hoarding great wealth could be offset by great charity.[17] Medieval marketplaces were filled with corrup-

---

6. Chroust, "The Philosophy of Law," and Wood, *Medieval Economic Thought* p. 17.

7. Viner, *The Role of Providence*, pp. 88–95.

8. Aquinas, *Thomas Aquinas on Faith and Reason*, pp. 114–201.

9. Jeffries, "Foundational Ideas."

10. Avila's *Ownership: Early Christian Teaching* traces the evolution of Christian thought on property.

11. Chroust and Affeldt, "The Problem of Private Property," p. 151.

12. Tollefsen, "Freedom and Equality."

13. Chroust and Affeldt.

14. Lapidus, "Norm, Virtue, and Information."

15. Wenzel, *The Sin of Sloth*, pp. 37–45.

16. Newhauser, *The Early History of Greed*. pp. 4–6.

17. Ibid, pp. 7–8.

tion, fraud, and violence.[18] Landlords taxed peasants to the point of deadly rebellion.[19] The Church made a fortune by selling indulgences (certificates for the forgiveness of sin), and practicing simony (sale of holy offices). Many clerics lived in abundance while communities in their care were ravaged by squalor, neglect, and poverty.[20] The combined forces of the Renaissance and Reformation shifted Western attitudes about economic matters, and laid the foundation for contemporary capitalism.

CALVIN MADE IT COOL

The Crusades, Black Death, new trade routes, and invention of new technologies produced an upheaval in Europe's class system.[21] In the 1340s, the Bubonic Plague killed at roughly one third of Europe's population.[22] The epidemic disrupted the social order by creating a ratio of laborers to employers that favored the workers.[23] As wages increased, so did tax revenue, which gave monarchs the capital to fight imperious, religious, and trade wars with great frequency.[24] New opportunities to invest in trade excited merchants and moneylenders. To many Christians, the new social and economic mobility confirmed that individuals were *not predestined for wealth*, but could acquire wealth by way of initiative, and that they could do so without endangering their souls. This was a major game-changer.

The social and economic movements of the 16th and 17th centuries were informed by new theologies.[25] Protestant theologians no longer reflexively defended the idea that peasants were divinely bound to their

---

18. Davis, *Medieval Market Morality*, pp. 1–2.

19. Bickle's *The Revolution of 1525* explores the Germany's Peasant war in which over 100,000 died, and Oman's *The Great Revolt of 1318* offers a look at the English Peasant Revolt in which at least 1,500 perished.

20. Lynch and Adamo's *Medieval Church* discusses the Church's corruption and its links to aristocratic and political dynasties. They note that, many sins were committed for the sake of divine order and salvation.

21. Sophisticated rudders, sail systems, maps, and compasses enabled trans-oceanic exploration and trade, and triggered competition for colonies and the expansion of the merchant class. See Parry, *Age of Reconnaissance*.

22. Ziegler's *Black Death* examines the Plague's origins and its effects on society, economics, and faith.

23. Cohn, "After the Black Death."

24. Voigtländer and Voth, "Three Horsemen of Riches."

25. Weber, *Protestant Ethic*. Also see Giogi and Marsh, "The Protestant Work Ethic."

landlords. John Calvin set off a moral revolution by preaching that accumulating wealth was not itself sinful, as long as one continually invested wealth in ways likely to bring about social well-being and goodness.[26] Whereas business was once regarded as a serious threat to the soul, Calvinism (Puritanism) reconciled piety and profit-making, thus, business was thus a sanctified enterprise.[27] Initially, Calvinism warned that the community would be destroyed if trade rather than self-sufficiency motivated work.[28] It also preached that enterprise undertaken for the sole purpose of enriching the individual rather than the community was sinful.[29] Both of these notions lost their luster as the American republic evolved.

The justifications we hear today for corporate behavior often use the Protestant work ethic as a touchstone. That is a tortured stretch of logic, if for no other reason than the fact that 18th century Protestants had no way of knowing how 21st century corporations would behave. The context in which the Protestant work ethic took root was very different than the context of today. Work was not even expected to be steady in the colonies and early republic. Farmers, the largest contingent of labor at the time, worked most arduously during planting and harvesting seasons, while manufacturing was often disrupted by shortages of materials and interruptions in transportation.[30] The bullish corporation with rights equal to that of a private citizen simply did not exist when the 13 colonies of the Atlantic coast took shape. Workers worked largely for themselves. There was no army of paid corporate lobbyists mobbing law-makers, and no stock-exchange brimming with ravenous investors.

At the dawn of the Republic, state legislatures believed that concentrations of wealth and economic power in private hands was by definition a threat to the public's well-being. As such, only state legislatures could charter corporations, and they did so with tough regulations of how many assets the corporation could accumulate, what documents had to be submitted for public review, and how many stocks would be issued. The state determined how long the corporation could exist, and what the company owed the community in exchange for the privilege of its existence. It also

---

26. Lipset, "Work Ethic Then and Now." Also see Bernhard, "Cotton Mather."
27. Tawney, Forward to *Protestant Ethic* by Max Weber, pp. 2–3.
28. Applebaum, *American Work Ethic*, p. 5
29. Frey, "Individualistic Economic Values."
30. Rogers, *The Work Ethic*, p. 19.

routinely denied limited liability status to corporate executives because it gave these executives an unfair advantage in the event of business failures.[31]

THE REPUBLIC TAKES AN ETHIC

No single creed or manifesto represents the Protestant work ethic. It was evolutionary and crept into the philosophical musings of Americans of all faiths.[32] Thomas Jefferson and John Adams blended it with Enlightenment principles, as they envisioned a republic populated by "sober, industrious, and frugal" individuals who would be charitable to those unable to work, and scorn those who were able, but preferred not to work.[33] Jefferson's disgust for sloth had little to do with original sin, and more to do with the burden society bore when the able-bodied refused to work.

Enlightenment philosophy of the 18th century is the cornerstone of the United States' Constitution, and it represents a pivot away from Puritan theocracy. It embraced the idea that humankind is reasonable enough to rule itself.[34] It set the social contract as the centerpiece of its ethos, and displaced the centrality of religion as the source of law. The social contract promotes mutual respect for the rights to life, liberty, and prosperity. Mutual respect in this context does not originate in the love of God, but in reason and the natural law, which promotes a "live and let live" attitude.[35] It was a type of reason bound to historical context.[36]

The Protestant work ethic did not purge classism and elitism from American society, nor did the Enlightenment erase prejudices based on social status, race, and gender. Though a great many fortunes relied on slaves who produced cash crops such as cotton, rice, indigo, sugar, and tobacco, the colonial gentlemen who profited from the plantation system generally did not identify with the common man. George Washington referred to farmers as "the grazing multitude." Other colonial leaders had similar thoughts.

---

31. Derber, *Corporation Nation*, pp. 121–126.
32. Weber, *The Protestant Ethic*.
33. Dienstag, "Serving God and Mammon," p. 507.
34. Ferguson's, *American Enlightenment* reveals how ideas about the natural law influenced the U.S.
35. Hulliung's *Social Contract* traces the ideologies development and application in U.S. history.
36. Tise's *Proslavery* explores secular and religious attitudes and assumptions that "justified" slavery.

John Adams referred to ordinary people as an easily excitable and vulgar "common Herd."[37] Alexander Hamilton expressed grave skepticism that the common public—whom he regarded as volatile and distracted—could ever be learned enough to contribute intelligently to their own governance.[38] Little wonder, then, that after the revolution, the "founding fathers," who were largely wealthy landowners, merchants, and lawyers, created a constitution that restricted the ballot to white males with property.[39]

Alexis De Tocqueville, the French diplomat who traveled to the U.S. in 1831, observed that the absence of an aristocracy, people in the United States readily embraced the notion that class mobility was a core democratic element, as was the notion that faith was linked to prosperity.[40] Ten years after De Tocqueville's visit, former Unitarian minister, Ralph Waldo Emerson sang the glory of self-reliance, and urged individuals to trust their own moral compass and capacity to master their own destinies.[41]

Evangelical Christians chimed in on the matter of mastering one's destiny, and sounded the news that faith paved the way to good fortune. Many exploited religion for their own profit and promoted the seductive myth that the truly faithful are pre-ordained to be rich. Tenaciously, Americans clung to the notion that the individual alone is master of one's economic outcomes, furiously rejecting the notion that external forces, such as laws or business practices were relevant.[42] In the 19th century, Horatio Alger, a Unitarian minister, sold millions of books about the downtrodden who lifted themselves into prosperity with their own determination, honesty, and hard work.[43] William McGuffey's readers were standard reading in public schools well into the 20th century, and explicitly glorified the virtues of piety, self-sacrifice, kindness, and self-sufficiency.[44] Secular literature

37. Wood, *Radicalism of the American Revolution*, p. 27.

38. Sheehan, "Madison vs. Hamilton."

39. Beard's, *Economic Interpretation* asserts that wealthy American merchants designed revolution and subsequent laws for their own advantage. Property requirements for voting were abolished in the early 1800s.

40. De Tocqueville's, *Democracy in America*, is regarded as an accurate portrait of the U.S. then and now.

41. Emerson, "Self Reliance."

42. Lehmann's *Money Cult* is a riveting history of America's romance with the "Gospel of Prosperity."

43. Scharnhosrt's *Lost Life* examines Alger's life and the influence of his work.

44. Westerhoff's *McGuffey* chronicles the life and works of this most influential American scholar.

proliferated and drew readers into the world of banal amusement and spectacular tales of villains and debauchery while religious ministers amplified the call to piety and salvation.[45]

The American republic prospered as it expanded west. Industrialism and a laissez-faire approach to business made entrepreneurs and investors rich.[46] At the dawn of the 20th century, Sociologist Max Weber lamented, "In the United States, the pursuit of wealth, stripped of its religious and ethical meaning, tends to become associated with purely mundane passions, which often actually give it the character of sport."[47] The industrial revolution proved that the Christian republic had no intention of using new wealth to create class equality. The Protestant work ethic did not liberate Americans from the notion that some people are destined to have, and some are destined to have not. The Protestant work ethic taught that wealth was a sign of God's favor, which fortified the resolve of entrepreneurs, and missionaries to spread their version of capitalism to non-industrial nations and to colonies on distant continents.

GILDED ETHICS

Presidents and Congressional members generally held corporate power at bay until the after the Civil War. After the conflict, corporations, or "voluntary contracts among private persons," enjoyed greater congressional favor.[48] The first steps toward endowing corporations with rights and privileges previously reserved for individuals were invigorated by a steady flow of corporate money into law-makers' pockets.[49] The rough edges of public fears were sanded away by welcomed conveniences and access to consumer goods made possible by industrialization.

In the Gilded Age, "captains of industry" transformed the United States into a formidable figure in global trade.[50] Their innovation and en-

---

45. Moore, "Religion, Secularizations, and the Shaping."

46. Josephson's *Robber Barons* discusses the careers of 19th century industrial titans, and how they secured favorable tax codes and rights to monopoly by way of lobbying and buying lawmakers.

47. Weber, *Protestant Ethic*, p. 182.

48. Ibid, p. 127.

49. Beatty's, *Age of Betrayal*, chronicles the bribery of the late 1800s and explores how the corruption seemed at the time to be a price society had to pay for increased production, and faster access to more goods.

50. Historians generally refer to America's Gilded Age as the era between 1870 and 1914.

trepreneurial leadership generally improved the quality of life for anyone with access to what they produced. They made fortunes while their employees typically worked 50 to 60 hours a week in dangerous conditions for low wages and no benefits. Farmers were impoverished by railroad fees. Industrialists often used their money to create monopolies that stifled competition and labor regulations.[51] Many industrialists scorned the laboring masses, and hired thugs to beat and kill strikers.[52] Outraged reformers warned that when civilization fell, it would be the fault of "barbarians from above," and not from below.[53]

Increasingly, ministers found ways to justify the naked pursuit of wealth.[54] [55] Evangelist Russell Conwell pontificated that there was nothing wrong with being rich. "Money is power," he announced, and "you can do more good with it than you could without it."[56] Sounding like Calvin on steroids, Conwell also declared that it was a Christian duty to get rich, because to "make money honestly is to preach the gospel."[57] Spiritualism, the New Thought Movement, and Christian Science promised that prayer could make one rich.[58] Millions flocked to novel variations of Christianity that promised to deliver them from poverty.[59]

Between 1870 and 1910, the top 10 percent of Americans increased their share of America's wealth from 70 to 80 percent.[60] Industrialization's bonanza left workers behind however, sparking interest in unions, socialism, and revolution.[61] Marxists called for a proletariat seizure of government would lead to equity in the distribution of wealth.[62] Many Protestants and Catholics, however, deplored the idea of a proletariat revolution, as

51. Folsom's *Myth of the Robber Barons* studies the complexity of industrialists' conduct.
52. Boyer and Morais' *Labor's Untold Story* and Ornstien's *Cass Counts* chronicle the Labor Movement.
53. Lloyd, *Wealth against Commonwealth*, pp. 494–513.
54. Dubisch and Michalowski, "Blessed are the Rich," p. 34.
55. Wauzzinski, *Between God and Gold*, p. 43.
56. Conwell and Shackleton, *Acres of Diamonds*, p. 20.
57. Dubisch and Michalowski, p. 36.
58. Bowler, *Blessed*, pp. 12–15. Conkin's *American Originals* surveys the variety of Christian movements that proliferated in the United States, and offers insights to the psychology and culture that fueled them.
59. Conkin.
60. Piketty, "About Capital in the Twenty-fist Century."
61. Currarino, "Introduction."
62. Marx and Engels, *Communist Manifesto*.

many believed that there was a divine design in the distribution of wealth and power.[63]

The Protestants' "Social Gospel" advocated a new urban ethic that called for fair wages, the abolition of child labor, the elimination of slums, and improvements in education and health care. Proponents of the Social Gospel, including Frances Peabody, William Gladden, and Walter Rauschenbusch[64] saw the Kingdom of God on Earth not in the form of theocracy, but in the form of caring and just communities.[65] Influenced by Enlightenment philosophy and adversely impacted by anti-Semitism in industry and politics, American Jews participated in social reform movements. Reformed rabbis prompted congregants to activate charity, and schools for Jewish immigrants proliferated. They helped people assimilate, while offering courses vocational skills, and home economics.[66] Like those who embraced the Social Gospel, progressive Jews were confident that Americans would ultimately unite to see that justice prevailed.[67]

Catholics weighed in on the labor question with the same passion as Jews who experienced discrimination in the work place.[68] In 1891, Pope Leo XIII issued *Rerum Novarum (On Capital and Labor)*, which defended private property while condemning the great chasm between rich and poor. Leo noted that poverty tempted the working class to be envious, violent, and revolutionary. He argued that workers had an obligation to give employers an honest day's work, and that employers had an obligation to provide fair wages and fair workloads, and that anything less was an assault on the family itself.[69] Other Catholics were more radical. Like all Catholics of his generation, Father Edward McGlynn of New York was taught that the faithful should see blessings in poverty. He rejected that notion, arguing that poverty could not be sanctified when it drove the faithful to

---

63. Gutman, "Protestantism and the American Labor Movement."

64. Rauschenbusch saw the Kingdom of God not celestial real estate, but as a way of life following transformations of conscience. See his: *Christianity and the Social Crisis* and *The Social Principles of Jesus*.

65. Morse's, *Church and the Working-Man* acknowledged class as a theological issue.

66. Evens, *Social Gospel in American Religion*, pp. 65–68.

67. Feldman, "Social Gospel and the Jews."

68. Higham's *Social Discrimination* explores anti-Semitism in the U.S. from 1830–1930, while Dolan's *American Catholic Experience* sheds documents American Protestant biases against Catholics and the papacy.

69. Leo XIII, *Rerum Novarum*, para. 15–20, 39–47.

resent God.[70] The pope excommunicated McGlynn for allegedly endorsing socialism. Others, such as Father Thomas McGrady, left the priesthood and became socialists as they found the Church's response to poverty incompatible with their faith.[71]

Robber barons of the Gilded Age frequently turned to science rather than theology to justify their attitudes towards work and wealth. Many saw Herbert Spencer's and Charles Darwin's ideas about the "survival of the fittest" as justification for social inequality.[72] Many asserted that laissez faire capitalism elevated man's nature, while government regulation and capitulation to workers' demands made men weak and effeminate.[73] Social Darwinists held that wealth was the product of hard work and self-discipline, and that the poor simply lacked these "biological traits."[74] The idea that only superior people should thrive complimented America's faith in rugged individualism and the Protestant work ethic.[75]

Steel magnate Andrew Carnegie said that competition was "best for the race,"[76] and argued that the concentration of wealth into a few hands was "clearly another step in the upward path of development."[77] He punctuated his beliefs in 1892 by slashing wages at his steel mill in Homestead, Pennsylvania and giving his partner, Henry Clay Frick, free reign to smash the resulting strike. Frick, who prided himself on his manliness and nerve, believed that only those who held stock in the business had the right to a say in company policies.[78] As striking workers and their families rioted, Frick coolly paid private guards to crush the strike by any means. Legally, he claimed, the only issue in question was his right to property.[79] At least

70. Shanaberger, "Edward McGlynn."

71. Dorn, "Comrade Father Thomas McGrady."

72. Social Darwinism is characterized by the belief that some people are a burden to society and slow social progress because they have inferior mental or physical traits. For a deeper look at American Social Darwinism and eugenics, see Black's *War against the Weak*.

73. Bannister, *Social Darwinism*, pp. 80–82.

74. Wyllie, "Social Darwinism and the Businessman."

75. See Davenport and Lloyd's *Rugged Individualism* for insights on these phenomena in America.

76. Hofstadter, *Social Darwinism*, pp. 30–34. Also see: Wyllie, "Social Darwinism and the Businessman" and Sumner's "What Social Classes Owe."

77. Carnegie, "Popular Illusions about Trusts," p. 144.

78. Standiford, *Meet You in Hell*, pp. 75–84.

79. Beginning in 1850, Alan Pinkerton's National Detective Agency served

16 people died in the crisis, which was emblematic of America's enduring conflict between management and labor.[80] As one historian noted, "What Frick and his fellow architects of corporate America did and said was readily accepted as the ethic of the business world, the dominant ethic of American society then and again, nearly a century later, in the time of Ronald Reagan."[81]

Like many industrialists, Carnegie believed that great wealth should be applied to great social progress.[82] They founded philanthropic organizations and gave money to public causes, but not always for reasons one might expect. Carnegie, for instance, did not base his charity on faith. Many industrialists, including Carnegie, funded research in eugenics with hopes of engineering a society void of "inferior" members.[83] They saw this gesture as a "venture in social betterment, not as an act of kindness as understood in Christianity."[84] They detested Christianity's appeal to charity because it sustained the lives of "unproductive" and "inferior" individuals.[85] Christians challenged social Darwinism's claim that only cold fierce competition could build great societies, and foster the advancement of civilization. As industrial tycoons were exploiting Gilded Age farmers and factory workers, Franciscan nuns and a family of physicians partnered to accomplish something extraordinary in the cornfields of southern Minnesota.

DO NO HARM

"My own religion has taught me to do all the good I could to my fellow man, and to as little harm as possible."[86] These are the words of William

---

government officials and industrialists as strike breakers, spies, and crime fighters. They were especially brutal against socialism and unions. The agency is now headquartered in Michigan and serves a global clientele. See O'Hara *Inventing the Pinkertons*. Also see Schreiner, *Henry Clay Frick*, pp. 69–85.

80. Krause, *Battle for Homestead*," pp. 5–6.

81. Schreiner, p. x.

82. Carnegie, "The Gospel of Wealth," p. 536.

83. Black's *War Against the Weak* is an astonishing account of how wealthy Americans worked with international scientists, including Nazis, to establish a means of improving the quality of the human race by way of birth control, selective "breeding" and sterilization.

84. Zunz, *Philanthropy in America*, p. 2.

85. Hawkins, *Social Darwinism*, pp. 142–144.

86. Blistein and Burns, *Mayo Clinic*, p. 27.

God Bless Our Cubicles

Worrall Mayo, who emigrated from England to the U.S. in 1846, and with his sons, William and Charles, created one of the world's most prestigious medical institutions, the Mayo Clinic. The Mayos' approach to medicine and patient care was a radical departure from business as usual in the late 1800s and the social Darwinism that so often characterized enterprise in the Gilded Age. It remains a powerful reminder that success does not require vicious competition, nor do exemplary organizations need to rely on gargantuan salaries and bonuses to draw the best and brightest employees.

The tornado that ripped through Rochester, Minnesota on August 21, 1883 left 37 dead and 200 injured. The small farming community had no hospital and so the Sisters of St. Francis, led by Sr. Alfred Moes, partnered with the Mayo father and sons team to care for the wounded in the old dance hall. Six years later, the partnership between the Mayos and the Franciscans produced St. Mary's Hospital. Several other buildings would be added to the Mayo enterprise over the next few decades, and several more partnerships would be cultivated for the advancement of medical research and education.

When St. Mary's opened, the scientific revolution was just beginning to have an impact on medicine. Most hospitals of the era were unsanitary places where folks went to die. Antibiotics were unknown, many physicians were quacks, hospitals lacked labs and libraries, and there was only a nascent understanding of anatomical systems and pathologies. The Mayo commitment to patient-centered care transformed not only the relationship between health care providers and patients, but the entire scientific approach to diagnosis and treatment.

William Mayo Sr. had been schooled by John Dalton, a Quaker, who was denied teaching positions in English universities because of his religion. Dalton taught Mayo chemistry and instilled in his student a firm reverence for the scientific method and social justice. The Quaker tradition held that one's social esteem should be based on the dignity of one's work rather than the class into which one is born, and that all individuals, regardless of gender, race, or background, deserved respect. The lessons reinforced Mayo's Anglican formation that urged him to always be of service to others, even when he was less than perfect in practice.[87] He thus became a natural ally

---

87. While progressive and philanthropic, the Mayos were men of their times. William Sr. was present in Mankato, MN when 39 Sioux warriors were executed for their part in Little Crow's War, 1862, and among the doctors who dug up the corpses of the dead so they could be used for dissection and study (Clapesattle, *The Doctors Mayo*, p. 77). The Mayos conformed to segregation, and did not hire African American doctors

of the Franciscan charism, which taught the sisters in training to be nurses to see the face of Jesus Christ in every patient.

The hospital's business model was essentially that of a ministry. Unlike the robber barons of the era, the Mayo brothers were committed to the idea that the spiritual care of their clients was as important as the material. They broke with tradition by establishing a new paradigm for medical interventions that replaced the individualistic model with cooperation and collaboration. In the individualistic model, doctors guarded their knowledge as to retain as many clients as possible as each paid fees for services. The collaborative model saw doctors constantly consulting with other doctors, nurses, and researchers, in order to better understand diseases, surgical procedures, post-surgical care, diagnostics, and preventative health care.

The Mayo doctors placed the patient at the center of their practice, which had both procedural and financial implications. To improve patient care, they developed sterilization protocols, kept libraries in their clinics so the staff could access current research, placed labs close to surgical rooms so biopsies could be done swiftly during surgeries, and invented numerous surgical instruments and procedures to improve patient outcomes. The clinic reserved a large share of its income for research, and regularly sent physicians across the globe to learn new techniques and to share what their own experiences had taught them. This was an extraordinary exchange of "secrets of the trade," and it was happening as medical specializations as we know them were just emerging.

The clinic also played Robin Hood to the poor, as it used fees paid by wealthy patients to cover the cost of caring for those without money. They offered free care to nurses, ministers, teachers, and state employees with meager incomes. The Mayo brothers vowed that the inability to pay for services would never compromise the quality of care, and believed that income should not determine health.[88] They had all the luxuries that other affluent entrepreneurs enjoyed, but lived on half of their income and placed surplus revenue and other assets in a trust for public use.

The Mayo Clinic's success is due in large part to the Franciscan sisters who demonstrated that compassion and self-sacrifice, including the vow of poverty, were not merely good for medical outcomes, but could be elements of a sustainable business model. The Mayo paradigm of service

---

until the 1970s. See: *The Mayo Clinic: Faith Hope and Science*, directed by Erik Ewers, Christopher Loren Ewers, and Ken Burns. (2018; PBS Distribution), DVD.

88. Clapesattle, *Doctors Mayo*, p. 378.

emphasized collaboration in a business world that was highly combative, humility in a business world that ran largely on autocratic dictates, and empathy in a business world that saw humanity as a pocket to picked and a cog in the machinery of production. The clinic earned it place as one of the best medical institutions in the world by insisting that professionals be excellent in character and craft, not by insisting that stockholders get rich.

A BEWILDERED HERD

Like several of America's "founding fathers," many 20th century business executives and elected officials lacked confidence in the average person's powers of reasoning. Journalist and social critic Walter Lippmann asserted that the average American was not up to the task of self-governance.[89] He penned in 1922 that people rely on stereotypes to steady our wobbly sense of self and judgement of others.[90] He also held that, while people believe that they are masters of their own will, they are the product of social norms and propaganda.[91]

Lippmann's opinions came in the wake of World War I, the catastrophe that killed over 10 million people, and wed militarism to modern technology.[92] The war obliterated the Austrian, Ottoman, and Russian empires, and triggered the Bolshevik Revolution.[93] It amplified doubts that humanity was naturally reasonable, good-willed, and capable of democracy. In the 1920s, the West endured economic devastation and psychological disorientation. Many placed their hopes in an elite of group of strongmen who would purge their countries of enemies within and enforce radical policies to make their nations great again.

Lippmann argued that, despite the glorification of democracy, people are not equally competent and not equally dedicated to working arduously

---

89. Lippmann, son of Jewish immigrants from Eastern Europe, was a founding editor of the *New Republic* magazine, originally progressive in its views, then more conservative during the Cold War. Lippmann coined the terms" stereotype" and "Cold War." See Steel, *Walter Lippmann*.

90. Lippmann, *Public Opinion*, pp. 5–7; 30–38.

91. Ibid, p. 64.

92. Sondhaus' *World War One* eyes WWI with a global perspective and attention to culture and prejudice.

93. Gerwarth's *Vanquished* explains how World War II was seeded in the failed peace of World War I.

for each other's well-being.[94] He complained that American education did not produce individuals who knew what "insiders" of businesses and finance knew, and so produced graduates capable of rising only to the level of "amateur executives" and mediocre managers.[95] The common citizen, he surmised, was unable to anticipate problems, effectively analyze them, propose solutions, and determine the implications of those solutions. "The public must be put in its place," he preached, "so each of us may live free of the trampling and the roar of a bewildered herd."[96]

In 1939 Freud joined the conversation about humanity's dismal nature and concluded that civilization was forever teetering between benevolent cooperation and mutual extermination. The super-ego—the cultural ideals, theologies, and ethical norms that guided the conscience—could not forever keep the id— the bestial side of human nature— in check.[97] Eventually, he argued, individuals will resent demands that they must sacrifice their appetites and conveniences for the sake of civilization.[98] Freud held that the commandment to "love they neighbor as thyself" was impossible to fulfill because there would never be enough love to neutralize the passions and aggression of human beings. He noted that, "Anyone who follows such a precept in present-day civilization only puts himself [sic] at disadvantage *vis-a-vis* the person who disregards it."[99]

Spiritual protagonists of the 20th century had their critics. Marxism, social Darwinism, and Freudianism challenged the notion that here was anything divine about the purpose of our lives. World War II, the Holocaust, the nuclear arms race, and wars of de-colonization during the Cold War seemed to underscore the folly of believing that human beings were much better than crazed primates hysterically trying to get all the bananas, and attacking anyone in the way.

LESSONS OF HISTORICAL LEGACIES

What does all this history of ideas have to do with us? Are we really a "bewildered herd" that must be managed because we lack reason? Are we little

94. Lippmann, *Phantom Public*, p. 28.
95. Ibid., 138–139.
96. Ibid., p. 145.
97. Freud, *Id and the Ego*.
98. Freud, *Civilization and its Discontents*, pp. 61–63; 81.
99. Ibid, p. 90.

more than hysterical primates embattled in bloody competition? Are we God's sacred creation called to a life of dignity and spiritual development? Are we paying for sins with miserable jobs? Are we abusing others because they are not "the fittest?" Do we believe that God owes us material wealth for our faith? Do we believe we must be charitable to all or only to those who "deserve" it?

There are at least two important lessons of this history. First, whether we are aware of it or not, modern American culture embodies every attitude towards work and wealth that has ever been espoused in Western civilization. Even when they contradict each other, our beliefs about labor, social class, charity, distribution of wealth, affluence, poverty, and corporate regulation that were normed into society hundreds of years ago still influence our thinking. Whether we are aware of our own assumptions or have consciously assimilated popular beliefs is another story.

The second lesson pertains to the fragility of our attitudes, values, and thoughts. We are social creatures, and as such, we are profoundly influenced by what others do and say. In the workplace, spirituality and moral ideals often melt away in the heat of peer pressure, especially when our status or income is threatened. In the 14th century, for example, many Christians burned Jews because it was rumored that Jews caused the bubonic Plague.[100] We may mock the ignorance of such superstition, but we too are capable of irrational thinking. Consider the ads we consume daily that tell us that if we buy a certain product, we will be happier, sexier, more powerful, and worthy of adoration. Consider the money we spend on things we do not need.

The narratives that rattle around in our heads at work influence our attitudes and actions, yet often remain subconscious. The workplace is frequently an environment in which people do more than complete a set of tasks for a paycheck. It is a place where we negotiate power and influence; it is place where we build a sense of self and judge ourselves against the failures or achievements of others; it is a place where we have opportunities to lift others up and bless them with our kindness and respect, or tear them down and batter their reputations and self-esteem. The workplace is therefore both a carnival of egos and a venue for ministry.

---

100. Cohn, Jr., "After the Black Death."

REFLECTIONS

1. Which of the following propositions best represents your beliefs and why?
    a. God wants us to work hard and struggle in the world because we are sinners
    b. God proves his love for us by allowing us to accumulate fortune while on Earth
    c. God has nothing to do with work or the workplace, because nature dictates that those who do nothing to earn a living will perish, and those who work hard thrive
    d. God calls everyone to be a co-creator of life, which means being responsible for our sustenance and helping others thrive as well

2. Identify the things relative to work to which you feel entitled, explain why you feel entitled to those things, and describe how those entitlements might contribute to or diminish your spiritual growth and integrity.

3. Think about an experience in which a co-worker made a mistake or revealed a lack of knowledge or skill, and determine whether your response was empathetic, charitable, judgmental, cynical, helpful, or punitive, and why.

4. Instructors: How can you help students detect the presence of social Darwinism, the Protestant work ethic, and the Gospel of Wealth in today's society, and explore their impact on our lives?

5. Instructors: What are your own biases relative to social Darwinism, the Protestant work ethic, and the Gospel of Wealth? In what ways might these biases "leak" into your curriculum and instruction, and what could you do to keep your instruction objective?

3

Dragging God into the Workplace

JESUS THE ENTREPRENEUR

THE IDEA OF BRINGING spirituality to bear in the workplace is nothing new, but it remains controversial. Contemporary efforts to bring spirituality into the workplace are the result of two distinct events. The first was the "Jesus Movement" of the late 1960s and 1970s that saw millions of Americans turn to Christian fundamentalism and recommit their lives to God by being "born again." They were motivated in part by a desire to restore social order and a sense of moral decency that they thought was ruined by anti-war demonstrations, feminism, race riots, gay rights, drug use, and open contempt for authority. Many looked to religion as a stabilizing and cleansing agent, and sought to remake society in the image of their interpretation of the Bible. Organizations, such as Jerry Falwell's Moral Majority, Pat Roberson's Christian Coalition, and James Dobson's Family Research Council, generated voter's guides and worked for political candidates who promised to restore Christian values through legislation.[1]

The second event was economic hardship in the 1970s and 1980s brought about by inflation, oil embargos, the cost of war in Vietnam, government spending on public assistance programs, and technological innovation that resulted in down-sizing, and outsourcing. Workers were

---

1. FitzGerald's *Evangelicals* examines evangelical ideology and political agendas in recent history.

agitated as their productivity increased and wages stagnated.[2] In that era, management took notice and began to explore "people centered" management.[3] Books with titles such as, *Managing with the Wisdom of Love*, and *Leading with the Soul* proliferated.[4] Ford Motor Company shifted away from its traditional belief that workers were robotic objects that would work faster and more efficiently with strident supervision, and moved towards the notion that when workers had their psychological and physical needs met, they were more productive.[5] A study of senior executives announced that, "We need to integrate spirituality into management," as "no organization can survive long without spirituality and soul."[6] Managers learned that respect for workers' needs improved motivation and was good for business.[7]

Others who wanted to infuse spirituality in the workplace took a more evangelical tone. The Faith at Work Movement (FAW) aims to bring religion into the workplace. It is Christian, but has no single creed, nor single executive leadership. It has multiple goals, strategies, theological perspectives, and many leaders.[8] FAW draws inspiration from Protestantism and the Social Gospel,[9] and from Catholic teachings.[10] Chuck Ripka's Riverview Community Bank of Otsego, Minnesota was once an example of FAW.

Ripka was a poster boy for the merger between evangelism and money lending. In 2004, he reported that Jesus said to him, "Chuck, I wanted to show you how to talk to people about me at work, and I wanted to prove to you that you would be able to do that and prosper." Ripka also claimed

---

2. Cowie's *Stayin' Alive* explores how class conflict over social reform, was exploited by conservatives.

3. Burack, "Spirituality in the Workplace."

4. See: Marcic, *Managing*, Bolman and Deal's, *Leading with Soul*; and Chappell's, *Soul of Business*.

5. Burack, "Turnaround and Renewal."

6. Mitroff and Denton, "A Study of Spirituality."

7. Cavanaugh and Bandsuch, "Virtue as a Benchmark."

8. Miller, *God at Work*.

9. Social Gospel Movement emerged at the turn of the 20th century, and asserted that Christians had a duty to activate the Gospels in labor reform, public education, and care for the poor and sick. It inspired Christian socialism and the Catholic Worker Movement. See Evans, *The Social Gospel in American Religion*.

10. Examples include Leo XIII, *Rerum Novarum* (The condition of labor), John Paul II, *Laborem Exercens* (On human work), and the United States Catholic Bishops' *Economic justice for all*.

that Jesus told him to "start a new bank based on Christian principles," and said that, "if you do all the things I want you to do, I promise I'll take care of the bottom line," and "cause such a rate of growth, the secular world will have to take notice."[11] The words attributed to Jesus echoed the familiar Protestant mantra that prosperity is evidence of one's strength of faith. The message had an odd theology. It was all about getting the secular world to notice Jesus, as if Jesus were saying, "Alright . . . OK . . . You were not impressed with what I did on the cross . . . raising the dead . . . a few miracles . . . fine . . . Will you notice me if I make this guy rich?"

Odd theology or not, people who thirsted for high-yielding investments gathered to drink from the anointed bank's well. The bank was different from other banks. Employees were sensitive to their customers' problems and they took time on the job to pray with them, even if it was just a quick blessing at the drive-through window.

When state regulators closed Riverview Community Bank in 2009, it had over $100 million in assets. Like many banks that year, it held loans backed by investments in real estate that plunged in value as the mortgage market collapsed.[12] The closure of Riverview Community Bank caused some to wonder whether God is actually concerned with the "bottom line," and if Ripka's message ever squared with what Jesus preached about money.

Ripka was not an ordained minister, but he understood that people yearn for a sense of security in the secular world. He had the courage to bring God into public discourse and the workplace, and espoused habits, such as communal prayer and compassion on the job, that many people liked.[13] He acknowledged that workers do not live by bread alone. This is no small matter in the American workplace. Even in our highly secularized society, 90 percent of Americans report that they believe in God, and 60 percent say they pray on a daily basis.[14]

Most employers do not integrate spirituality into the workplace as did Ripka. Many enforce policies that are intended to eliminate religious discrimination on the job through training in religious diversity and honoring employees' right to participate in religious rituals. These actions represent institutional responses, which do not require employers or employees to be deeply committed to anyone's well-being or dignity; they simply mandate

---

11. Hoffman, "Feds Close," lines 1–8..
12. Serres, "Regulators Close Otsego Bank," lines 3–7.
13. Ripka, *God out of the Box*.
14. Reilly, Sirgy, and Gorman, *Work and Quality of Life*, p. 430.

that behaviors do not discriminate or give the appearance of discriminating. Institutions, however, cannot create policies and hold individuals accountable for every behavior under the sun, nor regulate private thoughts. Institutions can comply with state and federal laws, but that is not the same as integrating spirituality into the workplace.

Management cannot do what spirituality is intended to do. Management is about orchestrating productive economic activity. Spirituality is meant to help us see the face of God in others, and to see our work as a ministry. This flies in the face of cultural norms that venerate certain faces and despise others, and that rank people by what they do for a living and how much money they make. The notions that God can be seen in everyone's face and that all work is a ministry have not always been easy for me to honor, but they are familiar and dear to me. They were central to the Benedictine and Jesuit spiritual formation I received in formal education. Currently, as the nation's leaders openly attack the dignity of others, model hateful partisanship, and allow corporate criminals to dodge legal consequences, I sense that new ethical norms have replaced the old, and wonder how long society can survive without empathy and cooperation.

GOOD OL' MIKE BOSKO

Mike Bosko (not his real name) was my classmate at St. Bridget School in Minneapolis, where we undertook the tutelage of Benedictine sisters and rounded off our lessons by going to Confession, attending Masses, and reciting the Stations of the Cross. Mike was mild boy with a broad, sleepy-eyed smile and kind manners. He often came to school wearing a uniform that had not been laundered or pressed for weeks. His blonde hair often looked as if it had been dipped in motor oil and dried by a hurricane, and his teeth were encrusted with yellow tarter. Mike frequently got lost when students read aloud. When called upon to answer the teacher's questions, would grin silently as his gaze met those of anticipatory classmates. He regularly picked his nose, placing whatever he fished from his nostrils neatly between his lips. Mike was always the last to be chosen when captains selected their classmates for kickball during recess, but he never complained. He laughed and cheered his teammates.

In our reading lessons, Mike was in the third track, which meant that he struggled laboriously to articulate words on a page that others eloquently read in seconds. He got lots of Cs and Ds on his report cards, and the priest who distributed them in class always whispered to him with a smile, "Mike you are a good boy, and I know you can do better next time." The teachers treated Mike with steady respect and encouragement. They saw that he got the after school help he needed to learn math and grammar, and they saw that nobody bullied on him on the playground or in the lunchroom.

Mike was one of God's children, and so was everyone else. The faculty reminded students that God created all of us for some special purpose, and that all of us had unique gifts to use as we made our way in the world. They taught us that as we grew up we would hear God calling us and then know the special purpose for which we were created. Our duty was to act, and to take up work for the love of God and for the sake of society's betterment. The nuns emphasized that all work could be the work of God, and that God did not care whether a person was a doctor, janitor, police officer, cook, or a bank teller. They assured us that, as long as we worked to the best of our ability and were kind to others, every job was a ministry.

I remember starring at Mike, and wondering what he would be when he grew up. I assumed that Mike would work in some kind of job that did not require a college degree. He would work at a gas station or a grocery store, I mused; but that was OK: he would get up every day just like me and go to work, and he would earn enough money to have his own little apartment and something to eat. I recall feeling comforted by the knowledge that no matter what Mike did, he was here because God wanted him to be here, and somehow he possessed all the gifts he needed to take care of himself and be the person God wanted him to be. He would go through the liturgical seasons just like me, and celebrate Christmas and Easter. When death came, he would go with faith and God would reward him. As a kid, I felt sorry that Mike struggled with his lessons and hygiene, but I had no doubt that he was equal with me before God's eyes and that God would never abandon him.

I often wondered about how Mike did in the world. I know that people sometimes single out people like him in the workplace for special abuse. Social Darwinism thrives. Some like to pick on the weak because it amuses them or because they think this impresses people they want to impress. Others take advantage of the tender and the meek, and exploit their labor and good will. Recently, I searched for Mike on the Internet. I saw that he died a few years ago and is buried in a military cemetery. He had been in the armed forces, but where? Vietnam? El Salvador? Bosnia? Iraq? I wondered. Did he rape and torture? Did he kill? Did he save lives? Did he believe that he was using his gifts to serve God? Did he love himself? Did he believe he was always in the presence of God? He was in his mid-fifties when he died. God bless him.

WE DON'T DO JESUS HERE

Believing that every job is a ministry is one thing, and actually being free to talk about work in that way on the job is another. I was reminded of this when I began my work at a public institution after working for many years in parochial schools. The winter break was before us and employees gathered around tables festooned with green and red cloths and decorations. There were heaping platters of international delicacies, bowls filled with vegetable dips and sauces, cold plates of shrimp, streaming trays of chicken, beef, noodles, and rice, and cleverly arranged assortments of candied breads and cookies. The mood was mellow and festive. Wine flowed and office mates chuckled away their fatigue as jazzy holiday music floated around us. I raised my cup at one point and happily chanted, "Merry Christmas!" A moment of silence followed as people collectively caught their breath and darted their eyes from one person to the next. A few looked stunned, as if thinking to themselves, "Didn't she get the memo?" A friend leaned toward me and whispered, "This is a public institution; we don't do Jesus here."

Chuck Ripka, the Benedictines, and staff at the Mayo Clinic got away with their proclamations of "Merry Christmas" because they worked in environments that normed the open celebration of faith. I was in an environment that normed silence on the matter of ecclesiastical affairs, and in which folks were hostile and dismissive towards those who were openly pious.

Many in the workforce take their spirituality seriously, but must pretend it does not exist when they get to work. For the sake of collegial cooperation and protecting people from discrimination based on religious affiliations and creed, many organizations permit employees to take time away from work to comply with religious obligations, and prohibit religious proselytizing on the job. The Equal Employment Opportunity Commission's *Compliance Manual* states that employers must consider whether an employees' expression of religious faith, prayer or proselytizing would be disruptive to others on the job or constitute harassment before prohibiting it.[15] The statement is slippery because the terms "proselytizing" and "disruptive" are subjective, and mean different things to different people.

Most employees do not read the entire EEOC manual. They take their cues for how to act in the workplace from what the human resource office emphasizes, and from the behaviors that are normed by co-workers. In some environments, people consider the casual reference to one's religious upbringing or experience as proselytizing, and in other environments, people do not make that assumption. Some people protest when members of work teams mention practices that come from religious ideas, even if the practices were purely secular in nature. Others welcome the ideas and see that they can be applied without theological overtones.

Strict prohibition against referencing the source of values and principles that inform our thinking process and priorities is challenging, but spirituality does not need neon icons or quotations from scripture in order to be effective. The effect comes when individuals are able to translate spiritual values and principles into universal values and principles. Putting our commitment to good will, respect for others, and support for the vulnerable into action is often more effective than putting it into words. Still, it is sometimes very frustrating to keep the inspiration for our actions in the closet.

Arguably, having to translate things into "politically correct" language is a form of discrimination. We are told not to take personally the requirements of political correctness, as they are well-intended and seek to foster inclusivity and social harmony. Admittedly, political correctness can feel inauthentic. Whether it is a betrayal of one's spirituality, however, is a matter of conscience.

POLITICALLY CORRECT

Political correctness has two faces. The first is benevolent. It puts the well-being of the community ahead of the wants of the individual. It is motivated by the desire to advance justice and to honor the dignity of divergent and competing perspectives. The second face is malevolent, as it can be repressive and applied capriciously. Political correctness can be exploited by people who want only to appear benevolent and thus remain in the good graces of those with power or access to resources. Political correctness lives

---

15. Equal Employment Opportunity Commission, *EEOC Compliance Manual*, pp. 77–78.

closer to the ego than spirituality. Political correctness often takes it cue from whatever consensus society reaches at a given time about right and wrong, while spirituality (ideally) takes its cue from universal and fixed principles and values.

It seems counter-intuitive that political correctness is not necessarily an ally of one's spirituality, but the two are not always destined for alignment. Despite the good intentions of people who enforce the use of politically correct language, set politically correct boundaries around conversations, or pursue politically correct agendas, political correctness can have adverse consequences and be co-opted for ignoble purposes. Francine, the woman who complained about Benji's driving tests' passing rate and "Rosie Rainbow's" agenda, believes that political correctness has gotten in the way of healthy professional communication and public safety. Scholars have observed when open conversation about bigotry are repressed, people become paranoid about what others are thinking, and skeptical about what motivates benevolent rhetoric.[16] As one scholar opined, "In some ways race was easier to understand and discuss when it was that obvious impetus for public water hosings and police dog attacks," and that political correctness has created the paradox wherein race does not matter and matters a great deal at the same time.[17]

Dr. Sally Satel reveals how political correctness has resulted in very bad health care outcomes as physicians and administrators flock towards popular trends and away from sound medicine.[18] Dr. Miriam Grossman echoed Satel's concerns, asserting that the unwritten rules that govern what doctors can talk about with their clients on college campuses leaves many students at risk for psychological distress, disease, and unwanted life changes.[19] Criminologist Thomas Gabor complained that the politically correct practice of ignoring race and other demographic features of offenders diminishes the ability of the justice system to find ways to reduce crime.[20] Others have explored the damage done to liberal arts education

---

16. Jackson's *Racial Paranoia* explores this phenomenon with profound vignettes and insights.

17. Ibid, p. 10–11.

18. Satel's *How Political* explains how adverse health outcomes result from misguided benevolence.

19. Grossman's, *Unprotected* discloses how trendy beliefs sustain public ignorance.

20. Gabor, "The Suppression of Crime Statistics."

when instructors glorify identity politics, and multiculturalism, while vilifying classics in Western literature.[21]

Being politically correct establishes one's credentials in a certain group at a given point in time and place. The esteem these groups extend to us can sometimes become more important that the spirituality we are trying to cultivate. As the definition of what is politically correct shifts from time to time, it makes a feeble cornerstone for our moral outlook.

Being politically correct on the job is not the same as being committed to spiritual growth, compassion for all who suffer, or unconditional respect for the dignity of each person. One can, for example, be politically correct and still inflict injury to others. Employers who hire individuals because they add to the diversity of the team rather add to the competence of the team may be putting the organization and all who rely upon its products and services at risk. In the case of the high school that awards diplomas to students because it is politically incorrect to withhold diplomas, the school risks sending young adults off to work or college who soon discover that they do not have the knowledge and skills required to achieve their goals. In the case of the lawmakers who seek a means of demonstrating their allegiance to powerful peers, they may vote for legislation that they have never studied, only to find that their vote helped to disenfranchise the people they promised to protect.

Political correctness can be smoke and mirrors. Organizations are sometimes able to hide their more odious offenses against justice and love of neighbor when they grab the headlines for a job well done. For example, a food corporation that increases the percentage of ethnic minorities and women in administrative and management positions may win lots of praise from politically correct consumers, but still produce food that contributes greatly to public illness because of its high fat and sugar content.

Being politically correct on the job signals our need to be part of the gang. Being spiritual on the job signals our need to be part of something bigger than the gang. Even when some our spiritual values mirror aspects of political correctness, spirituality differs from political correctness inasmuch as it ultimately answers to God and not to the majority of the day.

Both spirituality and political correctness are intended to keep our egos in check and to steer our conscience toward justice and respect for others. Neither one is an absolute prophylactic against errors of judgment or egotistical biases. It is possible that in order to activate spirituality in the

---

21. See the essays contain in Newfield and Strickland, *After Political Correctness*.

workplace, one may have to assess one's own devotion to being politically correct. Spirituality might require one to speak critically of prevailing political correctness. Evaluating the benefits and detriments of political correctness necessitates a steady routine of prayer, discernment, and consultation with spiritual mentors. We may discover that spirituality is hard work, and that it is much easier to conform to somebody else's conscience. We may discover that we are a deeper well of humanity than we thought we were.

REFLECTIONS

1. To what extent does your workplace openly respect the influence faith and spirituality have had on your life and your work, and does the organization's respect or disrespect for spiritual formation matter to you and why?

2. In what ways could your work be considered a ministry, and how could you improve the way you approach it as a ministry?

3. How has political correctness affected your thinking and communication with others about your values, beliefs, thoughts, problem-solving, and relationships?

4. What do you think are the key differences between politically correct thinking and your spiritual convictions and commitments?

5. Instructors: To what extent does your curriculum integrate students' personal reflection on their epistemological development and vulnerability to public opinion and peer pressure?[22]

6. Instructors: To what extent is your curriculum determined by political correctness? What are the adverse effects of political correctness in academia and what are some strategies for overcoming the adverse effects of political correctness in academia?

---

22. Epistemological development refers to the way a person's understanding of what constitutes knowledge, how knowledge is created, and what criteria is important in assessing credibility and reliability of knowledge is refined by way of experience and education.

4

Song of the Whistle Blowers

SACRED NARRATIVES

THERE ARE MANY WAYS to integrate spirituality into the workplace. Some are more dramatic than others, and some are more dangerous than others. The conflicts we encounter on the job vary, and certainly responding to a co-worker's violation of personal space is different from responding to corporate exploitation of public money and trust. Regardless of the issues, those who choose to engage their spirituality to right what is wrong are often invited to use their prophetic voice. That may sound rather dramatic and sensational, but using the prophetic voice simply means that one has the courage to call attention to the gap between the organization's espoused ideals and values and what is actually practiced. Ideally, the prophetic voice calls others to heal wounds, seek justice, and extend compassion to the weak and wounded.

Prophetic voices are not always the loudest voices, and those with wise prophetic insights are not always highly visible or publically revered. Sometimes prophetic voices are manifest in what a student says to a teacher, or in what a homeless person says to a stranger, or in reflections shared between friends. In using one's prophetic voice, one does not always know which memo, phone call, or conversation will be the one to give hope to others, or inspire a change in behavior. Prophets sew lots of seeds, but are not always around to harvest the crop.

Engaging our prophetic voices is risky. Sometimes individuals who bring their spirituality to bear on their work lose their jobs, their reputations, esteem in high places, their friends and family, and sometimes, they even lose their lives. Society teaches us which causes are worthy of sacrifice and which are not worthy. The prophetic individual is the one who assesses how well society's priorities and agenda are with the love of God and neighbor.

What follows is a discussion about three individuals, Karen Silkwood, Bennett Omalu, and Roy Bourgeois, who all took the prophetic path as they spoke truth to power. None of these individuals began their careers with the intention of becoming famous or revolutionary. Their stories are remarkable because they illustrate the power of awareness and the profundity of incremental growth in the courage to speak truth. They are extraordinary inasmuch as they exemplify how everyday decisions bring the love of God to bear on the world.

ABALONE ON ROCK

Nearly 50 years after she was found in a smashed Honda Civic several yards off the road in a muddy stream, Karen Silkwood's death remains mysterious. The 28-year-old had been a laboratory analyst for Kerr-McGee Nuclear Corporation, inspecting plutonium pellets and fuel rods used in nuclear reactors. On November 13, 1974, after just about 26 months on the job, she was scheduled to meet with a union official and a *New York Times* reporter to present documents confirming that Kerr-McGee had falsified records pertaining to the quality of fuel rods and plant safety. Her death was ruled an accident. The files of documents she had with her at the time of the wreck never surfaced.[1] In 1979, the Oklahoma City federal court found Kerr-McGee liable for negligence and personal injury and awarded Silkwood's estate $10 million. Kerr-McGee appealed and later Silkwood's parents were forced to accept a $1.38 million in a settlement that did not require the company to admit wrong-doing or guilt.[2]

At the time of Silkwood's death, Americans were frazzled by the Vietnam War, the Watergate scandal, and civil rights' crusades. Inflation was up and conflict in the Middle East produced increases in the cost of oil, lubricant of the U.S. economy. Scientists and politicians alike confidently huffed that nuclear power was a clean and endless source of energy. The credibility of those assertions was challenged by 25 years research on the hazards of

---

1. Rashke's, *The Killing* is a biography that accepts the theory that Silkwood was murdered.
2. Oliver, "Firm to Settle Silkwood," lines 1–3.

radioactive substances. The credibility and morality of the government was suspect in those days.³ Put simply, in the 1970s, Americans were not in the mood to believe everything authorities said.

Friends said that Karen was not a rebel by nature, but "stood up for what she believed in, and was as tenacious as abalone on a rock."⁴ She graduated from high school with stellar grades. She volunteered at a hospital, and earned a degree in medical technology in 1965. At a time when many young adults were in the streets agitating for peace and civil rights, she was a young mother in trouble. Her unfaithful husband drank too much and mismanaged the family's income. Determined to build a stable life, she took a job at Kerr-McGee in Crescent, Oklahoma in 1972. She was divorced and her ex-husband had custody of their children.

The Oil, Chemical, and Atomic Workers union (OCAW) that represented Silkwood and her co-workers launched a strike in the fall of 1972. Picketers were replaced by local boys barely out of high school who thought that $3 dollars an hour was good money. They were given little training. They were not told that plutonium is 20,000 times more toxic than cobra venom, and so when they returned to work on their farms, they were unaware that they had been exposed to highly toxic materials.⁵ Work conditions at Kerr-McGee resembled work conditions of Henry Frick's and Andrew Carnegie's 19th century factories. They were strenuous, with twelve-hour shifts, seven-day work weeks, and constant threat of exposure to hazardous materials. Kerr-McGee had incentives to cut corners, to lie about the quality of pins and rods it manufactured, and to bend the numbers when measuring contamination in the workplace. Kerr-McGee was already the nation's largest uranium producer with one billion in assets, but wanted more.⁶

Silkwood's documentation of the plant's accidents, distribution of substandard rods, poor training, and indifference to the worker's health were the notes of a trained professional with a degree in medical technology. Still, because she wanted the company to take responsibility for the dangers it presented to the public and to its employees, she drew scathing criticism.

3. DeBenedetti's *American Ordeal* traces formal protests against war and nuclear proliferation back to the 1940s and 1950s, during which prominent scientists, clergy, and concerns citizens confronted American militarism and raised serious questions about American morality.
4. Rashke, p. 7.
5. Rashke, pp. 14–15.
6. Kohn, "Malignant Giant," para. 16–19.

Her cause generated division in the ranks of Kerr-McGee's employees. Some quietly supported and encouraged her, while others accused her of poisoning herself, endangering their jobs, and of being a rabble-rousing drug addict. Silkwood's personal life made her professional accusations the target of ridicule. She had sex outside marriage, she liked to drink, and sometimes took Quaaludes—a sedative legally prescribed for her. Despite her imperfections, Silkwood is remembered as a "Good Samaritan," who genuinely cared about public health and the safety of her co-workers.[7] Many believe that her death was part of a conspiracy to silence her.

Silkwood's story underscores corporate intolerance for criticism of its operations. Her prophetic voice—the critic of the status quo—was seen as a threat to productivity and profit. She was the modern version of strikers who were beaten and killed as they protested in Homestead, Pennsylvania back in 1892. Silkwood's actions went beyond those of an employee who did not want to get cancer from exposure to radioactive particles; she challenged the time-honored unwritten law that entrepreneurs must be free to do whatever they believe is necessary to stay in business. Reaction against Silkwood proved that the captains of industry in the 20th century were just as ferocious about employees' obedience as were the robber barons of the Gilded Age. In 1971, former President of General Motors, James Roche, lambasted critics with the language of Cold War paranoia:

> Some critics are now busily eroding another support of free enterprise—the loyalty of a management team, with its unifying values of cooperative work. Some of the enemies of business now encourage an employee to be disloyal to the enterprise. They want to create suspicion and disharmony, and pry into the proprietary interests of the business. However this is labelled—industrial espionage, whistle blowing, or professional responsibility—it is another tactic for spreading disunity and creating conflict.[8]

Spirituality is also concerned with the "proprietary interests of the business." It sees that the interests of the owners, managers, and employees as the same, because each has an interest in what is good for society. In our form of capitalism, "proprietary interests" are frequently severed from humanitarian interests. Roche's reference to "prying" into "proprietary interests of the business" suggest that a great wall divides the entrepreneur from consumers and workers, and that the entrepreneur's interests

---

7. See Rashke, *Killing of Karen Silkwood*, for biographical details.
8. Roche, "The Competitive System," p. 141.

are more important than all others. Roche's exaltation of loyalty suggests that employees shall have no other gods before the company. As "espionage" "whistle blowing," and "professional responsibility" are synonymous to Roche, he leaves no honorable way for employees to express legitimate concerns for their own or the public's well-being. The contempt that Gilded Age robber barons had for reformers lives on. A 1987 study that found that 84% of whistle blowers in the private sector had been fired, and 75% of whistle blowers in government jobs were demoted.[9] Thirty years later, whistle blowers still lose their jobs, and suffer devastating consequences including alienation from friends and family, a damaged reputation in the industry, and loss of homes and pensions.[10]

Silkwood's ordeal confirms that inhumanity in the workplace is often systematic, and that sometimes those within the organization work with external agencies against the best interests of humanity. In the case of Kerr-McGee, the company had very friendly relationships with the Atomic Energy Commission, which set what some say were dangerously high thresholds of safe exposure to radioactive contamination, and the Office of Occupational Health and Safety, which many argued were lax in their approach to hazards in the plant. Silkwood's story reveals the cozy relations between the Kerr-McGee's executives and those who kept the status quo intact, including: the doctors who gave distorted health information to company's employees; the managers who harassed employees with impunity; the regulators who looked the other way; the attorneys who vilified unions and activists; and, the lawmakers who failed to pass legislation that would have protected employees and communities from Kerr-McGee's machinations when it was just a small oil empire breaking into the business of uranium mining.[11]

Silkwood's actions on behalf of public safety and corporate integrity were not overtly based on religious doctrines. Silkwood is not known for preaching justice in the name of Jesus, or for leading prayer meetings that called for civil disobedience. She offered no theological argument for her actions; yet, she refused to be a member of the "bewildered herd," and

9. Bennett, "Trading Cards," p. 24.

10. Alford's, *Whistleblowers* contains several stories that illuminate the daunting and feudal power of corporations, and their treatment of those who expose their wrong-doing.

11. Rashke's narrative presents abundant detail on these relationships.

raised a prophetic voice against willful public deception and disregard for human life.[12]

HELMETS AND HALOS

Since he was a boy, Bennet Omalu knew that he wanted to spend his life in serving God. He ultimately did that with a microscope in one hand and a prayer in the other. His father, a Nigerian assistant director of mineral resources, was devoutly Catholic and instilled in his seven children the virtues of self-sacrifice, hard work, gratitude, humility, honesty, courage, and integrity. It would have been easy for his father, Oba John Donatus Amaechi, an expert engineer, to join Nigeria's corrupt bureaucracy, but instead he became a revered Igbo village leader known for his wisdom and generosity. He endowed his children with faith and sent them to universities for advanced degrees.[13] This was no small matter.

In the 1960s and 1970s, Nigeria suffered a horrific civil war. Christians who adopted Western culture populated the southern region, while Islamic tribes who lived in quasi-feudal societies that hated Western culture populated the north. When the British relinquished the colony of Nigeria, tribal leaders competed for the oil-rich region. In 1967, the southern region succeeded and became Biafra, but was unable to access its oil and thus could not obtain the weapons, medicine, and food needed to survive. Nigerians took advantage of the situation by raping and slaughtering ethnic minorities in the south. The war created a famine in which over two million people died.[14] As bombs fell on the region in September 1968, Bennet was born in an Ibo village near the delta.[15]

Following directives from his father, Omalu became a physician. He moved to the United States in 1994 for post-doctoral studies in medicine. Omalu idolized America, home of truth and integrity—a country always busy improving itself. He despised the corruption of Nigerian culture, arguing that it "steals our dignity from us as human beings and degrades us

---

12. Grant, "Whistle Blowers."

13. Laskas' *Concussion* contains rich details about Omalu's family and their role in his pioneering work.

14. De St. Jorre's, *Nigerian Civil War* traces the source of war and documents the rise and fall of Biafra.

15. Laskas, p. 26. Also see Uzokwe's *Surviving Biafra*, a gut-wrenching account of the Nigeria Civil War.

to the level of animals, and not the children of God that we rightfully are."[16] Looking to study under one of America's most brilliant forensic pathologists, Dr. Cyril Wecht, Omalu made his way to Pittsburgh, Pennsylvania, and in 1999, began his career at the Allegheny County Coroner's Office. Omalu also joined St. Benedict the Moor Catholic Church in Pittsburgh, where he befriended Father Carmen D'Amico. The priest ultimately provided the spiritual support Omalu needed for his fated battle with the National Football League (NFL), which began in an ordinary autopsy of an extraordinary athlete.

After Mike Wester's body was wheeled into the autopsy room, Omalu stood beside the deceased former center for the Pittsburgh Steelers and began his work with prayer. He said, "Mike, you have been misjudged. It is not right. They do not understand. We have to prove them wrong. Please help me. Guide me to the truth; let me use my education to establish the truth. Let us vindicate you."[17]

Webster was 50 years old when he died in September 2002. Friends and family reported that he had been acting crazy, and that his personality had changed dramatically after he retired. He suffered bouts of incoherence, disorientation, and violent outbursts. He would disappear for days. People took advantage of his mental incapacities and exploited him financially. His wife divorced him. Webster often used a Taser to render himself unconscious so he could at least find peace in sleep.[18] Doctors ruled that Webster died of a heart attack, but during the autopsy Omalu kept thinking about Webster's state of mind, and whether Webster's behavior was caused by brain damage. Omalu ordered Webster's brain to be "fixed—" set in formaldehyde— so that the fragile, gelatinous brain matter would be firm enough to slice and study under a microscope. His colleagues protested. On the surface, the brain appeared normal.

Webster's cerebral tissue showed that his brain was peppered with tau material, a protein that forms tangles when nerve cells experiences trauma. Tau gums up the mental machinery, and under the microscope looks like Alzheimer's disease. Since 1973, scientists were aware that boxers who had been repeatedly hit in the head suffered changes in their personalities and often became irrational and violent.[19] Autopsies of boxers' brains showed

16. Laskas, p. 45.
17. Ibid, 97.
18. Fainaru-Wada and Fainaru, *League of Denial*, pp. 29–30; 47–49.
19. Corsellis, et al., "The Aftermath of Boxing."

external signs of trauma, such as atrophy and swelling, but Webster's brain looked normal on the surface.[20] Omalu documented damage that could only be seen with the aid of a microscope. This discovery was monumental.

For years, the NFL asserted that football did not cause dementia or lethal changes in personality, and medical experts echoed the narrative because they lacked evidence to the contrary. Omalu confirmed that players were experiencing psychological trauma and deterioration in health because of damage that did not meet the naked eye. Webster had answered Omalu's prayers and revealed the truth about his death. Elated at the prospect of sharing his discovery and of preventing such injuries in the future, Omalu published his first article on Chronic Traumatic Encephalopathy (CTE) in 2005.[21]

Like many faithful prophets, Omalu was demonized for his work. Physicians in the employment of the NFL, journalists, and franchise owners accused Omalu of sloppy science. Evan after he reinforced his findings with additional autopsies from other football players who had gone mad and self-destructed, he was reviled by NFL executives, and mocked by parents who dreamed that their sons—the stars of peewee football—would one day become professional players who made millions. Prohibited from speaking at conferences that addressed the CTE, and the target of vicious racial slurs, Omalu never retreated from his convictions that football is not good for the brain, and that the NFL knew this and lied about it for decades.[22] His work ultimately led to changes in helmet technology and rules of the game.

Omalu admits that his discovery and advocacy for change cost him a job and his reputation. It rattled his confidence in America's love of truth, justice, and compassion. It magnified the agonizing reality that corporations as big as the NFL can control the popular narrative even if they lie and put people in harm's way. He thought about how others marginalized and reviled him and wrote:

> "Who are you?" is the underlying question, the accusation that follows me wherever I go. Does it follow me because of the color of my skin or because of the nation of my birth? Perhaps...
>
> I never sought this life. God placed me here. I believe that all that brought me to this place came as a direct result of the hand

---

20. Ibid, p. 152.

21. Omalu, et al., "Chronic Traumatic Encephalopathy." See: Frontline Interviews, "Dr. Bennet Omalu."

22. Omalu, *Truth Doesn't Have a Side*, pp. 165–175; 281–282.

of God leading and directing my life. Who am I that the One who created the cosmos would bother with one so small? The answer is much larger than football.[23]

Omalu pondered whether it was vanity or ego that drove him. "No," he concluded to himself, "You were just the messenger. You were God's tool."[24]

Omalu's work made the headlines, but he did not see that as a sign from God to rest on his laurels. In 2017, Omalu was one of two forensic pathologists who resigned from California's San Joaquin County Coroner's Office subsequent to the discovery that law enforcers routinely tampered with the bodies of individuals who allegedly died in accidents. Omalu asserted that Sheriff Steve Moore pressured him to alter findings in the autopsies of individuals who had altercations with police officers.[25] He stated that the Sheriff "seems to believe that every officer involved death should be ruled an accident because police did not mean to kill anyone."[26]

Omalu and his colleague, Dr. Susan Parson, found themselves working in an environment where people distorted the truth in order to preserve a positive relationship between the public and law enforcers. They autopsied individuals whose hands had been severed from their bodies for the purpose of "identification," and had difficulty accessing vital information regarding the circumstances surrounding deaths. When Parsons and Omalu formally contested Moore's directives, he retaliated and bullied them, leaving no doubt that under his administration, it was impossible to conduct objective medical investigations that met the standards of best practice.[27]

Omalu consciously devoted his life, his career, his mind, and his heart to God. His devotion was not passive, nor was it limited in its expression to attending Mass and saying prayers. His persistence in speaking truth to power, and stubbornly refusing to retract his research are examples of spirituality in action. The little things, however—things he did far from public view—are the ones that illuminate the spiritual possibilities of every moment. He spoke to the diseased as he conducted autopsies. As if in prayer, he communed with them and thanked them. For him, not even saws, scalpels, and formaldehyde could reduce the human being to an object—a

23. Ibid, p. 16.
24. Ibid, p. 214. Also see Frontline Interview, "Dr. Bennet Omalu."
25. Egel, Chabria, and Garrison, "Hands Removed, Findings Changed."
26. Ibid.
27. Ibid. Readers will find a copy of Omalu's resignation letter at this site.

thing without dignity and sacred purpose. Time invested in seeking the truth never stopped being holy. His work was a ministry.

Omalu regularly attended Mass before he went work, and visited Fr. Carmen in times of depression and doubt. This is pro-active spirituality. Omalu's spiritual maintenance made it possible for him to endure the wrath and vilification of his fellows. It steadied him to stay the course of integrity and compassion, and fortified his courage. It helped him be aware of the little things that make up the big picture of integrity and love of neighbor on the job.

AWAKENED BY ORPHANS

Silkwood and Omalu were whistle blowers in the classic sense, as they complained about the organizations in which they themselves worked. Roy Bourgeois' whistle blowing had other dimensions. Initially, Bourgeois was concerned with what appeared to be few bad apples in the barrel of otherwise good U.S. military apples. However, as he learned about U.S. interventions and covert operations abroad, and saw the horror and carnage they created, he began to see that something about the barrels themselves was rotten. In time, he saw that those barrels included the Pentagon, Congress, the State Department, and Catholic Church. Ordained as a Maryknoll priest in 1971, Bourgeois was excommunicated and expelled from the priesthood in 2012. Remarkably, after 40 years of serving the poor and working to end genocide in Latin America, he was not chastised as a Marxist agitator (which he was not), but for supporting what some consider to be the outlandish proposition that the Catholic Church should ordain women as priests.[28] His journey illustrates the power of stories to change lives.

Bourgeois came of age in Louisiana during the early years of the Cold War. With dreams of making a fortune in oil industry and someday raising a family, he was also a patriot.[29] He finished the Navy's Officer Candidate School in 1962, and in 1965, he volunteered for duty in Vietnam. There, his eyes were opened to war. While delivering materials to an orphanage, he met children maimed by land mines, bullets, and Napalm. He saw what the death of their parents and the terror of war did to their ability to trust

---

28. Roberts, "Roy Bourgeois," lines 8–22.

29. Hodge and Cooper's *Disturbing the Peace* is the basis of much of this chapter's narrative on Bourgeois. For another layer of biographical insights, see Masse, *Inspired to Serve*, pp. 77–101.

others and to feel the joy of living. When he returned to civilian life in 1966, he still supported the war, but thought that he might be of better service as a missionary, and thus returned to Vietnam as a minister.

In 1969, the story of the My Lai massacre broke. Over 400 Vietnamese civilians were raped and slaughtered, and witnesses were told to keep quiet. Bourgeois' faith in the war was so shattered by the event that he discarded a photo of himself and Cardinal Spellman, the once powerful cold warrior who assured Catholics that God demanded total victory over communism and that U.S. troops were "soldiers of Christ."[30]

Following his ordination, Bourgeois went Bolivia, where he helped establish schools, medical clinics, and a cooperative of women who made woolen goods for sale abroad. He learned that the poor were of little consequence to those who controlled the country, and that missionaries were tolerated as long as they preached to save souls, and not to empower peasants with literacy and economic justice. Gustavo Gutierrez's liberation theology was gaining popularity at that time, and those who espoused it were routinely vilified by the Church and military juntas.[31] In 1976, Bourgeois was taken by Bolivian police, beaten, and prohibited from calling anyone. The militia demanded the names of reformers. Fellow Maryknoll priests rescued him, but the experience hardened his resolve to make political activism a part of his ministry.

Back in the U.S., Bourgeois worked in New York and Chicago, where he continued his education by taking seminars and talking with men and women serving in ministries at home and abroad. He was arrested in 1979 for protesting a Chicago Arms Bazaar. It was the first of many arrests that landed him in jail for trespassing and vandalism.

The 1980s were especially brutal in Latin America where the U.S. thrust many of its last Cold War daggers into the bodies of innocent civilians and ministers trying to help them. On March 23, 1980, Archbishop Oscar Romero, who had repeatedly begged El Salvador's junta to stop murdering civilians, and asked President Jimmy Carter to stop funding El Salvador's militia, was shot dead as he celebrated Mass. Two months later, Bourgeois was arrested for pouring blood onto the gates of the Pentagon in protest of nuclear stockpiles and U.S. support for Latin American dictatorships. On

---

30. Zimmer, *Vietnam War Debate*, p. 14. Cooney's *American Pope* is a lively biography of Spellman.

31. Gutierrez's, *A Theology of Liberation* asserts that the Gospel calls the faithful to build societies based on social justice, wherein people are liberated from exploitation of all forms. Juntas are military councils.

December 4, a Catholic lay missionary, Jean Donovan, and three nuns, Ita Ford, Maura Clarke, and Dorothy Kazel were beaten, raped, and murdered by El Salvador National Guardsmen. The women had cared for refugees and orphans. In the eyes of the junta and their U.S. allies, they were revolutionaries and communist dupes.[32] The women were among the 8,000 who were slaughtered in 1980 by El Salvador's militia, who gave their victims no formal indictments, no due process, no legal representation, and no decent burial.[33]

By 1981, the terror in Latin America gained public attention. In April, CBS's Bill Kurtis brought Bourgeois with him to El Salvador. Kurtis was after a story about the civil war that would be fair to the counterinsurgency, but all Fr. Roy could see in that objective was the denial that the U.S. was enabling cold-blooded murder. Convinced that if Americans knew what was happening in their name, they would stop the violence, Bourgeois disappeared for several days with guides who showed him how things were. The priest's family and friends thought he had been kidnapped and killed. When he returned to the U.S., Bishop John Cody of Chicago fired him from his diocese. Bourgeois retreated to a Trappist monastery to contemplate his ministry. The faces of the poor followed him, and he could not shake his desire to make the faces of the poor and oppressed visible to others. As if to amplify Bourgeois' pleas to end funding for the juntas, El Salvador's militia shot, dismembered, and decapitated over 900 citizens—mostly women and children—at El Mozote on December 11, 1981.

By 1981, Bourgeois knew that Latin American dictators and militia were trained with U.S. taxpayers' money at the School of the Americas (SOA). Over the next decade, it became clearer to him that the massacres and terrorism in Latin America were not the actions of rogue soldiers, but were part of a grand U.S. agenda to retain control over the region.[34] In 1983, he was arrested for protesting at Fort Benning in Georgia (home of the SOA) and sentenced to 18 months at a federal work camp, a difficult incarceration during which he meditated on God's mercy and presence in the world. Upon his release, he returned to public ministry. In July 1986, just one month after Congress gave Nicaragua's Contras a $100 million dollar

---

32. The U.S. repeated delayed requests for inquiries into the murders. Government officials blamed the victims and were disinterested in bringing the killers to justice. See: Bonner, "The Diplomat and the Killer."

33. Markey, *A Radical Faith*, pp. 1–2.

34. Holden and Zolov's *Latin America* chronicles the U.S. agenda for South and Central America with scores of documents from the 18th, 19th, 20th, and 21st centuries.

aid package, news of the Iran-Contra scandal broke. The news confirmed that the Reagan administration had lied about trading arms for hostages in order to fight a war that it said it was not fighting.[35] In November, Bourgeois was arrested gain, and the U.S. Catholic Bishops published, *Economic Justice for All*, which presented a clear moral objection to the abuses of capitalism, and vindicated many of Bourgeois' objections to U.S. policies.[36]

On November 9, 1989, the Berlin Wall fell. The Cold War was gasping its last breath, but the killing went on south of the border. On November 16, six Jesuit priests, their housekeeper, and housekeeper's daughter were all murdered in San Salvador. Less than a week later, Congress continued its funding of El Salvador's regime, adding millions to what ultimately amounted to over $4 billion dollars of aid to the junta between 1979 and 1991.[37] The murders prompted Congressman Joseph Moakley (D-MA) to create an investigative commission,[38] and the United Nations' to conduct its own inquiry.[39] Both found that the majority of officers responsible for the murders were trained at the SOA. Bourgeois embraced a new objective: close the SOA.

FATHER PRESENTE

In 1990, Bourgeois rented a three-room apartment located 30 yards away from the entrance of Fort Benning, home of the SOA. He and other activists began the SOA Watch, dedicated to educating the public about the SOA and closing it. Each November, the organization led demonstrations at Fort Benning. People marched holding white crosses with the names of the murdered and disappeared, and as their names were called out in

---

35. Walsh's *Firewall* traces the arms deal, its cover-up, and explores their consequences and implications. Also see Alterman's *When Presidents Lie*, pp. 238–292.

36. United States Catholic Bishops, *Economic Justice for All* was released as Pope John Paul II' campaign to end communism was underway. The Pope had been in Louisiana when Bourgeois was imprisoned in Oakdale, but refused an invitation to visit him. Pope John Paul II opposed liberation theology, which he associated with Marxism, and distanced himself from clerics who even appeared to sympathize with it. See Quade, *Pope and Revolution*.

37. McKinney, "Twelve Years a Terror," p. 21.

38. Schneider's, *Joe Moakley's Journey* documents how people underwent transitions in their empathy and understanding of U.S. hegemony and leveraged their faith to advocate for the poor and oppressed.

39. Buergenthal, "The United Nations Truth Commission."

Gregorian chant, the crowd solemnly chanted in response, "presente." I recall the searing emotions that ran through me as I participated in this ritual. As I watched Bourgeois, I felt his sincere reverence for the dead and the terrorized. To me, he was "Father Presente," a man for whom ordination meant never leaving the broken, the despised, the poor, and the oppressed behind. He was always with them.

Bourgeois was arrested three more times during the 1990s, as the juntas continued to commit atrocities, and as U.S. officials continued to tell the American public that the SOA had nothing to do with torture and the slaughter of innocents. In 1997, 45 Tzotzil Indians, mostly women and children, were murdered with bullets and machetes in Acteal, Mexico. They were accused of supporting revolutionaries. The following year, Guatemala's Bishop Juan Jose Gerardi, author of a report that documented 400 massacres in his country, was assassinated.[40]

Between 1993 and 1999, Congressman Joseph Kenney (D-MA), Moakley, and others introduced bills that would either cut funding for the SOA or close it altogether. With the approval of Congress, the SOA changed its name to the Western Hemisphere Institute for Security Cooperation (WHINSEC), and its administrators vowed to adopt a curriculum focused on human rights and fighting drug trafficking. Critics say that the new name has not radically altered U.S. objectives in the region, and that Latin Americans still live amidst poverty, gang violence, corruption, and government indifference to human rights.[41]

Bourgeois' 40-year journey of faith took him to places where he sometimes doubted God. He confronted authorities who took the side of terrorists in the name of God and democracy. He remained a priest in the Catholic Church at a time when many Catholics were coming to the conclusion that the Church was little more than a bastion of superstition and repression. His own prophetic voice evolved incrementally as he witnessed extremes in human suffering, and opened his heart to the voices of the persecuted. He was willing to change his mind about what was right and wrong even when powerful officials ridiculed, imprisoned, beat, and dismissed him. His ministry kindled popular support for changes in U.S. operations in Latin America.

In 1994, President Bill Clinton signed the North American Free Trade Agreement (NAFTA). Bugle Boy, GAP, J.C. Penny, Sears, K-Mart, and

40. Human Rights Office of the Archdiocese of Guatemala, *Guatemala, Never Again!*
41. Blakeley, "Still Training to Torture?"

Wal-Mart and dozens of other corporations headed south of the border to cash in on cheap labor. On the bright side, poverty dropped in the region from 41.6 percent in 2003 to 25.3 percent in 2012.[42] On the dark side, elections were still manipulated, poverty was still acute, and gang warfare over drugs produced a homicide rate in Latin America that is many times the size of the U.S. and Europe, as its population represents eight percent of the world's population and 38 percent of the world's homicides.[43] Additionally, loans from the International Monetary fund pumped Latin American debt up from US$ 220 billion in 1980 to US$ 762 billion in 2000.[44] Pressure to remediate the debt led countries to reduce government funding for social services and human development, and to privatize public utilities such as electricity and water.[45]

NAFTA and its 2005 companion, the Central American Free Trade Agreement (CAFTA) were designed to give the U.S. significant advantages in economic enterprises, and not to transform Latin America into a fully developed modern nation. Neoliberal policies allow U.S. companies to sue nations that they believe impose unfair regulations, and CAFTA has forced Latin American farmers into bankruptcy, as they cannot compete with imported agricultural goods produced with the help of U.S. government subsides.[46] Adding to the misery, the defoliants sprayed over farms to kill the coca plants that make cocaine also kill fruit and vegetable crops, and leave rural residents with respiratory problems and other illnesses.[47]

Roy Bourgeois saw the poor as people worthy of dignity and compassion, while neoliberals— as represented by the World Bank—see the poor very differently. In its 2015 report, the Bank noted that prosperity is related to a person's knowledge, skill, and opportunities, and opined that "behavioral factors" play a role as well. Chronic poverty, it argued, pressures people and influences "their state of mind and decision making process in a more pronounced way than for wealthier people."[48] The report said that in order to escape poverty, people must have access to services, such as water,

---

42. Vakis, Rigolini, and Lucchetti, *Left Behind*, p. 8; 62–70
43. Daily Chart, "Latin American Homicide," lines 1–5.
44. Livingstone, *America's Backyard*, p. 192–193.
45. Booth, Wade, & Walker, *Understanding Central America*, p. 9.
46. Ibid, p. 298–314.
47. Livingstone, pp. 176–187.
48. Vakis, Rigolini, and Lucchetti, p. 9.

electricity, shelter, education, and health care. It also stated that the desire to escape poverty is often sabotaged by a socially normed lack of ambition.

The World Bank is correct in its assertion that "behavioral factors are especially important in understanding chronic poverty," but for reasons that go beyond its own explanations. The Bank criticized the behavior of the poor themselves, but not that of the bankers and industrial titans who determine who has access to resources necessary for self-improvement. It did not address the impact of U.S. imperialism, civil war, government corruption, dictatorship, and terrorism. The World Bank calls attention to how chronic poverty influences a national state of mind, and pressures people to think in certain ways. It is remarkably silent, however, on how chronic greed influences a national state of mind, and pressures people to think in certain ways.

The Bank's report did not explore what happens to hope and aspiration when, decade after decade, people go hungry, fear persecution, and bury the dismembered bodies of their loved ones left to rot in jungles or garbage dumps. Bourgeois and his associates understood that it is possible to beat self-respect and self-esteem out of people so thoroughly that they no longer believe that God created them for a sacred purpose. They see that it is possible to batter the human spirit so badly that people see life as an ordeal to survive either by being docile in the face of abuse, or by selling one's services to murderous regimes and thugs.

ONE SONG, ONE SPIRIT

The stories of Silkwood, Omalu, and Bourgeois are very different, but they are each examples of activating one's conscience. Silkwood is like the cook at the local Café who is troubled by falsified reports to the state health department, or the trucker who refused to distribute expired food, or the professor who says that the common practice of inflating grades is perpetuating ignorance and intolerance. Omalu is like the scientist who stands by his or her research that proves the existence of global warming, or the engineer who warns that the city's plans to build towering office buildings on landfill is a disaster waiting to happen, or the psychiatrist who asserts that violent video games and television programs contribute to children's anti-social attitudes and behavior. Bourgeois is like the advertising agent who learns that by promoting a certain product he or she is injuring the public, or the lobbyist who learns that Congressional members have no intention of honoring promises or following the law.

Silkwood, Omalu, and Bourgeois all had something in common. Each wanted to protect the well-being of others, and wanted people to know the truth. Each persisted with their cause despite threats against their well-being, punishment, and public ridicule. Each allowed their consciences to be transformed by the suffering of others.

Not all of us are called to be a Silkwood, Omalu, or Bourgeois. Most of us who activate spirituality in the workplace will probably not make the national news or influence national policies. However, whether the issue is a co-worker who persistently leaves dirty dishes in the lunchroom or dirty governments that dish out lies about the corpses by the side of the road, the principles of truth, good will, empathy, humility, and accountability are relevant. Silkwood, Omalu and Bourgeois teach us that regardless of whether the issue is monumental or miniscule, people are often tempted to be paralyzed by doubt and criticism. We are all tempted to disengage our interventions when things get tough. It is important to know why.

REFLECTIONS

1. What do Silkwood's, Omalu's, and Bourgeois' experiences teach us about integrity in the workplace and leadership?
2. Do you identify with any of these individuals and why?
3. Do you have a Father Carmen or spiritual advisors in your life, and do they help you cultivate the spiritual assets that are necessary in activating your prophetic voice?
4. Who are the prophetic voices in your workplace? How are they treated and how do you treat them and why?
5. How do you determine which behaviors at work and in society should be contested?
6. Instructors: In what ways do you facilitate studies of modern-day prophetic voices in our nation's business and governance and explore their impact?
7. Instructors: to what extent do you integrate studies of society's prophetic voices and their impact into your curriculum and prompt students to develop their own prophetic voice?

5

Get Off Your Cross

A FEW BARS OF KUMBAYA

TOMMY ALWAYS BEAT UP Eddie on the playground. Eddie had learned that it was not nice to hit people, and so the school bully routinely clobbered him to the cheers of other children. Then along came Sr. Mary Benedict with a boxing manual in one hand a rosary in the other. She gave Eddie boxing lessons and taught him how to bob and weave. Most importantly, she gave him permission to hit Tommy. I remember seeing that scene from the film, *The Bells of St. Mary*, when I was a child and wishing that Sr. Mary Benedict taught at my school.[1] The only advice about fighting that my peers and I got at St. Bridget's was to report hitting and meanness to adults. As I recall, that was only satisfying as long as teachers and principals imposed consequences that everyone agreed were truly awful, but fair.

In my youth, I assumed that nuns were too holy to fight. I had heard plenty of stories about how saints took a beating for their faith without reciprocal blows. I knew that many died and that it was O.K. because they would be rewarded in heaven. Through the eyes of a Catholic child, faith was supposed to help people endure the pain of victimization and cruelty, especially when fighting for a just cause. The abuses and injuries that we experienced were often portrayed as an opportunity to spend time on the cross with Jesus, and to suffer for our sins. On the cross, we were humbled

---

1. *Bells of St. Mary*, directed by Leo McCarey (1945, Los Angeles, CA: RKO Pictures, 2003), DVD.

and penitent, but there was a dark side to that perspective. On the cross, we were also passive towards those who hurt us and we were out of the way of those who wanted to create a world very different from a world wherein love of neighbor prevailed.

It is possible to use religion as a weapon against our spirituality. When creeds, doctrines, and theological teachings aim to deny the dignity of persons, or teach people that God wants them to remain silent in the face of inhumanity, religion assaults the spirit. When religion encourages the faithful to justify exploitation, or the exclusion of individuals from God's grace, it assaults the spirit. There are many ways that religious notions can cripple or corrupt our spirituality, and four ways in particular can be very problematic. The first is when we use religion as an excuse to retreat from the hard work of being God's co-creator, and thus diminish potential of spirituality to bring the Kingdom of God to bear on Earth. The second concerns our judgement of judgment, the third regards willed ignorance, and the fourth is perfectionism.

Robert Augustus Masters argues that one of the myths people have about spirituality is that it is supposed to help us avoid pain, conflict, and responsibility for our own growth.[2] He labeled such behavior as "spiritual bypassing," and observed that it is a way of excusing ourselves from our own development. Masters states that spiritual bypassing is fueled by the expectation that spirituality is supposed to make us happy, and that happiness is defined as the absence of all negative emotions and experiences. The problem with spiritual bypassing, he notes, is that it uses faith as a means of dodging psychological development, which is essential to spiritual maturity. It leaves the faithful with the notion that spirituality is all about "rising above" conflict, pain, and suffering, rather than facing them head-on and working through those things to heal our psyches and alter the courses of our own dysfunctional behavior.

Spiritual "by-passers" often seek peace at all costs. They easily bend to unreasonable demands because they cannot tolerate conflict or the threat of losing someone's respect or affection. They are often hypersensitive to anger, emotionally detached, and present an exaggerated sense of well-being and positive affect. Masters noted that many spiritual by-passers have "delusions of having arrived at a higher level of being."[3]

---

2. Masters, *Spiritual Bypassing*, p. 1–8.
3. Ibid. p. 2.

In the workplace, this approach to spirituality sometimes leaves co-workers with the impression that one is sanctimonious or arrogant. Masters notes that spiritual by-passers also prematurely offer forgiveness to offenders. While this practice may calm tensions on the surface, premature forgiveness does little to increase the offender's awareness of how his or her behavior affects others. Further, it often leaves the offended or injured without an apology, and co-workers without a shared sense of accountability and what is expected going forward.

Spiritual by-passers often go to great lengths to avoid judgment or at least appear to be non-judgmental. They are what Masters calls "blindly compassionate."[4] Blind compassion represents a form of unconditional tolerance for hurtful and dysfunctional behavior. Some are motivated to blind compassion because they assume that everyone in the workplace is doing the best they can and are genuinely good-willed. Masters finds that many are blindly compassionate because they believe that any form of judgment is wrong and, by definition, sinful.

Spiritual bypassing ensures that we stay nailed to our own crosses. Up there on the cross, we might hum a few bars of Kumbaya and feel sanctimonious, but we are not doing much to improve the workplace. With our hands fixed to the bloody beam, we can no longer use them to lift ourselves out of unhealthy patterns of behavior, nor help others change what is unpleasant or unproductive in the workplace.

SPIRITUAL PIRACY

Our judgment of judgement may be well intended, but it can get us into trouble. It is easy for religious and spiritual people to be blindly compassionate and co-dependent in part because we have been taught that judgment always leads to bad things. Having been raised Catholic and washed in the progressive waters of Vatican II,[5] I understand the spiritual obligation to temper judgment. I also understand the terrific pressure Americans feel to be politically correct, and how that has magnified people's fear of judgment. I am not convinced, however, that all judgement is the devil in disguise. It seems that once we have been convinced that our judgment

---

4. Ibid, pp. 21–27.

5. Wilde's *Vatican II* explores the key documents produced by the Vatican Council (1959 and 1965), the significance of the Church's shift in thinking about Catholic social activism, and the conflicts it produced.

is evil by definition, it is easier for others to pirate the ship of our own conscience.

My heart still warms when watching Spencer Tracy as Father Edward Flanagan in the film *Boys Town*, as he announces, "There is no such thing as a bad boy."[6] Flanagan gave others the benefit of the doubt, hope, and honorable ways out of conflict. Flanagan, however, was no pushover. In his world, there was intervention and accountability. In order to get to those things, somebody had to decide right from wrong— somebody had to make a judgment. The priest understood that if he was to nudge boys down the moral path of life, he would have to distinguish that path from all others.

The assertion that it is politically or morally incorrect to make judgements is a form of spiritual piracy. Such assertions hijack one of the things that makes human beings unique in the process of co-creation with God, and that is our conscience. Endowed with the capacity to know right from wrong, good from evil, functional from dysfunctional, and healthy from unhealthy is a blessing and not a curse. This capacity makes it possible for us to decide which courses of action are aligned with God's invitation to love and serve others, and which are not. It enables us to determine whether people are using religion to hurt us or to protect and nurture us.

Judgement has a bad reputation because so many people associate it with intolerance, ultimatums, and arrogance. This is understandable because so many of us have abused the gift of judgement. "Discernment" and "discretion" may be more delicate words for judgement, but in the end, these behaviors are all about making a choice.

Judgement often arouses anxiety because so many of us still think dualistically and fail to see the complexities of matters. In the dualistic paradigm, there are always winners and losers, and what is right and what is wrong is obvious and simple. While religious doctrines often defend dualism, spirituality urges our hearts and minds to consider the complexities of human nature, morality, motives, and contextual factors when distinguishing right from wrong or good from evil. Spirituality often arouses dissonance in our conscience as we witness the gap between institutional doctrines and the love of God that extends beyond what human institutions can grasp. Spirituality invites the faithful to see the orphan first and the bishop second.

---

6. *Boys Town*, directed by Norman Taurog (1938; Beverly Hills, CA: MGM, 2011), DVD.

WILLED IGNORANCE

The American theologian, Reinhold Niebuhr, penned in the 1930s, "God, grant me the serenity to accept the things I cannot change, the courage to change the things I can, and the wisdom to know the difference."[7] It is a powerful prayer. It became a popular prayer among those recovering from addiction, dysfunctional family dynamics, and toxic work environments. It is a prayer that sees sin in the world and yet, does not pray for perfection, but for progress.

The Serenity Prayer hinges on awareness. It generally addresses matters that are immediate to us, and not things that are hidden. We do not generally petition God for the serenity to accept, or courage to change something that is not known to us. The phrase, "wisdom to know the difference" is nothing short of a prayer for our minds to be open and inquisitive. It is the part of the prayer that asks for help in overcoming ignorance.

Ignorance is one of the greatest challenges to spirituality in the modern world. Paradoxically, we possess technology with which to communicate with each other, instantly and globally, and yet, we know so little about each other. Inundated with social media, news, human interest, and advertising, we are frequently misinformed about or wholly oblivious to the world around us. We often prefer "echo chambers" and sound bites, and dislike studied and thoughtful analysis. The echo chamber—the media space in which everybody shares the same opinion and reinforces a common point of view—is a social security blanket. Echo chambers may validate us, but they do not always educate us. We are vulnerable to believing things that are popular but not true. Editorial spins in news reports, censorship, and our own lazy habits of information seeking and critical thinking often leave us ignorant of why the world is as it is.

"The wisdom to know the difference" may stimulate our imaginations. Consider the daily newspaper, for example. It has a whole section devoted to sports, but not even a page devoted to the daily contact between lobbyists and government officials. Why? Arguably, lobbyist's achievements have a greater impact on the public's well-being than the local team's standings in the playoffs. Generally, we hear about lobbyists only when something sensational happens to them, and even then we are likely to get only tidbits of news about matters before the next spectacle steals the headlines.[8] We

---

7. Zaleski and Zaleski, *Prayer*, p. 127.
8. For highly insightful documentation of how new media operates and why the

rarely think about the people who decide what is worthy of our attention, and the implications of their decisions for our own conscience and morality.

Our ignorance is not wholly the result of secular news corporations and rogue websites. Parents do not always cultivate their child's intellect and civic engagement, and schools do not always offer critical pedagogy. We as individuals often take root on the couch and find no excitement in reading great books or attending lectures, conversations, or film presentations. Every temple, church, and mosque has the potential to be a classroom where local leaders may facilitate study groups and speaker events featuring local professionals and scholars.

Spirituality invites the faithful to roll up their sleeves and do the work of God in the material world. What we learn about the world makes all the difference as to what shape that "work of God" will take. Roy Bourgeois' journey teaches us that information can be transformative. Had Bourgeois never encountered the orphans of Vietnam, he might have finished his military career ignorant of what effect U.S. policy had on the poor of Latin America. He might have never helped Americans to question whether their patriotism was truly aligned with the love of God. Had Bennet Omalu never contested the thoroughness of an autopsy report, many more athletes may have been fatalities of invisible injuries.

Arguably, learning about the world in which we live and about who controls our access to information are as important as prayer and fellowship. Knowing what others experience and need places us in a better position to love our neighbors in a way that *they need to be loved*, which is sometimes different than the way *we think they ought to be loved*.

DEATH BY PERFECTION

Sometimes the faithful excuse themselves from leavening the love of God into the world because they see themselves as a realist rather than an idealist. I recall a conversation in which a co-worker chided my idealism and said, "You can't take the spots of a leopard." The message was clear: my expectations were too grandiose for what the institution would bear, and I had better change my attitude. I thought about my co-worker's comment many times. I have wondered whether there would have been any Civil Rights Movements or an end to the Cold War if people believed that

---

public should care, see Bagdikian's *New Media Monopoly*, Ebert's *New Media Invasion*, and Goodman's *Democracy Now!*

leopards could never lose their spots. I have often wondered whether idealism or realism is the greater enemy of spirituality.

Idealism is associated with the tendency to represent things in perfect or pure and unadulterated forms, and the expectation that perfect or utopian ideals can be achieved in human relationships, endeavors, and organizations. Idealism also pertains to the practice of living according to what one idealizes.[9] Idealism can inspire individuals and communities to achieve great feats of humanity, and it can provide them with objectives that represent improvements over existing norms and conditions. Idealism can also infect individuals with intolerance and impatience that alienates others and sours their interest in worthy causes.

In contrast to idealism, realism is associated with the tendency to be practical or pragmatic about matters, and to reject that which is visionary in nature.[10] Realists often adjust to what is manifest or real and act according to what is expedient rather than what is perfect or ideal. Realism can help people see things as they are, without romanticizing things.

Neither the idealist nor the realist has a corner on God's love, nor is one necessarily more moral than the other. The realist, for instance, may justify murder by arguing that it is collateral damage regretfully incurred in the act of self-defense, while the idealist may justify murder with claims that genetically inferior people will ultimately prevent civilization from becoming the utopia it was meant to be. In the end, both ideologies can be lethal.

In some ways, idealism is natural to my generation, the baby boomers. We were weaned on crusades and optimism. We were told that it was our moral and patriotic duty to right every wrong, heal every wound, satisfy all hunger, and enlighten all ignorance.[11] In my youth, I assumed that religious people were idealists. My Catholic formation reinforced secular beliefs that if we all really wanted to make the world a better place, we could. I once thought realism was a coward's way out of doing God's work, or laziness disguised as pragmatism. A wiser conclusion would have argued that both

---

9. Idealism." Merriam-Webster Dictionary. Retrieved from: https://www.merriam-webster.com/dictionary/idealism.

10. "Realism." Merriam-Webster Dictionary. Retrieved from: https://www.merriam-webster.com/dictionary/realism.

11. Gorzycki's *Caesar Ate My Jesus*, Steinhorn's *Greater Generation*, and Light's *Baby Boomers*. address the idealism baby boomers learned and the disillusionment felt when leaders seemed to abandon the idealism.

realism and idealism are morally neutral by definition, and take their ethos from those who embrace them.

Perfectionists are rarely at peace with themselves, and so peace with others can be elusive. Some appear to be motivated by colossal egos, but many are insecure and have low self-esteem. Perfectionists often presume they know perfection from God's perspective. Their concept of perfect often leaves little room for the spirit to work, and sometimes justifies force and coercion. This may produce conformity without achieving progress.

Getting off the cross and giving ourselves permission to activate spirituality in our lives is tremendously liberating, but it does require tremendous faith and skill. We need faith that we remove the nails form our own hands, God's grace will be with us, even when we make the mistakes humans are bound to make when we take responsibility for our world. We may benefit richly from committing ourselves to life-long learning for the sake of refining the psychological and spiritual skills required to steady our feet on rough and rocky roads.

REFLECTIONS

1. To what extent are you keeping yourself "nailed to the cross" by way of "spiritual bypassing," fear of judgement, ignorance, or perfectionism? What prevents you from releasing yourself?

2. Would you describe yourself as an idealist or realist? Why? What roles do idealism and realism in your spiritual growth and in your interactions with others at work?

3. To what extent do you seek information about controversial behavior, troublesome policies, or adversarial points of view in the workplace? How would you rate your openness to such information and what might be areas of growth?

4. What might be some viable strategies for promoting civic and global awareness through your church, synagogue, temple, or mosque, and what might be some appropriate objectives for promoting this?

5. Instructors: To what extent do you teach students how to locate in depth information and analysis of world events and ideas? How do you improve students' critical consumption of news and critical thinking? To what extent do you collaborate with others on campus to ensure that every student has media literacy?

6

Spiritual Rubber on the Material Road

EMOTIONAL TRAPS

MOST OF US WILL probably not undertake interventions in the way that Silkwood, Omalu, and Bourgeois undertook them. The conflict that most of us are likely to encounter on the job are more likely to be those related to job security, advancement, fair compensation, and interpersonal relationships. Whether we are contesting the nation's foreign policy or confronting harassment on the job, however, we are all vulnerable to emotional traps that prevent us from taking action when we should. Emotional traps are feelings and beliefs that often entangle us in dysfunctional behavior. They neutralize our will to intervene when we or others are being abused. They may include fear of judgment, feelings of doubt or intimidation, and denial of the severity of events.

Management consultants Kathrine Crowley and Katie Elster state that emotional traps are formed by internalizing the expectations others have for us and making them the centerpiece of our responses to conflict.[1] The emotional trap evidenced in unresponsiveness and acquiescence to the hurtful and unreasonable demands of others. The trap is set when others violate our boundaries or sense of professional integrity and we are so consumed by guilt, fear, and conflict over our feelings about it, that the feelings paralyze us. Emotionally trapped employees often cope with distress and

---

1. Crowley and Elster, *Working with You*, pp. 2–4.

conflict by mentally checking out or displacing their anger, anxiety and frustration onto others.

An emotionally trapped worker might be unable to set limits with a co-worker who persistently crowds his or her workspace, or incapable of confronting the supervisor who habitually and publically ridicules employees. Many tolerate bad behavior—bullying, gossip, histrionics, harassment, excessive negativity, and unreasonable demands on employees—because they want to appear pleasant and charitable. Many do so because they are afraid of retaliation, getting fired, or loss of friends. Their behavior resembles what Masters called "spiritual bypassing." Getting out of emotional traps requires a conscious effort.

Crowley and Elster suggest four strategies for getting emotionally unhooked in real time while on the job:

- Pause to physically calm the body, take deep breaths, and maintain self-care off the job
- Mentally take account of what is happening, what part one plays in the conflict or situation, what part others play, and identify alternative solutions
- Verbally acknowledge the problem and engage in conversation that does not assault others personally, and is aimed to find a mutually agreeable way forward
- Engage business tools, such as organizational policies, job descriptions, documentation of behavior, or contractual agreements to motivate change when other strategies have not resolved issues

These are practical and viable strategies, and they may or may not produce desired results. They represent actions that focus both on the disturbing behavior of others, and they place the responsibility to alter unpleasant or dysfunctional dynamics on the ones who are being injured or offended. Those who use these strategies do not need to be especially religious people, but I believe that there are advantages to integrating spirituality into such interventions.

A DEEP SPIRITUAL BREATH

Activating spirituality when responding to distress or conflict on the job offers two advantages. First we add another layer of sensitivity to our awareness and regard for others. The added dimension is the steady awareness that our co-workers—adversarial or not—are ultimately our brothers and sisters who, like ourselves, are called to a sacred purpose. We may begin to detect the motives behind our co-workers' behavior, and actually empathize with their insecurities, struggles with self-esteem, or lack of skill. We may even discover that we have behaved in ways we find objectionable and that we need to change. Second, when we activate spirituality in the workplace, it helps us acknowledge that jobs that require us to inflict injuries on the public or exploit employees may be jobs not worth keeping.

Taking a deep spiritual breath also enables us to put our work in perspective and to recognize that sometimes we bring too much ego to the workplace. When we get tangled up in who gets the corner office, or who gets promoted, and who has the supervisor's ear, we are often tangled up in ego. When we thrive on the flattery or deference people offer because of our profession or title, we are tangled up in ego. We are challenged to see that titles and degrees do not make us Gods. It is possible that the janitor who cleans the office toilets is a far better conduit of God's love than the executive who uses the toilet, because all day long the janitor is humble, kind, helpful, and cheerful to all he meets, while the executive is haughty, rude, demanding, and mean to all he meets. The janitor may enjoy spiritual serenity that is elusive to the executive for no other reason than the executive expects his job to establish his stature and identity in the world, and the janitor does not.

Crowley and Elster tell a story in which an employee, Susan, attends a meeting during which another employee, Tracy, takes full credit for Susan's work. Susan is struck by rage and shuts down, effectively disengaging from the meeting.[2] Crowley and Elster tell readers that Susan swallowed her anger and "got hooked" into passivity and did nothing to improve the situation. They suggest that Susan could "unhook" herself by: 1) calming down and engaging in the meeting; 2) psychologically freeing herself by embracing the assertion she need not be intimidated by her co-worker; 3) speaking up at the meeting and telling the group that when she first came up with the idea, Tracy was excited; and, 4) using a business tool, such as sending an e-mail to the group that summarized the meeting and acknowledged that people seemed pleased with her ideas.

The four steps Susan could take to unhook herself from anger and passivity in the face of unfairness are practical, and they represent an initiative

---

2. Ibid, pp. 3–6.

of self-care. None-the-less, Susan's actions may not have gone in the best direction. Susan did not directly communicate her thoughts on the matter with Tracy, and that smacks of passive-aggressiveness. In addition, Tracy may not take the hint that her conduct was inappropriate and thus, in the future, the matter may resurface.

The four strategies Susan might take to unhook herself might solve her problem with Tracy, so why bother with adding a spiritual dimension? First, if Susan actually thought deeply about Tracy's actions, she might discover that Tracy may be in distress. Perhaps Tracy is insecure and feels compelled to compete even when competition does not win much. Perhaps Tracy is in her early sixties and fearful that managers are trying to push her out of her job. Maybe Tracy is new to the job and does not understand the protocols of professional courtesy. In any event, it is important for Susan to identify the assumptions behind her reaction to Tracy, and consider what it would mean for Tracy to have an honorable way out of conlcit.

A second reason to infuse the situation with spirituality is to keep one's ego in check. Susan may have learned important things about herself had she channeled some of her reflection on her role in the meeting toward her own motives and expectations. Tracy clearly stepped on Susan's toes in the meeting, and when others step on our toes, we learn from investigating why it hurt so badly. Perhaps Susan was angered because *she* is the self-serving corporate climber in the group. Perhaps Susan was jealous because Tracy did a better job presenting her ideas. Perhaps Susan expects her job to fulfill emotional needs to be loved and revered by others—needs that are not filled in any other part of her life—and so habitually interprets others' actions as either a sign of personal acceptance or rejection. If this were the case, Susan might benefit from adjusting in her own attitudes and behaviors, so that she did not depend so much on the workplace to satisfy her psychological or spiritual needs. She might benefit from joining a spiritual community or working with therapists who could help her discover healthy ways of thinking about and meeting emotional needs. She might also learn how to forge agreements with others with whom she shares her innovations about how innovations will be shared and managed.

SHAME, SHAME, SHAME

Upon learning that I grew up in a Catholic household and attended Catholic schools for 16 years of my life, some of my friends have said, "So, you grew up in the church of shame, eh?" We laugh and on occasion have debated whether Jews or Catholics suffered more from guilt complexes. We share stories of how guilt and shame kept us "in our place," and how it aroused self-hatred and self-doubt. In hindsight, I am unconvinced that the experience of shame was all bad. Yes, I was embarrassed when I was confronted by teachers and elders who exposed my wrong-doing, meanness, or selfishness, and yes, it made me uncomfortable about myself. Catholicism provided an honorable way out of shame, however, and there was always hope for a clean slate and self-improvement.

In Catholic tradition, the sacrament of Reconciliation—or Confession, as it was known in my youth—was a means of restoring character and healing relationships. The truly contrite admitted their sins, vowed to amend their ways, and undertook penance. The sacrament is meant to renew one's commitments to moral decency and to foster maturity of conscience. In the sacrament of Reconciliation, the individual is brought back into alignment with God and the community. They are rededicated to humility and self-discipline.

The trouble with shame is that it is so often stripped of its restorative properties, as many people use it to attack the dignity of the person or to destroy someone's self-esteem and reputation. Recently, shame has gotten some bad press, and some see it as politically incorrect. Others are exasperated with elected officials and pundits who try to out-shame each other in public discourse.[3] This does little to sharpen our view of common needs and to build consensus. Shame seems to be more effective when it is a personal response to transgression, rather a weapon of scorn and judgement. To ban shame from the resources our psyches have to keep our egos in check, however, leaves us with one less psychological experience that monitors our spiritual development.

Both civilization and spirituality depend on shame.[4] As a psychological phenomenon, shame acts as a barometer of wrong-doing. It arouses regret when people act indecently or cause injury to others, and often suppresses the desire to repeat the offending behavior. As a cultural phenomenon, shame reinforces the norms and values most revered in society. In social settings, such as the work environment, shame may act as a prophylactic

---

3. Mark Thompson's *Enough Said* examines the increase in aggressive civic rhetoric, and Zompetti's *Divisive Discourse* explores extremism and distortion in public narratives and debates.

4. Locke's *Democracy and the Death of Shame* explores Western civilization's veneration of shame and the social consequences of shamelessness.

against bad behavior if there is a shared sense of what individuals owe the community and what constitutes the common good. The breakdown of consensus on the common good is a disaster for society, because when it breaks down people literally become shameless.

As a spiritual resource, shame alerts us to the disparity between our professed love of God and the way we treat our neighbors. It arouses empathy by provoking our imaginations so that we might sense the hurt our behavior has caused. Spiritually mature individuals do not fear or resent shame; they are humbled by it and welcome its lessons. Effective approaches to shame keep shame in perspective. Roy Bourgeois and Bennett Omalu, for example, had reasons to shame others that were clearly lying to the public and causing people to suffer. Instead, they prayed for their adversaries and criticized their practices and behaviors, not their persons. Ironically, both were publically shamed by their own supervisors and made to appear unfit for their professions. Both saw that shame as attempts to break their spirits and abort truth. Both refused to be silenced because they answered to a power greater than the Pentagon and NFL.

Effective activation of spirituality in the workplace depends in part on our willingness to avoid behaviors that shame, and readiness to be shamed without retaliation. In activating spirituality on the job, one might assess how shame operates in the workplace, and take steps to disengage from shaming dynamics. Initiating interventions, exiting the gossip gallery, and extending courtesy to office mates who have been shamed are small but important blessings.

WALK ON WATER

A friend once poked fun at my strident approach to institutional reform. The well-deserved jab was aimed at the altitude of my ideals. She said, "Well, the rest of us don't walk on water, but you seem to." I chuckled, "*Oh yah, you bet'cha . . . I do walk on water, and so do most Minnesotans—but we have the good sense to wait until winter when the lakes are frozen so yah don't fall through da ice!*" Effective interventions in the workplace require good timing, and taking risks that might result in what we thought were unachievable miracles.

Knowing when the time is right to dissent or intervene requires much discernment. In some instances, even when individuals are patient and careful, the timing is never perfect for all concerned. How do we know when the lakes are frozen enough for ice-fishing? Sometimes we drive onto the lake and see if anything around us cracks. People, however, are not water, and so driving over them to see if they crack is not a good idea. Those who want to initiate change or blow the whistle on foul play are best served by their conscience, and the honesty of their own personal inventories that indicate their readiness to proceed with matters without malice. Readiness concerns one's commitment to the greater good of all, and the willingness to face the obstacles and criticism. Good timing is often influenced by the immediacy of crisis, and the greater crisis that may follow if nobody intervenes, as illustrated by a modern plague.

While making rounds on his first day at San Francisco General Hospital in 1981, Dr. Paul Volberding met his first HIV patient, who presented with Kaposi Sarcoma, a rare cancer. The AIDS crisis was in its infancy then, but it was not long before SF General and hospitals across the country saw overwhelming numbers of patients, mainly gay men, succumb to the disease.

By 1983, Volberding found himself in a crisis. Patients with AIDS drew condemnation from religious conservatives who spewed that the disease was God's way of punishing people for their sins. Many in the health care professions were terrified of coming into contact with AIDS patients and refused to work with them. With the help of Drs. Constance Wofsy, and Donald Abrams, Volberding co-founded of Ward 5B, a special unit at SF General to treat and care for AIDS patients.[5] The doctors were criticized and ostracized, but ultimately created what became a model of AIDs care and intervention that was replicated throughout the country.[6]

Volberding grew up in rural Minnesota, near Rochester, where he daily completed farm chores and was raised in the Lutheran faith. He believed in "callings," the inner voice of a higher power or God that compels one to undertake a certain cause or enter a certain vocation. He held that his work was a ministry.[7] In doing so, he applied patient-centered care to a population that many believed deserved no care at all.[8]

---

5. Cicneros, "Thirty Years of AIDS."

6. See Cochrane's *When AIDS Began* for a chronology of the epidemic and national reaction.

7. Talbot, *Season of the Witch*, pp. 390–393.

8. Pogash's *As Real as it Gets* documents the extraordinary humanity of medical pioneers who made SF General a world renowned model of AIDS treatment and care, as they faced public scorn and funding shortages.

When asked about the deciding moment when AIDS became an important issues in Volberding's life, he noted that he was impressed by how the gay community sprung into action and how easy it was for the medical community to work with grassroots organizations. He also said, "But I still think the vivid memory of my first patient was the real spark for me."[9] He was a lot like Omalu and Bourgeois who saw humanity first and job descriptions second.

SPIRITUALITY GROUNDED INTERVENTION

Business courses and human resources training routinely teach people to document events and communications, so that in the event of a conflict or need for intervention there exists a substantial and accurate account of matters. Documentation represents an important aspect of preparedness to intervene, and it certainly has legal ramifications, but bringing spirituality to bear requires more than pen and paper. The other aspect of preparedness concerns one's the state of mind and attitude. Being in a state of calmness, open-mindedness, and empathy is important. Sometimes, even the most justified and well-rehearsed interventions fall through the ice because it is clear that those petitioning for change harbor vengeance and demonstrate little to no empathy for those involved.

Not everyone involved in interventions reach a state of spiritual centeredness. In working with others to prepare an intervention, it is important to explore everyone's motives, feelings, assumptions, and attitudes, and to evaluate the potential for those things to contribute to a reasonable and gracious resolution. It may takes months before those involved reach a psychological state of calm and spiritual serenity. In some cases, those involved may best prepare themselves by getting psychological or spiritual counseling.

Spiritually mature interventions and dissent are driven by four cardinal values. The first is a sincere and deep respect for the truth. The second feature is a genuine empathy and valuing of all stakeholders in all decisions and conflicts. Third, spiritually driven dissenters and interventionists embrace humility, and fourth, they value open and respectful communication. These values often get lost in formal education and in our on-the-job training, and we frequently wait until a crisis erupts before we think about these values. Making it our mission to think about these values and discuss them

---

9. San Francisco AIDS Foundation, "The View from Here," para. 11.

with others who are equally interested in maintaining a healthy workplace may prepare us for a crisis, and may even help us prevent them.

In valuing truth, one seeks a thorough and accurate grasp of the facts and why they are important. Since truth is often subject to interpretation, to value truth also means to seek multiple perspectives on matters, and seek these perspectives with equal interest and respect. Truth is vital to creating visions and goals. Truth is indispensable in our assessment of the workplace and estimations of our own character and conduct. As the cliché goes, "If it ain't broke, don't fix it." Its lesser known sidekick is, "It ain't possible to fix things that you don't admit are broken."

Having empathy for everyone—especially one's adversaries—is not easy. Empathy is not always popular in the workplace because it runs contrary to cultural and company norms about the "competitive edge." To value empathy is to reject the notion that people are objects. Empathy enables us to anticipate how others are impacted by our behavior, even if those others are not yet born or not of our own species.

We sometimes forget the power of empathy, and that this power can be used for better or worse. Modern advertising, for instance, became a multi-billion dollar industry because its creators and designers were extremely empathetic. Ad agencies study the consumers' motivations, anxieties, fears, fantasies, and emotional needs. They use what they learn to create slogans and images that manipulate those feelings and needs, and to get us to buy what they want us to buy.[10] We have the choice to crawl inside other people's heads for the purpose of manipulating their spending habits, voting preferences, and self-esteem, or for the purpose of cultivating compassionate executives, honest workers, and good neighbors. We choose.

Empathy requires discernment. My friends and I sometimes shake our heads and roll our eyes over the number of times we have been bamboozled by a stranger's sad song. There are people in the world who exploit empathy, and the wisdom of discerning healthy boundaries to our generosity speaks to us against the ills of compulsive care-taking, co-dependence, and self-annihilation. Having empathy for others does not mean that others are always right. It is sometimes wise to consult with others, such as a spiritual

---

10. The pioneers of modern propaganda include Edward Bernays, nephew of Sigmund Freud, who used psychoanalysis to manipulate the public. He got rich teaching tobacco merchants how to pitch cigarettes to women and advised corporations and public officials on matters from consumerism to covert activities. See: Bernays', *Propaganda* and *Public Relations*. Tye's *Father of Spin* chronicles Bernays life and birth of public relations.

advisor or good friend when we struggle with the questions of when to share and when to conserve our resources and ourselves.

Humility is an attitude and a state of mind that is characterized by peace with the idea that one dos not have all the answers. To value humility in the workplace is to accept the reality that one is a part of something greater than oneself, and that could be the reputation of a family-own business, or the public's safety and wellness. Humility paves the way to growth as it allows us to admit that we do not always know what we need to know before we take action.

Author Stephen Covey has written much about leadership and asserts that humility is the "Mother of all other virtues."[11] Covey notes that the opposite of humility is pride, which is manifest in the perpetual assertion of one's will. From a spiritual perspective, humility is what makes possible the transformation from a material creature wholly consumed by material concerns to a conduit of the love of God. In humility the determination to gratify the ego recedes, and in its place steps compassion, charity, mercy, patience, good will, and genuine happiness for other's success and achievement. The absence of humility in leadership invites dysfunction and misery. Employees might go without deserved recognition and praise, without steady stewardship, and without reasonable accommodations.

Activating spirituality in the workplace pertains to the way we discipline our thoughts and engage our hearts in the process of listening and speaking. What follows is a short list of strategies that may help us bring spirituality to bear on our interactions and conflict resolution:

1. **Keep the Faith**. Be confident in the existence of God or a power greater than yourself that is benevolent, directs us to love one another, and frees us from the burden of omnipotence.

2. **Exercise Gratitude Always**. Be grateful for opportunities to grow intellectually, psychologically, and spiritually even if the lessons are painful and difficult.

3. **Seek Counsel**. Explore your concerns, your evidence for grievances, and the scope of your intervention to ensure these things are reasonable; rehearse interventions to ensure that your word choice and tone are gracious and welcoming.

---

11. Covey, *Principle-Centered Leadership*, p. 54.

4. **Respect Time and Place.** Secure an appropriate time and place to introduce concerns, keeping in mind the damage that can be done when having spontaneous confrontations in front of others. Stick to the time allotment to which you agreed, and be open to continuations of discussion based on mutual interest and need.

5. **Never Assume.** Avoid making assumptions about what others think, do, or say. Be mindful of how your own perspective may color your reaction to what you hear.

6. **Avoid Sarcasm.** Refrain from making sarcastic remarks and adding levity to the conversation as these things may signal a lack of sincerity or respect. Remember than one person's humor is another person's insult.

7. **Be Empathetic.** Demonstrate empathy for all points of view and remain open to options that allow others an honorable way out of conflict. Express authentic interest in others' well-being and be explicit in about how you understand competing perspectives. Be ready to respect those who are not ready to take a stand or get involved with matters. Remain open to sharing leadership and decision-making.

8. **Shame Not.** Be mindful that it is possible to call attention to mistakes, errors in judgment, hurtful behavior, and disregard for policy without shaming somebody's sense of self by focusing on behavior and the consequences of behavior rather than somebody's character, motives, or personality.

9. **Use "I" Statements.** Keep the conversation focused on your own experiences by using "I statements" that represent your own feelings about specific behavior. It is one thing to say: "This unit would be the best in the company if you didn't screw up every spreadsheet you touch!" It is another to say: "I have read your spreadsheets carefully and I am concerned about the accuracy of the data entry." It is one thing to say: "Everyone in the office thinks that you are a rabid sexist pig." It is another thing to say, "I am uncomfortable with the comments you make about women, and I feel disrespected when I hear what you say about women's bodies and personal relationships."

10. **Focus on Progress.** Remember that the point of intervention is not to create a perfect workplace, it is to make progress. The intervention may be the beginning of important shifts in the workplace's culture,

but people might need to experience things more than once and to sit with their conscience for a while before they are ready to make changes in their attitudes and behavior.

11. **Relevance.** Stick to the relevant issues and avoid dragging problems that are irrelevant into the matter; be faithful to the original scope of concerns and avoid speculation about problems outside that scope.

12. **Accept Consequences.** Be willing to accept the consequences and results of your actions even if you believe they are not fair or reasonable. Allow for people to have their own feelings and thoughts about the matter. If ideas of retaliation or revenge come to mind, explore what fuels them and discern what these ideas may reveal about the need to temper your ego and expectations. If termination is the outcome of conflict resolution, keep in mind that it may be a blessing in disguise.

REFLECTIONS

1. Think about a conflict you had with someone and explore what it taught you about yourself. Consider the source of the conflict. What was at stake for you? What was at stake for others? Did you accurately define the conflict and assess its significance? Consider the feelings you had at the time and determine you were more interested in preserving your pride or in preserving open dialogue and reaching mutual understanding. If you had to repeat the experience, what would you do differently? How and why?

2. Would you describe yourself as a humble person? Why? Would others describe you as a humble person? Why?

3. Review the short list of strategies that help us integrate the love of God and neighbor into our interventions, interactions, and communication in general, and identify which ones you feel you have consistently practiced, and which you have not. Explore the ways you may be able to increase the consistency of practice in all items on the list.

4. Instructors: In what ways could you integrate studies of and reflections on the strategies in the short list at the end of this chapter into your course curriculum? What campus resources may be able to help you with this endeavor?

5. Instructors: How could you design lessons so that students could rehearse interventions and improve their ability to communicate in the midst of conflict?

7

Quit the Weasel

ROSEMARY AND THE EVIL SPIRITS

LET US IMAGINE THAT all the individuals in the stories presented so far took the appropriate steps to speak out against unfairness, incompetence, or abuses in the workplace, and did so with a great deal of empathy and good will towards all. Imagine that Betty the accountant spoke up against the pressure to retire that she and her senior co-workers experienced. Imagine that Jeff politely and rationally contested the restructuring of his unit, and that Francine brought her concerns about standards of competence to high level management with accurate documentation and a sincere desire to protect the integrity of the staff and public safety. Imagine that each person followed designated protocols and did so in prayer and examination of conscience. Imagine that after all that, they were all denied the resolutions they sought. It does not stretch our imaginations to conjure these unfortunate outcomes. They happen all the time.

The interventionist is wise to be prepared for an unsympathetic audience, and the whistle blower in the workplace is wise to be prepared for rejection. We work in organizations created by human beings and that means they will embody all the virtues and vices humanity has to offer. Many of the decisions that managers face present the choice between satisfying someone's immediate personal interests and satisfying the long-range interests of the organization or the community it serves. There will always be tension between these interests. Workers might place their confidence in human resources departments or in unions and expect them to advance their causes, but human resources and unions often do not as they represent many interests besides that of the employee.

Human resources departments administer benefits and help employees strategize for retirement, but they also exist to protect both the rights and needs employee and the organization. Human resource experts are responsible for sustaining the productivity of the organization and defending it against the irrational or unjust demands of its employees. They are not obligated to ally with every worker who files a grievance. They are required to facilitate the grievance procedures with objectivity and deference to established protocols. Their primary duties relative to grievances are to distinguish the legitimate grievances from the illegitimate, and to resolve disputes as close to the source of the conflict as possible in a timely manner.[1]

Unions by definition have an obligation to be the employee's advocate. Their utility is widely known in matters where collective actions have resulted in strikes and forced negotiations with employers. Unions are limited in the capacity to serve employees, however, because their advocacy operates within the context of contracts and organizational bylaws over which they may not have control. Unions are also limited in their ability to protect the integrity of the profession because they frequently defend employees based on the employee's tenure rather than the employee's competence. In addition, the efficacy of both human resources and unions depends to some extent on the competency of their representatives. In one case, a union representative was asked to assist an employee who needed to know how to respond to an abusive supervisor. Lacking knowledge of grievance protocols and of the unit in which the employee worked, the union representative offered little help. She did, however, assure the employee that if she placed a Rosemary plant near the entrance to her office, it would "disperse evil spirits."

Spirituality is not supposed to free us from conflict and difficulty on the job, it is meant to help us maintain our dignity and integrity in the face of conflict and difficulty. Spiritual capital includes the ability to be patient not to rush judgement, open-mindedness, willingness to see all sides of conflict, genuine good-will for others, and humility enough to see one's own part in conflict. Using spiritual capital does not always prevent us from being fired. Sometimes there are just too many weasels in the henhouse for

---

1. Cole, *Personnel and Human Resource Management*, pp. 443–444.

us to nest our eggs safely, and sometimes we tap our spiritual capital when it is too late to salvage our careers.

HOMEMADE QUICKSAND

For numerous people, leaving their jobs is a sign of failure and humiliation. Leaving one's job can be a daunting prospect—even terrifying—especially in times of economic recession. Many people are traumatized by the idea of changing jobs because they rely on their careers and positions to define their self-worth and buttress their sense of identity.

Many people who want to leave their positions and find a new job do not because they lack confidence in their ability to do so or because they are lazy. Instead of finding someone who will assist them with job searches, getting a resume in order, and rehearsing job interviews, they wallow in self-made quicksand. In that situation, the unhappy worker has two problems. First, he or she is miserable in the workplace. Second, he or she is now convinced that his or her unhappy situation is inevitable and unchangeable. While the first problem might originate with others at work, the second problem originates with the worker.

We are ready to mix our own batch of quicksand for many reasons. One is because we believe that gratification must be instant. Another is the belief that organizations must adjust themselves to the individual's preferences, and failure to do so means that the organization is unreasonable, uncaring or bigoted. Many have missed wonderful opportunities to work in healthy environments because they lack the patience to seek options. Another batch of quicksand results from an irrational sense of loyalty. That leads people to remain in jobs long after the work environment has damaged their well-being. Other folks rationalize their own misery on the job as "God's will," as if a heavenly accountant kept tallies of how we paid for our sins.

Among of the cruelest and most tragic varieties of quicksand are those of our own personality disorders, flaws of character, and the refusal to get help when we need it. Individuals who compulsively abuse others, lack appropriate boundaries of behavior, or who are chronically angry or anxious often need to seek treatment as part of the terms of an employer's agreement to retain the toxic employee. Many who suffer from behaviors, such as a "pervasive pattern of instability of interpersonal relationships, self-images," and "impulsivity," undermine their own success in the world because they do not recognize their own self-destructive tendencies.[2]

The existence of weasels on the job—those who take credit for our work, gossip about us, or sabotage our advancement—are trouble enough for the average worker, but for workers who are psychologically fragile, the weasels can be doubly demonic. As Mark's story illustrates, the courage to get help is sometimes more important than the courage to contest our adversaries.

Mark Donovan (not his real name) was raised Catholic in a blue collar Chicago neighborhood. He took his religion seriously in his youth, dutifully taking the sacraments and serving as an altar boy. Finding his passion in literature, Mark aspired to become a teacher and relished the idea of awakening adolescents to universal themes in the human story, and the lessons of tragedy, comedy, innocence, war, heroism, and virtue. He earned his degrees and Ivy League credentials while working his way through college and living in a cheap, dilapidated rental unit. When he landed his first job as an English teacher, he was in his glory.

After his first year on the job, Mark's administrators decided that he was not a good fit for the school, and they did not offer a second contract. It did not take him long to find another job, where he worked for two years with colleagues that he described as stupid and banal. He ultimately was fired because students and parents complained about his temper. While at his third job, Mark regularly contested his departmental chairperson's leadership. Eventually, the disagreements became shouting matches that reverberated down long corridors. Mark and his chairperson exchanged harsh words as their faces reddened in rage. Both men lost control of their emotions, and both men hurled insults about each other's masculinity in each other's faces. The chairperson reported these episodes to the principal who calmly tried to reconcile the two. After repeated attempts to find an honorable reconciliation, the principal decided Mark that had to leave the school. The chairperson retained his job and eventually ascended into an administrative role, which vindicated Mark's cynicism about the "good old boy system."

The principal who facilitated the conversation between Mark and the chairperson asked each individual to speak about their part in the conflict and to the way forward. The agreements brokered by the administration

---

2. American Psychiatric Association. *Diagnostic and Statistical Manual*, p. 707-708.

were doomed however, in part because the chairperson was a popular figure on campus and Mark was not. Mark's promises to refrain from confrontation melted in the heat of what he perceived was persecution. He appeared constitutionally incapable of controlling his anger and sarcasm, and rejected the validity of other's perspectives.

Had Mark undergone intensive therapy or sought spiritual counseling after his first dismissal, he might have located the source of his defensiveness and chronic anger in time to salvage his teaching career. He may have avoided the humiliating rounds of dismissals from jobs and frustrating job searches. He eventually landed in psychoanalysis, where he faced rage against his father who physically and mentally brutalized him since birth. Mark's father saw no merit in Mark's interests, and nothing Mark ever did was good enough.

Mark was ultimately struggling not only to be the brilliant writing and literature teacher that he was, he was struggling to find a sense of self that was whole, sacred, and worthy of respect and love. Mark read the chairperson's responses to him and all the criticisms of students and parents as an assault on his existence. He had become his own worst weasel. He could not separate criticism for his pedagogical approach from his person. His expertise in the language arts was perhaps the one thing in his life that made him feel proud of himself. He struggled to see that critiques of his standards and communication style were intended to help him work effectively in the community, and not to insult his mastery of language arts.

EMOTIONAL INTELLIGENCE

Mark Donovan prided himself on being a very rational man, but even the most rationale and highly educated can have blind spots that destroy them like characters in a Greek tragedy. In his book, *Emotional Intelligence*, Daniel Goleman explores the phenomenon whereby highly intelligent people are not always successful in their endeavors because they lack "emotional intelligence."[3] Goleman stated that emotional intelligence is concerned with the capacities to: persist in times of distress; control impulses; delay gratification; remain focused despite distractions; empathize; feel hope; read other people's feelings; manage other people's feelings; and, accurately map a social environment by recognizing who was associated with whom and who cared about what. Goleman drew largely from Peter Salovey, whose list

3. Goleman, *Emotional Intelligence*, pp. 33–38.

of characteristics of emotional intelligence emphasized self-awareness, introspection, and the ability to discern personal strengths and limitations.[4]

All of the things Goleman and Salovey associate with emotional intelligence are relevant to spiritual development. First, emotional intelligence concerns the individual's relationship with oneself and with others, which is central to the faithful's invitation to build loving and just communities. Second, emotional intelligence invites people to embrace many of the same virtues that are commensurate with spiritual maturity. These include delayed gratification, self-discipline, hope, empathy, self-awareness, and strong sense of what parts of our selves require growth and maturation.

Emotionally intelligent people do not necessarily have to believe in God to dodge the weasels of the world or quit the weasel within. Mark Donovan, however, was among those who believed that people were created for the purpose of caring for each other and building a better world. He was a Catholic baby boomer who's potential to love himself and others collided with his father's fists and fury, and with monolithic stereotypes of what it means to be a man in our society. Mark did not tap his spiritual capital when, arguably, he needed it the most.

Mark's story bears witness to the reality that we sometimes bring our "emotional baggage" and spiritual wounds to work with tragic consequences. Paradoxically, while the workplace is an environment in which we may contribute to the healing and wellness of others, it is not the responsibility of our co-workers or employers to provide what only professional therapists and spiritual counselors can provide. Individuals who do not get professional help when they need it leave open the possibility that employers have little option other than to dismiss individuals who disrupt the workplace.

THE VIRTUE OF MALADJUSTMENT

In quitting the weasel, we may have to endure accusations that something is wrong with us. If we work in an environment where "weaselism" is the norm, then as we disengage from our own "weaelitis," others may see us as disturbed or unhinged. Those who believe that we were created for a sacred purpose that finds its highest expression in peace, love, and justice are often ridiculed, because they do not feel compelled to congratulate others for their wealth and fame, or worship at the altar of convention.

---

4. Salovey and Mayer, "Emotional Intelligence."

Those who are awake to their spiritual selves and acutely aware of the disparities between the values and virtues that society espouses, and the values and virtues by which society lives, sometimes feel alien to the world. Reverend Martin Luther King, Jr. observed that people who strive to close the gap between espoused and lived values and virtues are sometimes accused of being maladjusted. He posited that such maladjustment was virtuous, and declared:

> Certainly, we all want to avoid the maladjusted life . . .
> But I say to you, my friends . . . there are certain things in our nation and in the world which I am proud to be maladjusted and which I hope all men of good-will will be maladjusted until the good societies realize. I say very honestly that I never intend to become adjusted to segregation and discrimination. I never intend to become adjusted to religious bigotry. I never intend to adjust myself to economic conditions that will take necessities from the many to give luxuries to the few. I never intend to adjust myself to the madness of militarism, to self-defeating effects of physical violence.[5]

King's words could easily be applied to our own personal inventories about life on the job. Sometimes we unconsciously make adjustments to things we find abhorrent. Sometimes we convince ourselves that we must adjust to beastly behavior at work because the office propaganda tells us that "weasels are people too." Spirituality invites us to examine whether we have replaced healthy conversations about behavior in the workplace with the unspoken agreement that "what is good for the bottom line is by definition moral and principled." It begs the questions of why people adjust to discrimination, greed, bullying, and incompetence, and what is at risk because we made adjustments.

UNDER THE RADAR

In my interviews with people, many of the individuals who offered their thoughts about work and the workplace confided that for the sake of self-preservation they have learned to focus only on their immediate duties and their personal attitudes. Some said that they learned to "fly under the radar," meaning that they do little to draw attention to themselves. They complete their assigned duties with care, keep quite during meetings, and

---

5. King, "Speech at Western Michigan University," pp. 17–18.

stay clear of office politics. They admit their conduct does little to change dysfunctional environments, but are satisfied knowing that they do a good job and are not contributing to unpleasant dynamics. They may have once been champions of initiatives and volunteered to serve on committees, but found that carrying the torch only resulted in third degree burns.

One of the weasels we may need to quit for the sake of our own peace of mind and wellness is the crusade. Many employees with good intentions undertake interventions or crusades for which they are psychologically and spiritually ill-prepared. In the process, they frequently experience resentment rather than empathy, cynicism rather than hope, and intolerance rather than patience and good will. They also alienate others including potential allies. From a spiritual perspective, the danger of the crusade is its potential to intoxicate our egos, and thus become the monsters we are trying to fight.

Some may insist that it is irresponsible under any circumstance to refrain from intervening in workplaces where people are routinely abused and there exists little accountability for high standards of productivity and collegiality. Some say that being passive under such conditions enables the weasel, and they are correct. On the other hand it is vital to understand that the weasel will always be with us, and that by grace we are given the capacity to discern which fight belongs to us in the moment and which ought to be saved for another day.

Despite the work of Jesus of Nazareth, Martin Luther King, Jr., Ella Baker, Fanny Lou Hamer, Helen Caldicott, Roy Bourgeois, Bennet Omalu, and Karen Silkwood, and all the men and women who have offered their lives for the cause of peace, justice, and decency, weasels live on.[6] It is compelling that when Jesus had the opportunity to lead a crusade against the Roman empire—an empire whose economy was fueled by slave labor and whose culture was as grotesque, violent, and obscene as it was technologically and artistically magnificent—he side-stepped the whole affair. His

---

6. King's role in the Civil Rights Movement is well known, but he was also a vocal advocate of economic justice and an opponent of American imperialism. Ella Baker was a key advisor and strategist of the Student Nonviolent Coordinating Committee during the Civil Rights Movement; see Ransby's *Ella Baker*. Caldicott's membership in Physicians for Social Responsibility revitalized the anti-nuclear movement; see Caldicott's autobiography, *A Desperate Passion*. Hamer, a poor sharecropper from Mississippi was among the most powerful and eloquent voice of the Civil Rights Movement; see Lee's *For Freedom's Sake*.

crusade, first and foremost, concerned the individual's commitment to love God and love neighbor.

There are at least three ways to quit the weasel. First, employees may participate in an intervention. Second, individuals can quit their own weasels by seeking psychological therapy and spiritual counseling in order to heal wounds and change behavior. Third, employees can quit weasels by finding new job opportunities within their careers or by changing their profession. None the options listed here are guaranteed to create a worker's paradise, but they might help individuals back away from debilitating depression, anger, hopelessness, and malice.

I have known individuals who have walked away from very lucrative careers in investment banking and industry because they could not in good conscience profit from what they believed were immoral business practices and objectives. I have known individuals who remained in such careers despite their knowledge of how their companies pillage public wealth, and contribute to human suffering on a massive scale. Every day, idealism and realism clash in the consciences of people who take spirituality seriously, and each must navigate their way to earn a living without making a mockery of their faith. To live in the spirit is to enter a constant state of discernment, controversy, and competing interests.

REFLECTIONS

1. What do you believe is the proper role of unions and human resources units relative to conflict resolution on the job, why do you believe these things, and what are the strengths and weaknesses of these convictions?

2. What kinds of behaviors might signal that you or someone at work is experiencing psychological or spiritual distress that warrants intervention, and what would be the ideal intervention, and why?

3. Reflect upon an experience where you felt exploited, abused or poorly treated in the workplace and identify the ways your own spirituality may have been used to sharpen your understanding of matters and respond in a healthy and charitable way to conflict and pain.

4. What are your own personal weasels? How do you know about them and what purpose do you think they have served? How have they

impacted others? What might be some strategies to quit your own weasels?

5. Instructors: To what extent do you help students understand the role of human resources and unions, and to identify strategies for using these entities effectively? To what extent do you help students create strategies for responding to unhelpful human resources and unions?

8

Geezers and Goslings

AGING INTO VULNERABILITY

A FEW DECADES AGO, most workers were confident that when they reached the age of 65, the age at which most qualify for Medicare, they could retire in relative comfort and security. That confidence is among the casualties of change in the nation's economic landscape. At present, many over age 65 find that they cannot afford to retire and so remain in jobs they do not like. Additionally, elders who want to quit their jobs and find new ones are sometimes stuck with the old job because of age discrimination in hiring processes. Many remain in the workforce because they love their work and the way it connects them to the community. Others are trying to survive after the 2008 recession destroyed their pensions.[1]

There is no shortage of debate on whether working past the age of 65 is beneficial or detrimental.[2] There is no scarcity of predators scheming to capitalize on the elderly's financial anxiety.[3] Stereotypes of the elderly portray them as crippled, crumpled, and cranky "old bags and geezers" who have lost their relevance, and who sap the energy of others with their endless complaints and dependence on others to get by.[4] Elders in the U.S.

1. Shawn, Kim and Jitendra, "Elderly Workers."
2. Burnes, et al., "Prevalence." See Senthiligam, "Pros and Cons" for a look at diverse aging experiences.
3. Hackard's *Wolf at the Door* provides a guide to identifying elder abuse and how families can prevent it.
4. Bergman, "Ageism in Childhood." Also see Brogden's *Geronticide* which explores

represent some of the most vulnerable of our society. In 2016, 14.5 percent of over age 65 lived in poverty.[5] About 20 percent of seniors over age 65 work, many because of the high cost of living and Social Security retirement rules, and others because their incomes are needed to support their grandchildren.[6] Many over the age of 55 work in low-paying jobs because they have been corralled out of their careers and cannot find high-paying jobs.[7]

Paradoxically, for as much as experts claim that we need the elderly in the workplace to keep the economy going, employers have an incentive to rid their organizations of folks over 50.[8] Seniors are expensive, they have health problems, and they sometimes lag behind youngsters in technological mastery. Ageism, the systematic stereotyping and discrimination against people based on their age, accounted for over 20,000 claims filed with the Equal Employment Opportunity Commission in 2013, and 64 percent of adults over age 65 say they have experienced or witnessed age discrimination on the job.[9]

For those over age 50 who are grappling with retaining jobs, finding new jobs, and retiring, it is difficult to say which is worse. Is it the boss that wants to fire elders or employers who will not hire anyone over age 55? Is it the economy that forces elders to work after the age of 62 because shelter, food, and health care are so damn expensive, or is it the politician who says that it is OK to spend billions on corporate subsidies and slash Medicare because our elders are so damn expensive?[10]

Operating on the "bottom line mentality," employers sometimes lose sight the humanity that stands behind the numbers. The spiritual factor that often remains invisible to management concerns the employee's sense of dignity. Employment is a source of dignity because it allows individuals to be self-sufficient and to contribute to the maintenance and well-being of society through their labor and taxes. Catholic bishops assert that

---

the systematic ways in which elders are not only marginalized from society, but treated in ways that hasten their deaths.

5. De Costa, "More and More Older Americans," para. 7.
6. De Pillis, "U.S. Economy."
7. Picchi, "The New Low Wage Reality," para. 4–7.
8. DePillis, "The U.S. Economy," para. 10–11.
9. Fleck, "Forced Out," para 7.
10. Federal spending on corporate welfare in 2018 was $150 billion, (J.T. Bennet, *Corporate Welfare*, p.1), while federal spending on Medicare was $589 billion.

employment is a basic right because all people in a just world should have the means to support their material existence. They state that the nation's first priority should be full employment with jobs that offer decent wages and working conditions.[11] The bishops acknowledge that unemployment often results in psychological damage to the unemployed. They note that the unemployed are blamed for their own fate because their skills are no longer a good match for the workplace.

Corporate boards, administrators, and managers are not obligated to honor the spiritual needs of employees. They must comply with federal, state, and local laws pertaining to wages, benefits, safety, and discrimination, but there are no state or federal laws mandating full employment. Despite laws against age discrimination, there are ways to muscle elders out of a job without repercussions. These include job elimination, job restructuring, denying promotions, isolating individuals in the workplace, decreasing departmental or project budgets, and reduction of responsibilities to the point where individuals feel useless and unwanted.[12]

Admittedly, when it comes to retirement, individuals can be their own worst enemy. Sometimes people do not plan well for retirement and save as much as they should have. Researchers conclude that certain personality types are more likely than other personality types to save for retirement. While "grasshoppers" like to feast and live for the moment, others are "ants" that are frugal and take time to prepare for a secure future.[13] In some instances, however, the odds are against the ants. Not all employees meet the employer's eligibility requirements for retirement plans. Not all workers can sock away thousands of dollars a year after paying for their education, health care, shelter, and all the incidentals that are necessary to support a family or to bear extraordinary financial burdens. Not all workers are rewarded equally for their labor. Despite the existence of civil rights legislation, U.S., ethnic minorities generally earn less than whites, and women generally earn less than men for comparable work.[14]

Age is more than a variable that may determine whether we hold our jobs for as long as we would like to hold our jobs. Age often determines what we expect from the work place and how we interact with others on the job. As folks in their 20s enter the workforce, they take their place alongside

11. United States Catholic Bishops, *Economic Justice for All*, p. 33–34.
12. Ballman, "Eleven Sneaky Ways," lines 1–19.
13. Ghilarducci, "The Real Reason People don't Save Enough," lines 1–13.
14. Brown, *Millennials and Retirement*.

folks over the age of 50, and then continue a ritual that has been going on for thousands of years. The ritual is the struggle of the old to understand the young, and the young to understand the old.

THOSE DARN MILLENNIALS

Much has been written about the conflict between baby boomers and millennials in the workplace. The scrapes and tiffs that pepper relations between boomers and everybody born after 1964 is just another chapter in the human story of how we learn to love the people those who brought us into the world, and those we brought into the world. Once upon a time, those born before 1945 thought boomers would bring civilization to ruin with rebellion, unrealistic utopian visions, sex, drugs, and rock and roll. Boomers now criticize the younger generation for their obsession with digital gadgets, their sense of entitlement, and casual approach to work. The beat goes on, as the cycle of each generation making the world in its own image is in motion.[15]

At present, the millennials, those born roughly between 1981 and 1996, are the source of much controversy about the direction the American workplace is headed. On one hand, millennials have been described as very diverse, optimistic, confident, cooperative, deferential to authority, and the hope of the future.[16] On the other hand, they have been characterized as indifferent to authority, narcissistic, highly dependent on directives, unmotivated, quick to espouse altruism, but not inclined to think about social problems or work for the government.[17] Some insist that millennials are not as bad as some say, and are more akin to older generations that previously thought.[18]

---

15. Time frames for each generation's birth years are roughly as follows: The Greatest Generation 1910–1924, Silent Generation 1925–1945, Baby Boomers 1946–1964, Generation Xers 1965–1981, and Millennials 1982–1999. See Zemke, Raines, and Filipczak's *Generations at Work* and Johnson and Johnson's *Generations, Inc.* for studies of generations in the workplace and insights to management.

16. Howe and Strauss, *Millennials Rising*, pp. 3–30. Also see Bannon, Ford and Meltzer, "Understanding."

17. Twenge, "Millennials." Also see Twenge, Campbell, and Freeman, "Generational Differences in Young Adults," and Twenge, et al., "General Differences in Work Values."

18. See Carmichael, "Millennials are Actually Workaholics," and Pfau, "What Do Millennials," para. 6–15.

In 2014, millennials represented 34 percent of the U.S. workforce, and they are projected to represent 46 percent by 2020.[19] Millennials bring a mixed bag of sometimes contradictory gifts to the workplace. They report that they value meaningful work and a sense of accomplishment more than they value making gobs of money, value structure in the workplace, and are very altruistic. Yet, research suggests that they are largely focused on their own agenda rather than society, highly dependent on frequent praise from supervisors, want employers to be flexible as to accommodate life-work balances, and express little commitment to staying with their companies for long periods of time.[20]

Studies also suggest that millennials are less religious than boomers, reflecting the overall trend in the secularization of the U.S. population. Whereas 83 percent boomer reported that they were affiliated with a particular faith in 2015, about 64 percent of millennials reported the same.[21] Increasingly, the younger generation does not lean on faith as a source of guidance in decision-making. In 2018, the Pew Research Center found that only 23 percent of younger millennials relied on religion for guidance, while 17 looked to philosophy and reason, and 46 percent depended on common sense.[22]

All statistics aside, it is very difficult to paint a whole generation with one brush, and unfair to stereotype every individual born between two given years. More importantly, spirituality transcends generations. It is universally concerned with the same purposes and principles, and with enduring questions about what it means to be human and good. Every generation faces obstacles to the development of spirituality, including the distractions of the material world, the thrill of ego's assertion, and the compulsion to justify anything to flee accountability. Every generation inherits the masterpieces and the messes of the parents, and every generation is the author of its own tragedies and triumphs. Every generation wrestles with what it has been told are universal beliefs and values, and is tempted to re-invent the wheel if for no other reason than to have bragging rights.

Among the greatest barriers to getting different generations to work effectively together is their inability to see themselves and their opinions objectively. Without objectivity, and honest and fair assessment of the good

---

19. Brack and Kelly, "Maximizing Millennials."
20. Ibid. also see Deloitte, *2016 Deloitte Millennial Survey*, pp. 4–7.
21. Pew Research Center, "Generational Replacement," see chart.
22. Pew Research Center, "Younger Millennials," see chart: Source of Guidance.

or bad that may come of initiatives, plans, resolutions, and policies is nearly impossible. The subjective view of the world often prevents people from recognizing that each generation's accomplishments were made possible in part by the previous generation's endeavors. Each generation takes time to mature. Acquiring maturity of character is not inevitable, however, and each generation will make the journey to virtue, wisdom, and humility only with the encouragement, instruction, and wisdom of elders who went before.

Humanity does not live on the wisdom of one generation alone. We have been successful in the business of civilization because we have been able to transfer culture from one generation to the next, and because our transfers of culture have mostly retained the valuing of order and organization. Many of the principles and values that sustain prosperity and pleasant workplaces are universal and enduring. Honesty, integrity, and respect for others are principles that are just as sterling in the era of Internet communication and jet travel as they were in the eras of block printing and travel by camel caravans.

Younger generations tend to rebel against older generations, and that is natural and healthy for autonomous and creative thinking. Events in recent history suggest that the rebellion of youth is far less dangerous to civilization and spirituality than the abdication of leadership in elders. Youthful rebellion normally conveys the proposition that there are great causes and principles for which to fight, and new ideals for which to stand. Many of my baby boomer peers who demonstrated for peace and who protested against oppression and discrimination did so because they believed that elders had failed to apply the values that elders espoused.[23] Elderly abdication of leadership conveys the notion that there are no great causes nor noble ideals—there is only the existential yawn, and no fundamental ethos worth protecting. The danger is that without great ideals, causes, and principles, we often become narrow and stubbornly self-serving in our thoughts and actions.

A VIEW FROM HR

Dan, former Human Resource Manager with three major companies in the defense and aerospace industries, supervised scores of projects and

---

23. DeBenedetti's *American Ordeal* and Watson's *Freedom Summer* eloquently make this point.

thousands of workers over his 40-year career. He also taught several management courses at the college level and has given countless hours of his time as a volunteer for charitable causes. In conversation, Dan revealed his thoughts about generational differences in the workplace, corporate and personal values, and whether current trends are putting our economy at risk. His observations provide considerable food for thought.

Baby boomers were raised by Depression Era parents, Dan stated, and that meant that they were raised to give the company your best, and to stay on the job as long as they could. Boomers understand the "politics of our work," he noted, which means they grasp the written and unwritten rules about raises, promotions, title changes, hierarchies, and communication protocols. "Boomers tend to value loyalty to the company and care about its growth and stability," he said, and "they typically don't complain about long work hours or having to rework something over and over until it is done correctly." Boomers, he said, also embraced the paradigm of "paying your dues" in order to advance in the organization, and they respect honesty, ethics, and hard work.

Dan indicated that millennials do not tend to value loyalty to the company, and are driven more by job titles that they believe will open the next door of opportunity. Millennials jump jobs with greater frequency than boomers, as they are motivated by and impatient about upgrades in pay and position.[24] Dan asserted that millennials have little to no interest in how things were done in the past; "They just come in and say 'this is how it should be done,' and expect that everyone will say 'yes.' " Millennials, he declared, are not driven by the big picture—they are not interested in "what we do—" as in the larger picture of the company's identity or meeting the needs of society—they are interested in themselves and their own career trajectory. Even when they seek new titles, he explained, "They want a title with no one to report to and nobody to report to them." Millennials work hard, Dan concluded, but, "They work hard only when they perceive some immediate benefit for themselves."

Dan said that millennials believe that they can multitask on the job and still be effective—something unheard of in the workplace decades ago when boomers entered the workforce. Millennials do have a lot to offer employers, he reported, then added that, "generations have to learn how to work together—companies have to learn how to respect the millennials' orientation to technology and social media, and millennials have to

---

24. Landrum, "Millennials aren't Afraid," lines 1–6.

respect company culture."[25] He said that older managers have simply been told to give the millennials whatever they want and to allow them to work while texting or surfing the Internet, as part of a strategy to give millennials incentive to stay with the company for a long period of time. Dan observed, "Boomers resent that the kids get everything they want and don't have to pay any dues, and then, even when the kids get what they want, they leave after a couple of years anyway."

Dan believes that many of the changes in corporate culture that occurred in his lifetime may be attributed to adjustments that administration and management have undertaken to accommodate the demands of younger generations' demands. He acknowledged that at some point businesses will have to set limits on accommodations because they may have an adverse impact on the company's viability. Without persistent investment in innovation and maintaining a competitive edge in the market, he noted, businesses in the U.S. are vulnerable to foreign investors, who may or may not have America's best interests in mind. Our business, he warned, might be bought up by enemies ready to take advantage of weaknesses that we created when we were cutting corners in order to make a fast buck.

Dan pointed to three critical variables that he believed are to blame for the deterioration of company loyalty, the value of paying one's dues, and making sacrifices for the good of the company. First, he acknowledged that boomer parents gave millennials whatever they wanted. Unlike boomers who had paper routes and part-time jobs at the local drug store, millennials got what they wanted without having to work for it. He also averred that millennials were largely protected from adversity as parents were quick to rescue their kids when they met with failure or conflict over everything from grades to a place on the starting line-up of little league soccer.

Second, Dan lamented that companies themselves have moved away from a family culture to being obsessed by the bottom line. "Companies once had a strong family culture," he claimed, "and that could be seen in the way they recognized and valued their employees and by the way they gave to charitable entities in the community—but now, they believe that if they save all their money and use it for incentives and bonuses, then employees can say, 'This is a fun place to work.'" When asked if this trend might change in the future, Dan was skeptical, citing changes in tax laws. Whereas tax breaks once gave corporations incentives to donate to hospitals, homeless shelters, and other charities, they now discourage such generosity.

25. See Deal, Altman, and Rogelberg, "Millennials at Work."

Dan asserted that the third factor contributing to changes in corporate culture is education. As a college professor, Dan encountered many students who lacked proficiency in mathematics, reading and writing. He believes that using appropriate English, syntax and grammar are important to undergraduates who want to work in corporate settings, because ultimately they will be asked to communicate effectively with peers, supervisors, and perhaps even represent their company to stockholders, the general public, and external regulatory agencies. Dan stated that when he raises these issues with students, they say, "If that is the case when I'm on the job, I'll just get my secretary to write something for me." When he suggested to other instructors that the department integrate writing skills more robustly into their courses, he was met with resolute disinterest and distain. "Not my job," said the professors.

Dan expressed concern over growing consensus in the professoriate that students' literacy is outside the scope of their responsibilities, and they believe that their most important job is to see that as many students as possible get college diplomas. He is also alarmed that so many instructors are telling students to "never stay more than two or three years in a job—keep jumping until you find the one you really want." This, he decries, sends the younger generation the message that job-hopping is normal, ethical, and wise, and it may be none of these things.

When I asked Dan about whether spirituality mattered in the workplace, he insisted, "Bringing God into the workplace is a problem because we need to respect diversity," and added, "Personally, it is OK to bring it to work, but not to flaunt it." He posited that spirituality matters in the workplace because it "brings honesty, ethics, and doing what's right . . . You don't have people who steal or take credit for other's work." He indicated that his own spirituality was important to his work ethic, and when he hired people, he "looked for diversity, ethical standards, honesty, and evidence of caring for others."

WHAT GOES AROUND

While it is interesting and perhaps even entertaining to compare and contrast generations in the workplace, what matters in the end is whether generations can reach a consensus about the highest purpose of their company, and for the community it serves. Building consensus is hard work, and requires humility, objectivity, and trust.

Each generation is shaped by forces they did not create, and each generation exerts forces that will shape generations to come. Boomers were shaped by dualistic thinking during the Cold War, wherein executives and managers were to be obeyed not questioned. It was a world in which people venerated honesty, hard work, and loyalty—in step with the Protestant work ethic, but often distributed rewards for such things according to race or gender—in step with social Darwinism. Many boomers advocated reforms to improve equity in the workplace in ways that would retain organizational reverence for honesty, hard work, and loyalty. Others found that if honesty and loyalty to both company and the public were compromised, they could make more money. When executives adjust their work ethic to be more attentive to the bottom line and the enrichment of their stockholders, and less attentive to the public's well-being, they essentially tell employees all along the "food chain" that entrepreneurs who are blessed with prosperity owe very little to the general public.

The dialectic between conservation and reform goes on. Each generation brings its anxieties and dreams to bear on the problems that society faces. Each generation provides the next with some sense of what conduct ought to be normed and which things ought to be valued above all others. Each generation chooses whether it will keep individualism in check, and thus determine whether future generations will live well or live at all.

Dan's remarks remind us that both family and institutional culture makes the world go around. Parents that instill a sense of entitlement and narcissism in their offspring should not be surprised to wake up to a world wherein selfishness is normed and criticizing it is politically incorrect. Corporations that exploit workers, commit fraud, and lie to the public for the sake of enriching stockholders should not be flabbergasted to find that employees lack a sense of loyal to employers, or that do not feel guilty when they steal from the till. Colleges and universities that produce graduates who are unable to comprehend complex text and who cannot compose a cohesive paragraph should not be astonished that taxpayers want to end their support for public education.

As for what might be gleaned from tensions between generations in the workplace, it is clear that in the workplace, all generations may benefit from accepting three premises. First, the workplace is about the big, picture, the organization's purpose for its existence, and its role in and obligations to society. When the big picture and purpose are limited to accruing profit in the short-run, the organization is basically telling society its commitment to the community's well-being is also limited. Second, regardless of our birth year, everyone benefits when workers experience a sense of family in the workplace, and everyone accepts the proposition that each can learn from the other. Third, unexamined deference to political correctness and avoidance of hard work, ultimately diminish our regard for high standards in the workplace.

Generational wars in the workplace are often exacerbated by the organization's failure to cultivate a strong commitment among employees to the organization's vision and objectives, and to keep the vison and objectives at the center of all matters from hiring to retirement. As Dan noted, the challenge of management is to accommodate young employees without negotiating to the point where the organization's core purpose and viability have been destroyed. All accommodations, whether they are undertaken on behalf of employers, customers, or stockholders have implications for everyone's sustainability. Dan recognizes the challenges the younger generation bring to the workplace, but he also see that elders have not always done a great job in keeping the common good in the forefront of their decision-making. He worries that executives in the older generation may be willing to adopt business practices that generate handsome profits in the short-run, while leaving the company vulnerable to ruin or take-overs in the long-run. A sustainable industry, he noted, has employees who respect the needs and culture of the organization, and has executives who respect the needs of the community that houses them, supplies them with educated and skills workers, and depends on their good judgement to protect the common good.

REFLECTIONS

1. Explore your assumptions and beliefs about people from generations different than your own, and discuss how these assumptions and beliefs have the potential to influence how you treat them on the job. Do these assumptions and beliefs mirror your convictions about human dignity and love of neighbor?

2. What are is the best criteria to determine whether an employee has a legitimate voice in the institution? Should employees enjoy unconditional freedom to express their beliefs, concerns, criticisms, and demands? Why?

3. Explore and identify your personal understanding of what you owe the company that hires you and what you believe the company owes you. What are the foundations of these beliefs and have they served you well in the workplace? Explain.

4. Students: To what extent do you accept or resist your institution's efforts to teach ethics, and teach you about social justice and responsibility? Why do you respond as you do?

5. Instructors: To what extent do you take seriously the ethical formation of students, and design courses that improve their empathy, moral reasoning, and commitment to serve causes higher than themselves? What evidence from assignments and assessments support your conclusions?

9

Leading for Loot

RUSTY RHETORIC

MANY OF THE INDIVIDUALS who were consulted for this book were asked directly, "What do you think has changed the most in the workplace over the last 50 years." Without hesitation, most replied that businesses executives seem greedier and more obsessed with pleasing stock holders than before. Many individuals complained that cost-cutting resulted in layoffs that left remaining staff to do the work of several people, and refusals to promote and reclassify individuals. Several grumbled about whopping disparities in pay for managers and laborers, and about outsourcing—the practice of opening factories abroad in order to reduce the cost of labor. Many voiced concern about hiring and promotion practices that prioritized diversity at the expense of high standards of competency.

When pressed in our discussion to identify the source of so many negative changes, most people pointed to leadership, not only in their own companies and institutions, but in public office. The moral of the story is that leadership matters. At present, there is no doubt that many people who are employed, unemployed, and retired are screaming for better leadership and greater accountability in both government and private industry.

Things have changed over the last several decades, and some of those changes have inflicted society with hopelessness and desperation. In general, the rhetoric that flowed from corporate America and the government after World War II fortified public confidence in executive leadership and faith in the wisdom of officials and administrators. At that time, whatever was corrupt about elections, industrial operations, foreign policy agendas, and government remained well out of sight of the average citizen. In 1953, when Charles Wilson, Chief Executive Officer of General Motors, declared that, "What was good for our country was good for General Motors," government and private industry enjoyed the reputation of being partners in patriotism and the advancement of the common good.[1] Moreover, many Americans assumed that patriotism was synonymous with a deep devotion to the well-being of each and every citizen. In those days, factory workers, teachers, janitors, and barbers could earn enough money to buy a home, a car, send kids to college, and retire comfortably. Today, that is not so easy, and public confidence in executive leadership is dubious.

Confidence in government leadership has been battered by what many believe is an increase in malicious political rhetoric and hate speech in social media.[2] Our confidence has also been eroded by what appears to be a sadistic dance whereby industries and banks bow and courtesy as they find new ways to reduce pensions, eliminate benefits, and increase the cost of everything, and whereby government do-si-dos in step to marshal tax dollars for corporate subsidies and bail-outs.[3]

During the 1960s and 1970s, as dissenters and reformers criticized national and local leadership, many believed that, if we could just get the warmongers and bigots out of power, then our society would be truly decent and truly democratic. At that point, many saw the problem of leadership as one defined by a few bad characters in high places. That view was very different from the contemporary cynicism, which holds that the problem of leadership is not a matter of a few mutts among the pedigreed, but a matter of an entire system gone to the dogs.

Not everyone saw dissenters and reformers in a positive light. In his philippic against the liberalism, Robert Bork, former Attorney General and U.S. Federal Court of Appeals judge, stated that, "The defining characteristics of modern liberalism are radical egalitarianism (the equality of outcomes rather than opportunities) and radical individualism (the drastic reduction of limits of personal gratification)."[4] Bork, who believed that

---

1. Patterson, "What's Good for America," lines 6–7.

2. See Chait, "Trump isn't Inciting Violence by Mistake," and Okeowo, "Hate on the Rise."

3. Bakan's *The Corporation* and Derber's *Corporation Nation* leave little doubt that democracy and decency are both jeopardized by our form of capitalism.

4. Bork, *Slouching Towards Gomorrah*, p. 5

morality was the foundation of culture, excoriated the "radical individualism" of feminists, gays, and minorities who championed "identity politics." This was a keen insight to the things that threaten civilization, but it was too partisan in scope. Bork did not apply the concept of "radical individualism" to corporate behavior, and so missed the opportunity to teach us about what happens to society when it is managed by individuals who put private fortunes above all considerations.

The 1950s "feel-good" rhetoric of politicians' and industrialists' does not feel so good any more. Since the 1970s, hard-working Americans have been assaulted by inflation, national debt, corporate greed, banking scandals, bailouts, and tax breaks for the rich.[5] Faith and confidence in leadership has lapsed, and political rhetoric is awash in vulgarity, cruelty, and blind partisanship.[6] Since the Vietnam War and Watergate scandal many Americans expect leaders to lie, and they are not disappointed. Tobacco industries lied about the relationship between their products and cancer.[7] President Reagan lied about human rights violations of juntas in Latin America and trading arms for hostages.[8] President Clinton lied about his extra-marital affairs.[9] President G. W. Bush lied about Iraq's cache of nuclear weapons, his relationship with Enron executive Ken Lay, and the effects of tax policies.[10] On it goes.

JUST SHUT UP AND GO AWAY

The relationship between public mistrust of politicians and corporate executives in high places and how we behave in our lowly workplaces may seem remote, but people keep telling me the two are intimately related. They assert that when leaders lack credibility, it breaks their spirits. The corrections officer reports that the state is committed to solving problems

---

5. Reich's, *Beyond Outrage* documents contemporary abuses of capitalism and their consequences.

6. Zvesper, "The Problem." Good reads on the quality and meaning of political rhetoric include: Derek Thompson's, "Presidential Speeches," Mark Thompsons' *Enough Said* and Lim's *The Anti-Intellectual Presidency*.

7. Orey's *Assuming the Risk* chronicles the legal battle to get the tobacco industry to tell the truth.

8. Alterman, *When Presidents Lie*, pp. 238–293.

9. Toobin's *Vast Conspiracy* documents Clinton's cat and mouse dalliances and their implications.

10. Corn's *The Lies of George W. Bush* is comprehensive and well-documented.

with trendy solutions rather than strategies involving systemic social reform because trendy is cheaper and has the look and feel of "innovation," and so he remains quiet when asked for his recommendations. The nurses who try to keep up with exemplary patient care while cost-cutting initiatives increase the ratio of patients to nurses often quit the profession rather let politicians who know next to nothing about best-practice in health care dictate the quality of care they give their patients. The professor reports that the chancellor is more interested in the numbers that graduate than he is in literacy levels of college graduates, and so avoids conflict by inflating his grades. The unspoken mantra is that, "When leaders don't care, workers don't care."

Many with whom I spoke also fervently wish that politicians and corporate leaders who have no enduring, deep, and sincere interest in the public's well-being, and no substantial expertise in their professions, would "just shut up and go away." They are not hateful people; they are people who are hurting and sick of hearing leaders make excuses for the hurt. Leaders who do not possess a deep store of knowledge about the operations they supervise lack credibility, yet they are legion in our organizations. Expertise and discerning stewardship are not always the criteria for ascending into leadership positions. Pliability and subservience to power-broker-brokers and executive atop the organization's hierarchy sometimes determines who gets to be prompted. A friend's story drives the message home.

Brandon's supervisor was, by his account, promoted to her position because she took directives well and demonstrated little interest in contesting the status quo, even when it showed signs of dysfunction. Brandon said, "As it turns out, this woman was not interested in innovation, and was super eager to comply with whatever administration wanted, because she knew absolutely nothing about how the system worked—it was not that she thought the system was so great that kept her complacent, it was the fact that she didn't understand the system itself!" Brandon confided, "This supervisor got little respect from the team because they knew far more than she did about technology and how quickly it was changing in the industry . . . Rather than dutifully follow directives, we started to do things the way we knew they would work, and then take the criticism later—if it ever came—for not following orders." I asked about what the poor choice in supervision cost the organization, and Brandon laughed, "You don't know all the costs—how many people quit, how much productivity was lost to fake sick days or disengagement, or how much we spent to fix problems we should have prevented, or how much data was lost or compromised—who knows?"

Leadership's rhetoric matters because what leaders say and how they say it is supposed to inspire us to do our best. At present, many Americans do not see the difference between shepherds and shysters. Recent surveys found that at least 80 percent of Americans do not trust their government,[11] and that, 63 percent believe that corporate executives are not at all, or only somewhat credible.[12] In 2016, just 56 percent of registered voted cast a ballot.[13] The day may come when democracy no longer exists because good people who really wanted to vote found that no candidate met criteria that was compatible with their conscience.

During the 1970s and 1980s, the U.S. lost some of its might in the global economy and hit several potholes alone the road of domestic prosperity. Several factors contributed to the nations' troubles, including: Nixon's removal of the U.S. from the gold standard in 1971;[14] the 1973 oil embargo;[15] and, the increase of well-made German and Japanese goods in the global market.[16] As citizens called for businesses to exercise greater social responsibility, economist Milton Friedman bellowed that the only obligation businesses had was to increase profits.[17] Inflation, wage stagnation, and relatively high unemployment persisted throughout the 1980s.[18]

To restore profit and global competitiveness, corporations created the "leadership industry."[19] Scholars, politicians, and corporate executives placed great hope that a "science of leadership" would produce a modern business paradigm that would secure "America's place" as the dominant force in the global economy, and enable steady market expansion. It was

11. Derek Thompson, "80 Percent of Americans Don't Trust Government," line 1–4.
12. Harrington, "Survey: People's Trust has Declined," para. 1–3.
13. Desilver, "U.S. Trails Most," line 1.
14. Nixon took the U.S. off the gold standard as foreign banks had more U.S. currency than the U.S. could back. One of the results of this action was inflation. See Matusow, *Nixon's Economy*.
15. The embargo was in part a retaliation against the U.S for supporting Israel in the Yom Kippur War, but the Organization of Petroleum Exporting Countries (OPEC) did have grievances about the low prices its oil fetched, and had other political conflicts with the West. See Venn, *The Oil Crisis*.
16. Weaver, *United States and Global Economy*, pp. 39–50.
17. Friedman, "The Social Responsibility."
18. Reed, "One Hundred Years of Price Change," para. 70–106.
19. Kellerman, *The End of Leadership*, p. 164.

a pivotal agenda. Rather than creating a modern business paradigm that fostered collective executive leadership on a global scale, American leaders sought preeminence. The neoliberal model for the world's economy gives significant power to the World Bank, which decides which nations will get loans under which conditions and how resources will be manufactured and distributed. The face of this neoliberalism are pacts such as the North American Free Trade Agreement, which universally give advantages to affluent countries and multinational corporations.[20]

Neoliberal economics is more than a framework for production and distribution; it is an ethos, and it is an ethos that has not dissuaded students from seeking a business degree. In 1971, about 11 percent of all master's degrees were for Business Administration, and by 2012, they represented 25 percent of all master's degrees.[21] Over the last 30 years, business schools, online leadership training, and management publications have multiplied. By 2017, 19 percent of every college graduates majored in business.[22] The proliferation of business degrees, however, has not necessarily improved our economy or our leadership.

THEY DIDN'T GET THE MEMO

Despite growth in the leadership industry, Americans have traveled over some bumpy roads in the last three decades. Our leaders have even taken us for a stroll into economic mine fields where they assured us that all was well, even as we lost our homes, our jobs, our health care insurance, our pensions, and our hope. The Savings and Loan (S & L) scandal that lasted from 1986 to 1995 saw the failure of over 1,000 (32.2 percent) of all savings and loans institutions in the U.S.[23] Those who orchestrated the calamity were able to do so because they convinced leaders in government that strong regulations and strident measures of accountability were unnecessary and detrimental to the economy.[24] Lobbyists vouched for the soundness of junk bonds and subprime loans. It took over $120 billion of tax-payers money to rescue their banks.[25]

20. Gill, "Leaders and Led."
21. Byrne, "Why the MBA is now the Most Popular," lines 4–8.
22. Hess, "The 6 Most Popular College Majors," para. 9.
23. Curry and Shibut, "The Cost of the Savings and Loan Crisis."
24. Day, *S & L Hell*, pp. 31–34.
25. Ibid, p. 9. Also see Stewart's *Den of Thieves* for details on how bankers and their

Following the disaster, a bevy of federal and state leaders shook their fists with righteous indignation, and modest legislation was installed to curb banking abuses and increase accountability.[26] Editorials warned that by ignoring the lessons of history, the economy was sure to stumble into new catastrophes.[27]

Apparently, some leaders did not get the memo. After the S & L scandal, investment banks pressured Congress for legislation that allowed them to perform spectacular feats of financial hocus-pocus at the public's expense.[28] Further, it appears that those who *did* get the memo did not take seriously the assertion that it was irresponsible and dangerous for bankers to speculate with debt, exploit low-income borrowers, and misrepresent the virtues of their policies. As early as 1998, Brooksley Born, former head of the Commodity Futures Trading Commission (CFTC), was already publishing reports to the CFTC and others, warning that the shadowy derivatives market could cause a massive economic meltdown. Her critics, Federal Reserve Chairman, Alan Greenspan and Treasury Secretary Robert Rubin ridiculed and dismissed her research and predictions.[29] A decade later, Brooks' forecast came true. She was the prophetic voice that tried to prevent a manmade economic disaster, and failed because leaders in high places were too arrogant to listen. The damage done by the 2008 Recession outdid the S and L scandal, as tax payers were tapped for the mind-blowing bailout of over $700 billion.[30]

Adding insult to injury was the puny list of convictions and prison terms for wrong-doing. *The Washington Post* chided Americans in general and the justice system in particular when it noted that, "It's shocking that for a crisis that drove the global economy off the cliff, caused millions of

---

Washington buddies made the S &L scandal and insider trading enticing and profitable.

26. The Financial Institutions Reform, Recovery and Enforcement Act, 1989 replaced the Federal Savings and Loan Insurance Corporation with the Savings Association Insurance Fund, and gave the Federal Home Loan Mortgage Corporation (Freddy Mac) and the Federal National Mortgage Association (Fanny Mae) greater responsibility for administering loans to low and moderate-income individuals.

27. See "The S & L Scandal's Cruel," and Konczal, "Robert Reich on Why."

28. For details on bank-friendly legislation that led to public ruin, see Hirsh's *Capital Offense*.

29. Roig-Franzia, "Brooksley Born," para. 17–26. Also see *The Warning*, a PBS Frontline documentary.

30. Herszenhorn, "Congress Approves $700 Billion," lines 1–4,." Also see Lybeck, *A Global History*.

people to lose their homes and generally spread mass human misery to almost every corner of the earth there is no defining prosecution," and not one leader of "the firms directly culpable for the catastrophe has been put in a prison-orange jumpsuit."[31] The *New York Times* noted that courts prefer settlements to court trials, and suggested that the courts have a difficult time keeping up with the complexities of Wall Street's operations and laws that apply to them.[32] That alone begs the question of why leaders pass laws that are so esoteric and complex that they cannot be readily understood by the average lawyer.

While hundreds of bankers went to jail as a result of the S & L scandal, just one Wall Street executive was sent to prison as a result of the Recession of 2008. Rather than litigate public trials in which bankers would be forced to disclose their practices, the Justice Department determined that it would be best for the public and banks alike if guilty parties would admit their wrong-doing, pay a fine, and quietly be re-assimilated into the gray ethos of Wall Street.[33] This paradigm of justice is not restorative. Homes, businesses, jobs, pensions, and college funds that were lost, remained lost.

Leaders who created the economic hell of severe recession for millions were not only free from incarceration, they continued to award themselves millions in exorbitant bonuses and salaries. Following the bailout, Goldman distributed nearly $1 billion in bonuses to 200 individuals (roughly $5 million each), while Morgan-Stanley split $577 million among 101 people (roughly $5.7 million each). Nine of the banks bailed out by taxpayers paid employees a grand total of $32.6 billion in bonuses in the wake of their collective loss of $81 billion.[34]

The unabashed greed boggles the mind. The complicity of law-makers in the disaster cripples our faith in democracy. When viewed through a spiritual lens, the conduct of the crisis' masterminds and those who made little effort in their legislative and judicial proceedings to criminalize such pillage suggests that shame has no meaning in our society. The pillaging and subsequent distribution of bonuses are examples of "radical individualism," what Bork called the limitless pursuit of personal gratification.

---

31. Irwin, "This is a Complete List," lines 17–21.

32. Buell's *Capital Offenses* exposes how banking laws and regulations are deliberately written to be confusing to law enforcers, and so complex that it is hard to determine the source of wrong-doing.

33. Cohan, "How Wall Street Bankers Stayed Out of Jail," para. 10–11.

34. Story and Dash, "Bankers Reaped Lavish Bonuses," full story.

Our inability to accept the proposition that the "radical individualism" of corporate entities can be just as devastating to society as the "radical individualism" of the individual is one of the greatest challenges to our spiritual maturity.

THE EXTRAORDINARY

Brian Tracy of the American Management Association wrote that, "Leadership is the ability to elicit extraordinary performance from ordinary people," and that, "Leadership is the ability to get followers."[35] If this were all that mattered regarding leadership, then we are all doomed. After all, Adolph Hitler had millions of followers, and "elicited" from them the "extraordinary" act of killing more than six million people.[36] The Reverend Jim Jones had thousands of followers, and achieved the "extraordinary" feat of getting 900 people to commit suicide in the jungles of Guyana.[37] Having followers does not make one a leader, and doing something "extraordinary" is not necessarily doing something right.

Both Hitler and Jones were charismatic leaders who had the ability to talk people into abdicating their own consciences. This is not leadership in the deepest spiritual sense because it nullifies the individual's capacity to act as a free agent capable of moral reasoning and discerning the will of God, or a higher power. The conscience is a vital medium between the individual and his or her sense of divine purpose and obligation. Subverting others' consciences is a means of diminishing their humanity and capacity to be a co-creator with God.

Literature concerning management is robust on the matter of best practice, but even the best authors routinely do not address love of neighbor and spirituality. These topics are quarantined away from secular affairs because, even in our classrooms, we have not yet learned how to talk about religion, faith and spirituality in a way that is objective and non-threatening. Rather than training professors and managers in the art of instruction

---

35. Tracy, *Leadership*, p. 7.

36. Rees' *Hitler's Charisma* explores the dark relationship between desperate people and the messianic individuals who offer them hope, and explains why so many gladly slid into the abyss of evil.

37. Guinn's *The Road to Jonestown* presents an in depth biography of Jim Jones, his tragic past, and study of the people who venerated him and followed him without question to their deaths in November, 1978.

that reference spirituality or faith, Americans prefer to completely sever the spirituality and faith from formative conversation.

For the sake of keeping peace, we dutifully refrain from discussing faith and spirituality in public classrooms. The irony is that peace is not maintained and indoctrination continues. Silence on the matter of faith and spirituality—or any other matter—can breed assumptions. Business programs stripped bare of an ethics curriculum tacitly indoctrinates future leaders and employees with the idea that moral reasoning is superfluous in economic matters. Removing the conversation about ethics, virtue, and spirituality in the classroom does not make the classroom—or any other venue—a morally neutral environment; it only means that prevailing secular beliefs will dominate the conversation, and become the moral paradigm by default.

MISSION IMPERCEPTIBLE

To prevent organizations from becoming the extension of a single personality, organizations create mission statements. The missions of organizations are very important as they establishes an ideological platform for all operations. Mission statements express the organization's sense of duty to society at large, and speak to its objectives relative to the community's needs and well-being. The credibility and safety of organizations comes into question when mission statements are not aligned with actual practice. The troublesome case of Well Fargo Bank provides an example. Here are its vision, values, and goals:[38]

> We want to satisfy our customers' financial needs and help them succeed financially. This unites us around a simple premise: Customers can be better served when they have a relationship with a trusted provider that knows them well, provides reliable guidance, and can serve their full range of financial needs.
>
> Five primary values guide every action we take:
>
> - **What's right for customers.** We place customers at the center of everything we do. We want to exceed customer expectations and build relationships that last a lifetime.

---

38. Wells Fargo, "The Vision, Values and Goals of Wells Fargo."

- **People as a competitive advantage.** We strive to attract, develop, motivate, and retain the best team members—and collaborate across businesses and functions to serve customers.

- **Ethics.** We're committed to the highest standards of integrity, transparency, and principled performance. We do the right thing, in the right way, and hold ourselves accountable.

- **Diversity and inclusion.** We value and promote diversity and inclusion in all aspects of business and at all levels. Success comes from inviting and incorporating diverse perspectives.

- **Leadership.** We're all called to be leaders. We want everyone to lead themselves, lead the team, and lead the business—in service to customers, communities, team members, and shareholders.

We want to become the financial services leader in these areas:

- **Customer service and advice.** After listening to and understanding our customers and their financial goals, we want to provide exceptional service and guidance to help them succeed financially.

- **Team member engagement.** Our team members are our most valuable resource. We want to be the employer of choice—a place where people feel included, valued, and supported; everyone is respected; and we work as a team.

- **Innovation.** Through innovative thinking, industry-leading technology, and a willingness to test and learn, we create lasting value for customers—and increased efficiency for our operations.

- **Risk management.** While working to set the global standard in managing all forms of risk, we want to serve customers' needs and protect their assets, information, and privacy.

- **Corporate citizenship.** We make a positive contribution to communities through philanthropy, advancing diversity and inclusion, creating economic opportunity, and promoting environmental sustainability.

- **Shareholder value.** We want to deliver long-term value for shareholders through a balanced business model, strong risk discipline, efficient execution, and a world-class team.

Leading for Loot

These statements are meant to assure the public that Wells Fargo really cares about people. In theory, according to these statements, everything that Wells Fargo does will reflect these statements. All that rhetoric about philanthropy, protection of privacy, understanding, respect and integrity sounded so heavenly... until the bankers from hell arrived.

Whatever one may think about Wells Fargo's mission, the company itself demonstrated that its own words sometimes have no meaning. In 2017, Well Fargo disclosed that it had created over 3.5 million fake bank and credit card accounts and enrolled about 528,000 people in online payment plans without their knowledge. Carrie Tolstedt, who headed the retail division of the bank during the years in which the fraud was committed, lost her job along with thousands of lower level employees, and had to surrender $47 million in Wells Fargo stocks.[39] In 2004, Tolstedt set aggressive sales quotas that she knew were untenable, and then ignored evidence that fraudulent accounts were created to meet the quotas.[40] Wells Fargo employees reported that managers constantly pressured them to increase sales, and then did nothing when they learned that employees were increasing sales by establishing bogus accounts.[41]

The fraudulent activities initially cost the bank over $6 million to compensate customers for illegally collected fees and charges, and $185 million in penalties.[42] Later, it settled a class action suit related to the scam for $480 million.[43] For over a decade, Tolstedt and her ambitious underlings stole money from and violated the privacy and trust of Well Fargo's customers, without having to spend a day behind bars for doing so. The banks' highly polished mission statement, as a friend noted, "Melted away like make-up on a clown's face in a downpour."

A RAGING FIRENADO

On occasion, a fire will be so intense that superheated air rising from the ground will produce a spinning whirl of wind as hot air meets cooler temperatures above ground. The twirling column of air looks like a typical tornado, but does not behave like a typical tornado; it behaves more like a

---

39. Crimmins & Freifeld, "'Best Banker in America,'" para. 14.
40. Cowley and Kingson, "Wells Fargo to Claw Back," para. 12.
41. Egan, "Workers Tell," para. 3–9.
42. Egan, "Wells Fargo Uncovers."
43. Peltz, "Wells Fargo Agrees to Pay."

"firenado." It does not jump like other twisters, but scatters flaming debris in all directions, and is very difficult to combat. Firestorms create their own weather by generating wind and heat and sucking air into the blaze. The weather they create is designed to keep the fire burning.

The business practices in the U.S. are like fire-generated weather. Decades of bankers' exploitation of vulnerable customers, monetization of debt, wild speculation in the market and real estate, dishonesty about the security and soundness of dangerous policies, and the collection fat fortunes in salaries and bonuses in the wake of bailouts has created a unique social and economic climate. The weather outlook has been dismal: cloudy ethical standards with a chance of gale force greed that could demolish the value of credit and currency on a global scale.

In 2012, about three years after the taxpayers floated a bailout for Goldman Sachs, Greg Smith, a former employee of the investment firm for nearly 12 years, publically announced that he was quitting the investment firm. He found he could no longer breathe the air in Goldman's climate. His complaint was simple: his conscience could not longer bear the burden of working for a company that explicitly conspired to make money even if it meant harming innocent clients and the general public.[44] Smith states that during the executive administration of Lloyd C. Blankfein and Gary D. Cohn, there occurred a decline in Goldman's sense of morality wherein leadership was measured by the extent to which one could persuade clients to buy financial products that were not profitable for Goldman, and to sell whatever would bring Goldman the biggest profit.

Smith acknowledged that there is nothing illegal about profiting from transactions with clients, but noted that the practice was a threat to clients' trust, and thus the company's long-term stability. He pleaded with boards of directors to terminate unethical employees, regardless of how much money they made for the company. Goldman rejected the petition.

In 2016, Goldman admitted that it defrauded consumers in its activities prior to the 2008 financial meltdown, and said that it would pay the government $5 billion for its errors.[45] Critics howled that justice had been evaded as the settlement inflicted no real penalty, nor compensated all of Goldman's victims.[46] The company wanted to play nice with

---

44. Greg Smith's, *Why I Left* documents Smith's conflict with Goldman and Wall Street greed.

45. Shen, "Goldman Sachs Finally Admits."

46. Dayen, "Why the Goldman Sachs" para. 4–9.

the government, and the government wanted to play nice with Goldman. President Donald Trump took four former Goldman employees into his administration: Dina Powell (Department of National Securities); Steve Mnuchin (Treasury Secretary); Steve Bannon (Chief Strategist); and, Gary D. Cohn—one of the men Smith blamed for creating Goldman's rapacious and predatory culture—(National Economic Council).[47]

Trump is not unique. Throughout history, presidents of all parties have appointed captains of industry, banking executives, and Wall Street lawyers. The problem is not that government relies on these experts. The nation needs such experts to help steady the economy. The problem is that many business executives want laws that tilt prosperity towards themselves at the people's expense, and that ensure that public money will bail them out when their machinations produce disasters. The marriage between government and corporations keeps the fiscal firenado in motion. The blazing spin of smoke and debris clouds our moral outlook. It produces a climate wherein everyone, regardless of wealth and creed, must choose between being their brother's keeper, or devouring their brothers before their brothers devour them.

Leaders are the gatekeepers of domestic tranquility and justice. In many ways, they determine the scope of monetary meltdowns, and decide which underbrush to clear and who is allowed to play with matches. The Recession of 2008 demonstrated that leaders—even the most highly educated—are capable of gross offenses against the innocent. As a result of the recession, global unemployment increased from 178 million to 205 million, and as many as 87 million were thrown into poverty, from which millions never recovered.[48] The sudden collapse of credit and value of assets hit the poor without pity, causing those already enduring deprivations to endure even greater pain and suffering, as access to basic necessities turned to metaphoric ash.[49]

People take notice when their leaders' moral compasses go haywire. They want to see whether meaningful consequences will follow, and they want to gauge the latitude of misconduct that society will tolerate. They want to know if they are in danger. They want to know if their leaders have deceived them and are indifferent to human rights.

---

47. Link, "The Wall Street White House," lines 1–9.
48. United Nations, *The Global Financial Crisis,* p. iii.
49. Ibid, pp. 49–74.

In the wake of Goldman's pyrotechnics, Journalist David Dayen observed that, "We don't have a justice system with the courage to convict everyone regardless of wealth and power," and so, "the wealthy and powerful will keep committing crimes."[50] Many believe that we also do not have a government with the courage to regulate everyone regardless of wealth and power. The Dodd-Frank Wall Street and Consumer Protection Act, 2010, sputtered towards radical reform. It aimed to make banks more resilient to failure, and to reduce the adverse effects if they did. Critics argue that the legislation is flawed because it gives banks and investment houses too much authority to regulate themselves.[51] The legislation did not drastically increase taxes on hedge fund profits, break up the hegemony of the few banks that command over half of the industry, prohibit commercial banks from engaging in high-risk speculation, or limit the practice of insuring investments as to curb incentive to manage them recklessly.[52]

As Congress debated the Dodd-Frank bill, JP Morgan-Chase, Wells Fargo, Goldman Sachs, Bank of America, and Citibank spent nearly $25 million on lobbying for favorable provisions.[53] In 2017, 439 lobbyists (four more people than the number in the House of Representatives at the time), representing commercial banks at home and abroad spent over $67 million in their effort to influence government policies, and that does not include the nearly $10 million that was spent by private equity and investment firms.[54] Lobbyists do more than meet with officials to pitch ideas; they often draft legislation and testify before committees.[55] They have access to lawmakers and influence that the typical American does not have, and their speech is protected. In the years leading up to and following the 2008 recession, they convinced law-makers that banks and investment firms could be trusted with a flame-thrower in a straw castle.[56]

---

50. Dayen, "Why the Goldman Sachs."

51. Born, "Forward;" Skeel, *The New Financial Deal*, pp. 1–18;" Fischer, "Dodd-Frank's Failure."

52. Collins, "The Big Bank Bailout."

53. Godwin, Ainsworth and Godwin, *Lobbying and Policymaking*, pp. 15–42. Drutman's *The Business of America* documents how corporations became politicized and government became corporatized.

54. Center for Responsive Politics, "Commercial Banks," chart: Annual Lobbying.

55. Fisher, *Strategic Influence*, p. 23–48.

56. Jeff Connaughton, lobbyist and Senate aid, reveals Wall Street's hand in law-making in *The Payoff*.

ANTHONY QUIT

Anthony Try, a banker at Wells Fargo, quit the company when the fraud hit the fan. He stated that illegal activity and the creation of fraudulent accounts was systemic and "engrained in the culture for a long time."[57] An anonymous former employee of Wells Fargo stated that managers explicitly directed bankers to create false accounts, and then to tell alarmed customers who did not authorize the accounts that there was a mistake. The former employee indicated that bankers complied with unethical demands for fear of losing their jobs. Following the scandal, some Wells Fargo managers closed fraudulent accounts in an attempt to make them disappear before the accounts could be investigated, as required by law.[58] The icing on the cake came in in March, 2018 in the form of a $4.6 million dollar raise for Chief Executive Officer of Wells Fargo, Tim Sloan.[59] He was paid $13 million in 2016, the year the scandal became public, and defended his raise claiming that just some, but not all the naughtiness occurred under his watch.[60]

Greg Smith and Anthony Try exercised their consciences and love of neighbor by walking away from their jobs. They took a hit for integrity's sake and sacrificed whatever financial security they had in their positions. The reality that there were probably hundreds waiting in line to take their places speaks to why leadership matters. Leaders decide the agendas, and agendas shape what companies want in their employees. Smith and Try publically disclosed their motives for quitting their jobs, and so demonstrated the potential for low level employees to expose corporate malfeasance.

Smith of Goldman Sachs and Try of Wells Fargo were, perhaps, gambling that bad press would inspire reform. That may be wishful thinking. Research finds that unethical conduct in the workplace is often ignored when the employee in question is highly productive and exemplary in performance.[61] That sort of reality situates employees in the constant state of temptation, wherein voices named and unnamed whisper, "I will give you wealth and job security if you would merely bow down and worship me."[62]

57. Ibid.
58. Popken, "Wells Fargo Hit," lines 1–11.
59. Melin and Nasiripour, "Wells Fargo Boosts CEO," lines 1–12.
60. Tompor, "Wells Fargo CEO Slams Criticism," lines 10–11.
61. Quade, et al. "I Don't Want to be Near You."
62. This is an oblique reference to Jesus' temptation found in Luke 4:1–13.

REFLECTION

1. What traits do you associate with good leadership? Do you think moral leadership can sustain profits in business? Explain.

2. Write a mission statement for your life. What beliefs about yourself and others influence your statement? How would you rate the sincerity of your mission statement? Why?

3. What obstacles do you think you might encounter as you pursued your mission? What are your most important allies and resources in pursing your mission and outcomes?

4. Should private corporations and public institutions be held to a greater standards of accountability than individuals? Explain your rationales.

5. Instructors: How do leaders in your discipline differ from the lay person? How do you help students understand what leadership means in your discipline?

6. Instructors: Does the leadership in your department or unit encourage the ethical development of instructors and students? What could you do to improve these things?

7. Instructors: How do you help students understand and evaluate the merits and detriments of making profit the bottom line of leadership? How could this improve?

8. Instructors: To what extent are you objective in your instruction about capitalism and its alternatives? To what extent do explicitly teach students to be objective in their assessments of capitalism and their alternatives, and in their studies of the economy and those who exercise great control over it?

10

All Hail the Grand Poobah

MANDATORY MERRIMENT

SHARON HAD A LUXURIOUS office, "princess parking" in the garage, a six-figure salary, and a birthday party every year. She was the preeminent "poobah." She had lots of power in a powerful organization. Staff members stayed up late the night before the event preparing salads, pies, cakes, and savory dishes. Some bought presents, others decorations. Supervisors chastised staff members who failed to attend the event, told them that they had better be punctual next time. They suggested that to do otherwise was essentially insubordination. No other staff members' birthdays generated parties and gifts, and even though the average staff member earned about one fourth of what Sharon earned, they dutifully spent lots of money on treats and gifts. The birthday gal did not know the names of all staff members, and typically did not socialize with them outside the workplace. According to one party-goer, "It seemed like we were medieval peasants paying homage to the landlord."

The ritual of celebrating leaders in our workplaces to the exclusion of celebrating others reminds us of who is in charge, and who is special among all others. Parties for poohbahs are not diabolical by definition, but they can be very political and unintentionally hurtful. For some, parties at work present an opportunity to court the favor of individuals who may be instrumental in their promotion or support for pet projects. Others may find it difficult to bring gifts and cheerful faces to a leader that has denied them promotions, or disrespected the staff. When participation is mandated and there is no honorable way out, workers are compelled to put on their "happy face," and behave in ways that are not aligned with their own sense of integrity.

In theory, it is nice to honor leaders publically. They are the ones that bear the burden of executive decision-making, and bear the brunt of criticism when things do not go well. They are the men and women who are supposed to possess the special knowledge and skills that it takes to keep the organization solvent and successful. They often take risks that other employees doe not have to take, and are often subjected to public scrutiny in ways that the typical employee is not subjected. These things deserve respect. However, when employees are compelled to attend ritual festivities under threat of adverse consequences, it can breed resentment.

As children, many of us were taught early in our lives to respect titles. We honored titles such as "Doctor," "Sister," "Officer," "Governor," "President," and "Rabbi" in part because these titles conveyed the notion that people who had them had your back. My generation was taught that people earned titles by being especially responsible and keenly attentive to the needs of the weakest. Of course, later in life we learned that some people were charlatans, and that some people got titles for reasons other than skill and character.

Since there are so many leaders in government, public service, and private industry who are incompetent, selfish, mean, and vulgar, the matter of what do with "poohbahs" today is difficult. The kid inside me—that little boomer who wanted to be a noble citizen and a good Catholic—wants to honor and respect leaders. That kid understood that to honor and respect titles was another way of saying to the leader, "I see the goodness in what you do, and I want to follow your footsteps because you are trustworthy, kind, and competent." As age and experiences wore away the downy naiveté of youth and idealism, the adult in me says to the leader, "I see the power you have, but I am not convinced that you are using it wisely, and, although I believe in the need for great leadership, I will not follow your footsteps because they are sometimes morally wobbly and headed in the wrong direction."

THE ULTIMATE APHRODISIAC

Many people want to be grand poobahs, but not necessarily good leaders. Some simply want power. Some believe they will be great leaders because

All Hail the Grand Poobah

they confused leadership with management. Others seek positions of leadership because they want a raise, a new title, a corner office, additional staffing and resources, a transfer to a better location, or more autonomy. Employees are often careful to hide their motives for power and privilege, so it often falls to managers and administrators to detect the truth of people's interest in leadership, and to decide whether the ambitious will do more harm than good to the organization in their ascent.

Power is associated with leadership, but power is not leadership. Power is both a means to an end and an end itself. Power is the capacity to exert and impose will. It is currency, and can be traded for favors. History reveals that one tyrant will tolerate another so long as a "balance" of power between them can exist. In the words of former Secretary of State, Henry Kissinger, "power is the ultimate aphrodisiac."[1] His summation may have described not only power's effect on those around individuals with power, but the self-stimulating properties of power as well. Lust for power can inspire people to do whatever it takes to experience the exhilarating sense of importance, control, and command. The behaviors that catapult one to the top are not always honorable. As one author opined, the fast track to executive heights requires one to flatter superiors, hide one's intentions, learn how to use and dispose of one's enemies, get others to do the work while taking all the credit, and ingratiate oneself to powerful people.[2]

The desire to acquire, aggrandize, and protect power by all means cripples the ability to lead because these goals take time and energy away from leading. Time spent on fortifying one's position could be spent on learning more about community needs, improving the employees' experience, and creating sustainable business operations. The quest for power also breeds paranoia and enslaves individuals to perpetual supplication of those above them. Typically, the greater the debt the newly empowered owe to "kingmakers," the greater the claim the "kingmakers" have to the newly empowered person's conscience and obedience. Those who place poobahs on pedestals can also knock them down. In recent history, two powerful men exemplified a lust for power that drove them to deadly and doomed courses of action. Their stories illustrate the hazards of believing that if one makes a bargain with one devil, he will have the arsenal he needs to defeat other devils.

---

1. Isaacson, *Kissinger*, pp. 365–370.
2. Greene, *The 48 Laws of Power*.

God Bless Our Cubicles

Lyndon Baines Johnson (LBJ) was sucked into the war in Vietnam in part because he feared the East Coast Establishment—the industrial and banking "poobahs," who he believed would destroy his presidency if he was not militant enough against communism in Southeast Asia.[3] He was haunted by a sense of inferiority to the Establishment and frequently discharged his insecurities in vulgar rants and self-destructive behavior.[4] LBJ's predecessors, Eisenhower and Kennedy, had deployed CIA agents and military advisors, to prevent communist North Vietnam from uniting with South Vietnam. Johnson did not want to be the first president to lose a war, nor earn the reputation of being soft on communism.

In 1964, getting Americans excited about sending their loved ones off to die in a land they could not locate on a map, and to kill people they never heard of was a major feat. The less-than-glorious Korean War soured American zeal for taking the offensive for an ideological cause. Fighting in responses to an assault, however, was another story. LBJ thus manufactured a provocation following an alleged torpedo attack against the USS *Maddox*, in the Gulf of Tonkin. In 1964, U.S. forces were gathering intelligence and attacking North Vietnamese forts near the gulf. The U.S. claimed, however, that the *Maddox* was fired upon for no reason. LBJ used the phantom attack to mobilize Congress for war. Despite contradictory reports about the attack, he muscled J. William Fulbright (D-AR), Chairman of the Foreign Relations Committee, to rally his cause.[5] Congress ultimately gave Johnson a blank check to wage war.

Within months of the Gulf of Tonkin Resolution, 1964, LBJ sent tens of thousands of U.S. soldiers to South Vietnam and commenced aerial bombing of North Vietnam. By 1966, revelations of outright lies about the war's progress prompted Fulbright to hold Senate hearings. Congress felt bamboozled about the war, and resented LBJ's reduction of Congress' role in setting foreign policy. The hearings exposed a hierarchy of dishonesty: Advisors lied to the President, the President lied to Congress, and everyone lied to the public. Believing the lies was at that time a way to prove one's patriotism and preserve one's reputation as a cold warrior.[6]

---

3. Alterman, *When Presidents Lie*, pp. 160–237, McMaster's *Dereliction of Duty* describes the 1960s political climate in which aggression and confrontation were hallmarks of both manhood and leadership.

4. Dalleck's *Flawed Giant* explores Johnson's character, neuroses, and their impact on his leadership.

5. McMasters, *Dereliction of Duty*, pp. 62–83.

6. Alterman, *When Presidents Lie*, pp. 184–230.

All Hail the Grand Poobah

Fulbright was not a hippie liberal in 1966, yet he became one of most daring opponents of the war. He was a scoundrel to many Democrats as he had supported segregation and he was a consummate politician who finagled behind closed doors and was reflexively loyal to presidents. He dissented because LBJ had offended his principles and sense of decency.[7] His contempt for the war inspired others to call for a halt to the bombing and for immediate peace negotiations.

In his darkest hours, Johnson could not understand what he surmised was betrayal. He cursed those who would not be subdued by his rants and pontification. LBJ's biographers map his passion for control, revealing a man who believed so much in his messianic persona that he was utterly destroyed when others doubted his wisdom and right use of power.[8] His successor, Richard Nixon, vowed to restore law and order, and to win the war with honor.

Nixon was an ambitious cold warrior who, like LBJ, fought feelings of inferiority in the company of the Establishment, and cultivated masculinity and combativeness as political assets and as credentials for executive power.[9] He believed that the CIA was an ally of the "Ivy League liberals" who "had always opposed him politically."[10] Nixon escalated the bloodshed. He covertly bombed Laos and Cambodia. He added 21,194 Americans and hundreds of thousands of Laotian, Cambodian, and Vietnamese civilians to the list of fatalities.[11]

In his book, *No More Vietnams*, Nixon defended his thesis that fighting against communism is always noble. He asserted that his use of the phrase "no more Vietnams" meant that the U.S. should never to allow itself to fail as it did in the Vietnam War. He stuns readers with the announcement that the U.S. "won the war," because it had attained "the one political goal for which we had fought the war," which was the right of the South

---

7. Fulbright's book *The Arrogance of Power* chastises America's use of its resources, talent, credibility, and strength to bully other nations and impose its agenda and values on others.

8. Dalleck's *Flawed Giant* is a searing look at Johnson's ambitions, personality, and relationship to power.

9. Cuordileone's *Manhood and Political Culture* explores politics as a projection of masculinity. Also see Cuordileone, "Politics in an Age."

10. Priess, *The President's Book of Secrets*, p. 59.

11. Lewy, *America in Vietnam*, pp. 442–452. Some estimate that over 2 million Asians died in the war.

Vietnamese people to "determine their own political future."[12] It is hard to imagine how one can "fail" in war and "win the war" at the same time. Since the U.S. supported the French attempt to re-colonize Vietnam after WWII, it is also difficult to accept the claim that the U.S. was at war to protect Vietnamese sovereignty. Nixon, a Quaker by faith, despised communism and argued that, "Communist peace kills more than anti-communist war," but never took up the matter of how many have died for the sake of American imperialism.[13]

Johnson's and Nixon's relationships with power were very different from Omalu's and Bourgeois' relationship with power. Johnson's and Nixon's relationship with power caused them to be very secretive and deceptive, and Omalu's and Bourgeois' relationships with power connected them with many communities and caused them to be transparent. Power was both a means and an end to the presidents, while power was largely a means to a larger end for Omalu and Bourgeois. The threat of losing the White House motivated Johnson and Nixon to prove to Washington power brokers that they were worthy of high office, while Omalu and Bourgeois feared no loss of office, and so were freer speak truth to power. The need for vindication drove Johnson and Nixon to delusion, and engaged them in linguistic shell games, wherein facts were fluid and truth was elusive. This was not the case for Omalu and Bourgeois. The need for vindication often drives people to destroy their critics. While Omalu and Bourgeois were troubled by their critics, they did not plot their demise as did Johnson and Nixon.[14]

THE TROUBLE WITH TRAITS

To educate and form good managers and executives, many professional organizations have identified the desirable traits and habits of a good leader. These are sometimes so broad and vague that they readily accommodate malpractice and abuse. Two lists that follow make the point. The American Management Association asserts that effective leaders execute the following practices:[15]

---

12. Nixon, *No More Vietnams*, p. 97.
13. Ibid, p. 17.
14. See Weiner's *One Man against the World* and Dalleck's, *Flawed Giant*.
15. Tobin and Pettingell, *AMA Guide to Management*, pp.227–339.

All Hail the Grand Poobah

- Link employees to strategy and operations as to clarify objectives and vital roles of each unit and team
- Develop a leadership pipeline by improving retention, mentoring, and succession plans
- Facilitate management development and training via formal educational opportunities
- Initiate solutions in the event of employee non-performance or low competency
- Link Human Resources operations to organizational vision and objectives
- Cultivate interest and enthusiasm for learning throughout the organization

At Google, a research team identified eight best practices for management:[16]

- Good coaching skills
- Ability to empower team and refrain from micro-managing
- Expression of interest in employees' success and personal well-being
- Consistently productive and results oriented
- Being a good communicator who listens to team
- Assisting with career development and advancement
- Has a clear vision and strategy for the team
- Has technical skills that enable the ability to advise and assist the team

Both of these lists are laudable, and while they are rationale in theory, the actions they espouse are not always practiced.[17] Many companies do not care much about mentoring, listening, caring, and the warm fuzzies of "people-centric" management. These practices require skills and resources that many organizations do not have. Management often does not trust that these practices will be profitable or practices that shareholders will value.[18] In addition, it is possible to follow the advice contained in these lists and still have a workplace that rains ruin far and wide. To be specific:

---

16. Birkinshaw, *Becoming a Better Boss*, p. xv.
17. Addady, "Study," lines 1–22. Also see Sgroi, *Happiness and Productivity*.
18. Birkinshaw, pp. 1–3. Also see Freidman, "The Social Responsibility of Business."

- Managers at banks and investment firms may be very effective at *linking people to strategy and operations*, so that individual brokers could understand with data-driven precision exactly what it was that executives wanted from them, and then use the links and data to deceive and fleece their clients.
- Lobbyists are good at *linking* government officials with donors with deep pockets, and thus exploit the capacity to link special interests that may exclude public interests.
- Managers of financial institutions have *developed leadership pipelines that were plain and simple*, but sometimes rewarded especially aggressive employees who were willing to violate public trust or break the law.
- Corporate administrators could be *very proactive in their dealing with nonperformers*, and dismiss only those who have a problem with the "profit-at-all-cost" paradigm.
- Leaders may have *refrained from micro-managing*, but only where it is concerned with accountability and preventing fraud and illegal activities.
- Boards of directors could *express interest in their employees' personal well-being* but saturate the distribution of bonuses at the highest level of the organization and leave lower level employees' salaries and benefits out of the equation.
- Leaders in business and government could *be highly results-oriented*, yet their results might be measured by the number of employees forced into retirement, or percentage of production outsourced, or what management was able to take away from unions.
- Industrial leaders and elected officials might have a very *clear vision and strategy for their teams*, and that vision might have very little to do with sustainability, social justice, consumer protection, or environmental protection. Visions are not automatically benevolent.

In some ways, expecting these practices to purge the workplace of abuse and dysfunction is like expecting a brigade of firefighters to extinguish a house fire with ice-cream cones. Nice, sweet, and cool do not solve all problems. Nice, sweet, and cool are not implicitly moral. Management strategies are inevitably flavored by the context in which they are applied, and strategies can be used for moral or immoral purposes. Some reject even the most reasonable and humane strategies when they do not square with "bottom line." The desire to maximize profits, enhance stock portfolios, and expand markets jams our spiritual frequencies. We have learned to live with the static, and the static garbles the difference between management and leadership. We suffer in the workplace in part because we have settled for managers when we need leaders, and, when we get leaders, we often resent their call for personal sacrifice and discipline.

VISION

Experts in leadership say that there are important differences between leaders and managers. While both might value the same things, such as team work and honesty, the primary function of the leader is to be a visionary, and the primary function of the managers is to be the "technician" or "mechanic" who oversee the implementation of the vision.[19] Leaders are supposed to conceptualize possibilities and discern the right way forward among all options; they must constantly educate others about their vision, adapt it to changing conditions and contexts, and translate it to constituents and stakeholders affiliated and unaffiliated with the organization.[20]

Many believe that the most important part of the business leader's vision is how well he or she sees a clear means of increasing revenue. The expedient path to profit, however, is not always a good one. In August, 2018, as firefighters battled the Mendocino Complex fire in northern California, Verizon, a leading provider of wireless communications, admitted that it "throttled" firefighters' Internet connections for profit. The Santa Clara County Firefighters' contract with Verizon was for unlimited data, but Verizon scaled back the access during the conflagration because it wanted three times the payment of the original agreement.[21]

Verizon's actions slowed the speed of communication among firefighters, making it difficult for emergency crews to manage evacuations and fight the fire. The inferno consumed over 400,000 acres, displaced thousands of residents, cost millions to extinguish, and killed one firefighter. Verizon's action was puzzling in light of its own mission statement, which announced, "Verizon delivers the promise of the digital world by enhancing the ability of humans, businesses, and society to do more new and do

19. Bennis and Nanus, *Leaders*, p. 21. Also see Gardner *On Leadership*, pp. 11–22.
20. Bennis, *Why Leaders Can't Lead*, pp. 14–18.
21. Redell and Intarasuan, "Verizon Admits it Throttled Firefighters," lines 1–18.

more good."[22] What does "do more good" mean when a company extorts clients that are trying to save lives?

Not all leadership is consumed by power or places private profit ahead of public well-being. Rick Roscitt created AT & T Solutions to serve the communication needs of fortune 500 companies. The business grew to employ over 5,000 in part because Roscitt was fiercely honest and knew when to admit to potential clients that his company did not have the resources needed to properly serve them.[23] Former Chairman of Merrill Lynch, John Tully, gained a reputation as the public's watch dog as regularly called brokers who earned over $2 million not to praise them, but to learn how they accomplished the feat and to prevent misconduct.[24] In 1982, when seven Chicago residents died after taking Tylenol capsules that were laced with potassium cyanide, James Burke, CEO of Johnson & Johnson, makers of Tylenol, issued a recall of 31 million bottles of the product at a cost of over $100 million (about $250 million in 2017 currency). He oversaw the introduction of new tamper-proof packaging, and then gave the public discounts for their purchases.[25] Apparently, the public appreciated the integrity. Stock in Johnson & Johnson that was worth $1.02 a share in January, 1982 bubbled up to $13.97 ten years later.[26]

Most books and articles about leadership punctuate the importance of vision in leadership. Vision is basic. Organizations need to have a clear sense of where they are going and why, and the ethos embodied in the vision is critical. John Gardner, Secretary of Health, Education and Welfare from 1965 to 1968, observed that one of the essential ingredients of effective leadership was a vision that respected values in society at large.[27] He acknowledged the challenge of creating visions in a pluralistic society riddled with competing interests. He contended that that without a mutual commitment to the common good, pluralism reduces civility to raw aggression and a survivalist mentality. He also acknowledged that as various groups compete to assert their interests above those of others, groups tend to focus on short-term outcomes rather than long-term objectives. Leaders

22. Verizon, "Mission Statement."
23. Capodagli and Jackson, *Leading at the Speed*, pp. 59–60, 79.
24. Neff and Citron, *Lessons from the Top*, p. 330.
25. Moore's, "Fight to Save Tylenol" walks readers through executive steps during the crisis.
26. Macrotrends, "Johnson & Johnson," see interactive chart.
27. Gardner, *On Leadership*, pp. 96–98.

are therefore pressed to keep organizations focused on long-term consequences, even when short-term profits are modest or meager.

Vision concerns what Professor Warren Bennis called "the management of meaning."[28] This task is about creating narratives about one's enterprise and how it benefits society. The management of meaning can either illuminate an authentic commitment to serve and protect the public's well-being, or it can feed the public specious propaganda about what is good for the people and how much the company cares.

Bennis found that many leaders fail to lead well because they capitulate to "the context," or the culture of their organizations, and so abandon the culture they assimilated in formal education and in their families.[29] His presumption is that families and formal education generally inculcate individuals with a strong sense of social responsibility and ethics. While this may or may not be true, Bennis does suggest that leaders often work for organizations that prefer that their leaders suppress their own inner voices and conscience. He recognizes that the context of our work can disorientate us from our own moral principles and create tension between our principles and organizational expectations.

In some instances, leaders face opposition to their visions because those visions do not mirror the legacies of previous leaders, or because opponents have sentimental attachments to certain traditions. Leaders must often decide between options that are popular but not essential, and options that are essential, but not popular. The university that is offered millions of dollars for capital campaigns is a case in point. The choice between building a world-class ice arena, for instance, and a health care clinic is more than a capital campaign matter, it is a moral issue. The arena may entice applications to the university, draw rent for recreational ice time, and dazzle alumni donors. The health clinic may also entice applications and impress alumni, as it facilitates on-site internships for nurses, physical therapists, dieticians, accountants, managers, and social workers. The clinic may also partner with community agencies to extend affordable care to veterans, the elderly, and the disabled. The decision ultimately represents the university's sense of its highest purpose and priorities, and the extent of its courage to "think outside the box."

---

28. Bennis, *Why Leaders Can't Lead*, p. 20.
29. Bennis, *On Becoming a Leader*, pp. 26–31.

A COURT GESTURE

Business organizations and universities are not the only entities that need leaders with crystal clear and panoramic vision. Ordinary folks need and want leaders with noble vision in all areas of our lives. People yearn for vision that speaks to future achievements, but they also yearn for vision in a different way. They want their leaders to envision them—*to actually see the people all around them*—to see their condition, their needs, their strengths and their limitations for what they are, and to feel moved to compassion by what they see. People crave the security of knowing that those who have real power in the world are always going to see the little guy and use power benevolently on his behalf. People generally understand that when leaders treat others as though they are invisible, their worthlessness to that leader is real.

Leaders need not say much to reveal their vision of others. They need not make speeches or write essays to convey their regard for their fellows. This was demonstrated in September, 2018 during the Senate hearings to confirm the Supreme Court nominee, Brett Kavanaugh. As the assembled were leaving the Senate chambers for their lunch break, Fred Guttenberg approached Judge Kavanaugh and extended his hand to introduce himself. Kavanaugh turned to see Guttenberg, and looked squarely at him while Guttenberg introduced himself as the father of a child slain at the Parkland School shooting.[30] Without a word, Kavanaugh turned his back and walked away from Guttenberg.

The episode aroused controversy. Some opined that the judge was right to turn away in order to maintain his safety in a politically charged environment, and some said the judge was just plain arrogant. It is hard to tell what Kavanaugh's inner voices were telling him as he looked into Guttenberg's eyes before he turned his back to him. It is also difficult to understand the argument that Kavanaugh did the right thing for the sake of his own security. After all, visitors to the Senate chambers are screened for weapons prior to admission, and Guttenberg was himself a guest of Senator Diane Feinstein (D-CA), who formally introduced him during the hearing.[31]

---

30. Rosenblatt, "Parkland's Victim's." para. 1–4." On February 14, 2018, Nicholas Cruz, age 19, used an AR-15 semi-automatic rifle to kill 17 people and wound 17 others at Stoneman Douglas High School in Parkland FL. The AR-15 fires 30 rounds in 15 seconds. Fully automatic rifles can fire hundreds of rounds in 15 seconds.

31. Mark, "Video Shows Brett Kavanaugh," bullets 1–5.

All Hail the Grand Poobah

From a spiritual perspective Kavanaugh's response to Guttenberg was a lost opportunity to let Americans know that he sees and is not afraid to see all those he would serve, and has empathy for their losses and their need for healing. Kavanaugh, a Catholic, probably knows something about the Church's call to welcome the stranger and comfort those who are afflicted. It would have taken him only seconds to take Guttenberg's hand in to his own and say, "Hello Mr. Guttenberg, I want to thank you for being here. I don't have time to talk now, but I extend to you my condolences and I will keep your daughter and your family in prayer. God bless you."

The image of the judge turning his back on a man who lost his 14 year old daughter, Jamie, to a hail of bullets as she was in school conjures much speculation. Was Kavanaugh afraid? Was he indignant because he thinks propriety is more important than spontaneous compassion? Did he believe that Guttenberg is beneath him, or unworthy of his attention?

Why does the exchange between these two men belong in this discussion? Supreme Court justices make laws that determine our quality of life. They have already decided that corporations are people and deserve the same rights of free expression regardless of their clear advantage to own media, control its editorial positions, and to influence political candidates with millions in campaign contributions.[32] They have the power to determine whether labor laws and regulations are legal. They have the power to decide whether our civil rights are violated on the job and whether the government has the right to violate our privacy. The Supreme Court may one day decide whether or not the public is entitled to any form of public assistance and to liberty itself. Put bluntly, the conditions that individuals impose on who has access to them in many ways define the perimeters of their compassion.

Arguably, a nation that is led by men and women who lack empathy is at risk for losing its own moral compass. When citizens believe that their suffering, their needs, and their dignity are invisible to those entrusted to shepherd and protect them, they naturally become distrustful. When trust is eroded, virtues such as self-sacrifice, mercy, tolerance, and charity do not seem so virtuous, but only the acts of fools willing to be exploited. The absence of trust and virtue is a threat to our sustainability.

---

32. *Citizens United V. Federal Election Commission* 558 U.S. 310 (2010).

SPIRITUALLY-BASED DISCERNMENT

The difference between visions that that foster love of neighbor and integrity and visions that do not foster love and integrity is not always clear. Human beings are capable of rationalizing anything, and so knowing the difference requires life-long learning and deep reflections on the consequences of our visions. Learning to discern and acquiring a sincere reverence for discernment are more than just ornamentation to one's spirituality, they are central to it.

Knowing the difference between visions that foster love of neighbor and integrity and visions that do not, and knowing the difference between the use of power for the common good and the use of power for private aggrandizement begins with a sound understanding of the human condition. This understanding is the first of four pillars of spiritually-based discernment. Leaders are often lauded for the way they accurately perceive the future, but it is their ability to see what is before their eyes, without the need to romanticize or distort what they see, that is vital. The spiritual leader makes no assumptions, but continually draws information from primary sources, including employees, stockholders, average citizens, customers, local public service providers, and lawmakers. The spiritual leader's vision beings with an honest inventory of what people are experiencing in the organization, in the community in which the organization operates, and what people experience as a result of the organization's activities.

A second pillar of spiritually-based discernment is empathy. Information gathered in inventories does not automatically arouses a sense of caring. Spiritual leaders are contemplative individuals who consciously direct their attention to how they feel about the people who will be affected by their visions. They have keen metacognitive skills, which enable them to monitor their own biases, detect their own limitations of understanding, and identify the conditions they place upon their own empathy for others. They are also able to perceive how their capacity to empathize may affect their judgment.

The third pillar of spiritually-based discernment is sound analysis. With information about the organization's discrete practices, leaders may discover the mechanisms of dysfunction or injustice. Analysis confronts assumptions. It may detect the source of a breakdown of trust between the organization and the general public, or determine why some parts of the organization work well while others do not. Fearless analysis of organizations allows leaders to see the extent to which the organization has allowed itself to be accountable to its employees and the community, and how it has or has not lived up to the promises of its own mission.

The fourth pillar of spiritually-based discernment is the belief that all individuals are endowed with material life for sacred purpose. This belief flies in the face of social Darwinism and the notion that the fundamental purpose of material existence is to thrive and survive. For some, the sacred purpose may concern the destiny of the soul in eternity. For others it may concern the worship of and obedience to God. For many, it concerns learning how to love and be loved, which is a purpose that may be activated in secular spaces as it is not contingent upon the belief in God. Leaders who embrace the assertion that all individuals are endowed with a sacred purpose approach empathy and justice in ways that go beyond what manmade laws are able to articulate. They understand that laws and policies must sometimes be supplemented with benevolent measures that underscore the employers' respect for human dignity.

Vision often that gets the least amount of attention in college business courses. Many courses address the matter of how to create profitable operations, but the study of how to construct and sustain a vision that places leaders in the position of public servant is frequently limited. Many courses focus on how students can one day be wealthy grand poobahs. As one professor noted, "It is widely assumed that the entire rationale for business courses is to teach students how to make money, and all other rationales line up far behind that purpose."

Business courses have their limitations, and empathy is not easy to teach. Ideally, for example, the well-instructed student who wanted to own and manage a company that made jeans would not learn how to do that in socially responsible and sustainable ways from a textbook. That student would go to where cotton is grown and spend time planting, caring for, and harvesting cotton. The well-instructed student would go to the factory where the cotton is converted into fabric, and work the heavy machinery for weeks, one after the other, to get a sense of the monotony, noise, air quality, and conditions of life in a factory. He or she would visit the dye makers, button makers, zipper-makers, and label makers to study their craft. He or she would spend several weeks making the jeans—measuring, cutting, ironing, and sewing fabric with precision and care, day after day, week after week. The well-educated entrepreneur would also live for a long while on whatever wages the lowest paid employee along the production chain earned. This might help the future executive develop strategies to build company loyalty and commitment to competent work.

After all this experience, the well-instructed student would probably have insights and knowledge that the classroom could never communicate. Ideally, if he or she were to ever become a grand poobah, he or she will have a strong sense of empathy for every person involved in the production of blue jeans, from those in dusty, hot cotton fields, to those who do repetitive piece-work in noisy and dangerous environments, to those who keep the records accurate for taxes, payroll, and insurance. The classroom, in any event, is a long way from field and factory.

REFLECTION

1. How do you define power and its proper use? When you think about power, how does love of neighbor and integrity factor into your convictions and why?

2. Identify a "grand poobah" in your world and evaluate your own attitude towards this individual. Do you understand his or her obligations? Are you more critical of this person than of others or yourself, and if so, why?

3. What criteria do you use to assess whether a business or industry or public institution has abused its power? What are the merits and limitations of these criteria? Why does this criteria work for you and what are the alternatives and their merits and limitations?

4. Reflect upon the four pillars of spiritually-based discernment. What do you think might be challenging about applying them to the business world? Do you believe these pillars are important in your life? Why? Do you believe that leaders in industry and public service should embrace these pillars? Why?

5. Instructors: to what extent do you explore what history, court decisions, and case studies involving businesses, corporations, and public institutions have to teach students about business ethics? How might you enhance the use of these sources and materials to help students understand cause-effect relationships, and the limitations and potential of human discernment?

6. Instructors: To what extent do you integrate the study of foreign policy and help students understand and critique the nation's concept of "Good Neighbor" and "Neoliberal economics?" How might such integration improve the quality of students' understanding of the world and what it takes to lead in the world? How could you improve the integration of foreign policy into the business curriculum?

7. Instructors: To what extent do you consistently explore the meaning of the common good in your courses on leadership and management? What impact do you think your integration has on students' beliefs and values, and is that impact meaningful to you? To what extent do you solicit the aid of philosophers and theologians in your own processes of curriculum development and instruction? How might such assistance benefit students?

11

Higher Education and Hire Education

GOD GOT EXPELLED

ONCE UPON A TIME, Americans imagined that the United States would have an educational system designed to maintain order and civility in a God-fearing democratic society. The schools would welcome studies in science and classical literature while still retaining a place for the worship of God, as was befitting of upstanding Protestants. Colleges in the 17th and 18th century were largely dedicated to preparing young men for their roles as public servants, and roughly 25 percent of college graduates prior to the Civil War were headed for the ministry.[1] Students were expected to be conversant in Greek, Latin, and mathematics. This vision of education gave way to the more traditional American expectation that education was all about improving economic efficiency and social equity.[2]

In 1870, less than 10 percent of Americans had a college degree.[3] By 2018, nearly 20 million students enrolled in college, and roughly 34 percent of U.S. citizens held a bachelor's degree.[4] The notion that higher education should be tailored for the masses evolved as did the nation's concept of citizenry and practical needs. Prior to the 1820s, the notion that individuals

---

1. Brubacher and Willis, "Beginnings." Also see Kimball, *Orators and Philosophers*, pp. 148–151.
2. Haveman and Smeeding, "The Role of Higher Education."
3. Statistia, "Number of Bachelor Degree," see expanding table.
4. Wilson, "Census: More Americans," lines 3–6.

had to be prepared to exercise the arts of liberty applied largely to white males with property. The institutions of higher education as we know them today are the result of democratization and the ascendancy of material concerns over spiritual concerns. As ethnic minorities, women, the poor, and working classes demanded civil rights, they expected access to college and the opportunity to improve their lives by way of acquiring professional skills and knowledge. While the U.S. population moved west and grew in numbers, its need for communication and transportation infrastructures, and new technologies for manufacturing and agricultural production increased. Practical needs elbowed aside the curriculum of classics, philosophy, rhetoric, and theology, and replaced it with engineering, agriculture, and science. In the late 1800s, these needs combined with modern scientific methods, to produce the research university as we know it today.[5] Out of respect for minorities who did not subscribe to the majority's religion, legislation gradually forced daily prayers and Bible readings out of the public classroom.[6]

Tension over the extent to which schools, colleges, and universities should engage in character formation and require students to undertake studies that reference the Bible as a source of teachings about virtue and values is an enduring feature of American education. The tension is fueled by fear that such curriculum will inevitably lead to intolerance and indoctrination. The problem reflects Americans' limited ability to see religion and spirituality in the classroom as anything other than proselytizing. The exclusion of conversations about religious ideologies from the classroom speaks to a lack of confidence in our ability to explore religious ideologies with objectivity and scholarly maturity. The expulsion presumes that when matters of faith arise, we are destined to be defensive and irrational, and will inevitably fight over which religion represents the one, true, and absolutely pure voice of God.

Many insist that schools and universities should sever discussions of faith and spirituality from the curriculum because they are personal matters. It is an argument that implies that, unless we share a consensus about what matters to our private lives, we should not talk about them in the classroom. The severance of personal matters from academic inquiry and debate is troublesome for two reasons. First, it is selective. At present institutions work very hard to ensure that, for the sake of "empowering" and

5. Goldin and Katz, "The Shaping of Higher Education."
6. Marshall, "Nothing New."

validating one's identity, students are encouraged in class to explore their personal beliefs and values. While it is generally permissible for students to discuss matters of sexual orientation, ethnicity, race, income, and family history, conversations about their faith and how it shapes their interaction with the world arouses much anxiety.

The second problem with the severance is that it removes the influence scholarship might have in the way students think about faith, ethics, and spirituality. Traditionally, scholarship is an antidote to intolerance. In theory scholarly analysis and critiques shield us from specious claims, biased thinking, selective reporting, and erroneous assumptions. Admittedly, an objective and academic cross examination of personal spiritual beliefs is not always comforting. When properly facilitated, however, such examinations have the potential to clarify personal convictions, foster tolerance, and fortify one's resolve to work for equity and justice.

It is irrational to hide religion and spirituality from students. It makes no sense to pretend faith is irrelevant to our public lives, because religion and spirituality are intrinsic to the American experience. Colonial laws drew from Christian scriptures. Missionaries claimed Native American land on behalf of monarchs who would Christianize the "heathen savages." Slave-owners and abolitionists both prayed to the same God to bless their cause. The anti-war movements, anti-nuclear movement, and Civil Rights Movement all looked to faith and spiritual teachings to guide goals and strategies. Utopian societies and urban reformers often leaned on religion as the cornerstone of their crusades. School boards across the country have quoted the Bible in their efforts to control their local school's curriculum and library holdings. Trying to understand the American experience—or even the human experience, for that matter—without appreciating the roles that religion, faith, and spirituality have played in social organization and moral development, is like trying to understand the dancer without hearing the music.

WHAT THE CULTURE WILL BEAR

Alisha taught Management courses in the School of Business at a large public university. Management majors were required to take a course in business ethics. To hear Alisha talk about it, one would think the course subjected students and faculty to a semester of medieval torture. "The students see it as a joke," she said, "and so they don't read assignments and they don't even pretend to be interested in class." Alisha added, "The instructors aren't really upset by the student's reactions because they don't like the class either. They try to avoid teaching that class, because they know students are just going to say what they think the professor wants to hear so they can pass the class." Alisha added, "Students have no problem telling the faculty what to teach and how to teach it, and they don't see the need for a class on ethics . . . So faculty ease back on assignments, because, you know, they don't want to have to deal with bad evaluations just because students hate the subject."

In response to the corporate and banking scandals of the 1980s and 1990s, colleges and universities that offered degrees in business and business related fields, such as accounting, leadership, management, and finance, added courses in ethics to their list of required classes.[7] They hoped that these courses would improve students' commitment to ethical conduct in business. The National Association of State Boards of Accounting and the Association for the Advancement of Collegiate Schools of Business chimed in and urged colleges and universities to require ethics courses, even though they knew that some student would resent the mandate.[8]

Instructors have mixed feelings about teaching ethics in business courses. Generally, business faculty strongly believe that business ethics courses should be a key element in accredited business programs, and maintain that effective business leaders are ethical. Many assert that ethics courses help students help students clarify their own values and become less dogmatic and more welcoming of diverse perspectives.[9] Instructors claim that ethics courses help students make effective moral decisions and inspire a positive attitude toward altruism.[10]

On the other hand, some say that business ethics courses have little impact on students' perceptions of ethical issues and ethical conduct.[11] Studies have found that a large percentage of students will opt for unethical alternatives when confronted with an ethical dilemma.[12] They also claim

---

7. Cordeiro, "Only Solution."

8. Bernardi and Bean, "Ethics in Accounting Education."

9. Dudani, "Stanford Panel Debates," para. 4.

10. Desplaces, et al. "Impact of Business Education," and Shurden, et al., "How Student Perceptions."

11. Waples, et al., "A Meta-Analytic Investigation." Also see Bloodgood, et al., "Ethics Instruction," and Ritter, "Can Business Ethics be Trained?"

12. Teer and Kruck, "Students' Responses."

that some business schools ignore ethics, encourage unethical behavior, and that business students are more likely than students in other majors to be selfish and unfair.[13] Inquiries also reveal that those who cheat in the classroom are likely to cheat in the workplace.[14] Researchers find that taking lots of courses in economics tends to increase students' levels of greed and indifference to its consequences.[15]

There are several barriers to the effective integration of ethics into the business curriculum. Instructors argue that ethics are too subjective to teach, and that college students will not change values and ethical outlooks that they learned in childhood. Many professors object to teaching ethics courses because they believe such courses are unprofessional or invade the privacy of instructors.[16] Professors also resist ethics courses in general because they believe they are subjective and aim to indoctrinate students.[17] Others say that studies in ethics are a waste of time because they do not translated well into the workplace.[18] Others hold that the workplace, not the classroom offers the best instruction on ethics.[19]

Ethics courses often stand alone and away from other courses associated with a given discipline. As one professor confided, "Even when we attempt to integrate ethics into all of the courses in our program, the effect is unsatisfactory, because instructors typically accomplish integration by devoting one hour out of 45 hours of instruction to address topics of honesty, discrimination, or some aspect of law—which is not the same as sustaining students' attention to a set of ethical principles throughout the course."

In his response to the question of whether higher education can teach morals, Derek Bok, former President or Harvard University, noted that to teach ethics in a given discipline requires not only mastery of the discipline but substantial training in moral philosophy or its equivalent. He opined that since the professoriate is typically trained only in one's discipline and not in ethics as well, instructors who teach ethics in their discipline

13. Melé, "Integrating Ethics." Also see Wolf and Fritzsche, "Teaching Business Ethics," and McCabe, et al., "Academic Dishonesty."
14. Lawson, "Is Classroom Cheating Related to Business?"
15. Wang, Malhotra, and Murnighan, "Economics Education."
16. McDonald, M. et al., *"Toward a Canadian Research,"* p. 48.
17. McDonald, G., et al., "Objections to the Teaching of Business Ethics."
18. McDonald and Donleavy, "Objections to the Teaching."
19. Beggs and Dean, "Legislated Ethics."

are often self-taught, "causing instruction to be irritatingly superficial or theoretical."[20]

In some respects, professors are doing exactly what is expected of them. Disciplines at the college level tend to be siloed. Institutions seek instructors who have expertise which is often defined as having mastery of a narrow aspect of the discipline. The assumption is that this type of expertise produces excellent teachers. This assumption fuels the belief that college instructors do not need training in pedagogy or knowledge of an eclectic nature, including epistemological and moral development.

Another reason why ethics, value formation, and studies in social justice live in the margins of college curriculum is because higher education is, to a large extent, a commercial enterprise. Students, the "buyers," do not want to spend lots of money on education, and they want required courses to be as few as possible. Administrations, the "sellers," do not want to spend a lot of money on training instructors to improve their pedagogical skills, and they want to attract as many "buyers" as possible. Instructors, who are essentially "customer service providers," want and need favorable course evaluations so they can earn tenure and promotions, have an incentive to wangle students' approval by making classes easy and fun.[21] Institutions want to increase persistence to degree, so administrators have an incentive to minimize course requirements and to retain instructors who are very good at "keeping the customers satisfied."[22]

Regardless of the ideals a university espouses, the curriculum is often shaped by unspoken rules about what the institutional culture will allow. The inconsistent or lack of integration of ethics into the business curriculum may represent the culture's dislike for interdisciplinary studies, or the faculty's sense of political correctness. It could also reflect institutional sensitivity to what the sources of grants and donations have to say about ethics.

20. Bok, "Can Higher Education Foster?"

21. Hacker and Dreifus' *Higher Education* documents serious flaws in college teaching and administration.

22. Bok's *The Struggle* and *Our Underachieving Colleges* explore what happens to learning when higher education adopts priorities that marginalize the quality of teaching and learning.

GET REAL

Ethics, empathy, social justice, and love of neighbor are difficult to teach. Even those with advanced degrees in moral theology, philosophy, and religious studies are profoundly challenged by the reality that individuals often learn only what their egos permit them to learn. In a society that is so wholly dedicated to the accumulation of wealth and oriented to commercial transactions as a way of life, instructors risk their popularity and appeal when they raise the specter of ethics in schools of business.

Much of our formal learning is concerned with dutiful material transactions, wherein students demonstrate something that the instructor values, and in turn are awarded grades that translate into diplomas. These transactions do not necessarily represent the most meaningful or profound experiences higher education can offer. Many of our most enduring and significant lessons come to us by way of watching what people do, listening to what people say, imitating people's actions, experimentation, and experiencing the consequences of our own effort, success, failure, or inertia. The effective teachers are the ones who bring these experiences into the classroom, and who make room in their course design for deep reflections on their meaning.

Students look for authenticity in their instructors. They want to know if the instructors are really present when they are in class, or are mentally somewhere else, thinking about their research or committee work. Students want to know the level to which their instructors are committed to their learning and well-being. They are sometimes astonishingly quick and accurate in their assessments of which instructors know their subject well, and which are "winging it," which ones are arrogant, which one's have eclectic knowledge, which ones are intimidated by students, which ones dislike students, and which ones sincerely respect students.

Authenticity in lessons is conveyed in numerous ways. It is represented by the amount of time and effort devoted to the exploration of a given topic. It is communicated in the instructor's affect and high standards of thought and introspection. It is communicated in the readiness of instructors to relate the concepts or principles of a given lesson to current events or the personal lives of students. It is also communicated in the way instructors talk about their own experiences. Authenticity comes through when instructors demonstrate their own capacity to be humble, learn from mistakes, and admit that they need others to see the whole picture, or to think through matters clearly. This is also true of good leaders and parents.

Students taking business ethics courses want to know if their instructors are "for real." In a world where there is much corruption, denial about corruption, and justification for corruption, students want to know whether their instructors are merely going through the motions of talking about ethics and values out of obligation, or because they are genuinely passionate about making the world a better place. When determining whether a teacher's commitment to ethical conduct is authentic, students often look to whether the instructor is accessible, the way the instructor listens to and responds to students' needs, and the transparency of grading. Like employees, students, crave fairness, explicit expectations, and consistency in processes and evaluations. By the same token, instructors look for authenticity in students' desire to learn. Such authenticity is characterized by class participation, completion of assignments, insightful questions, community engagement, deep rather than superficial responses to questions, and the capacity to relate what is learned in the classroom to social conditions, events, and personal experience.

LIBERAL ARTS ON THE LINE

Students' sense of ethics and common good are vulnerable because many colleges and universities have diluted the liberal arts curriculum. To increase persistence to degree and attract new students, many institutions of higher education have reduced general education requirements and replaced traditional survey courses with "electives" chosen from a "domain" of study. For example, rather than having all first-year students take two semesters of U.S. History and one semester course on the U.S. Constitution, students may take three courses of their own choosing from the smorgasbord of options to satisfy requirements in the domain of Social Sciences.

In many instances, the smorgasbord approach produces significant gaps in students' understanding not only of their society, its ideals, its laws, but in the students' understanding of the human experience and civilization itself. The smorgasbord curriculum places students at risk for not learning much about the liberal arts, which are studies that, in theory, prepare one to assume the dispositions and values befitting one who exercises liberty. The presumption of a liberal arts education is that tolerance, respect for diversity, an inquisitive mind, and reverence for the common good are all essential to democracy.[23]

23. Seifert, et al., "The Effects of Liberal Arts."

Many of the courses that satisfy requirements are so narrowly focused that students do not learn much about the place of the subject in liberal arts education or in the human experience. For example, students may take a course on the art of Andy Warhol, to satisfy requirements in the domain of the arts. Students may hear excellent lectures on Warhol's life and works, but learn very little about the function of art in civilization, the tensions between the artist and society, and the role of art in fostering humanity, critical thought, or a sense of aesthetics, and why these things matter. While satisfying graduation requirements, many college courses do little to get students into the deep end of the pedagogical pool, where cognitive and epistemological development are explicitly fostered.

The American Council of Trustees and Alumni (ACTA), a nonpartisan advocate of the liberal arts, studied the general education requirements of 718 U.S. colleges and universities. The institutions in their study enrolled 6 million students and included Ivy League and top research universities as well as small private and state colleges.[24] The inquiry concluded that general education requirements are faltering in their cultivation of civic literacy, mathematical proficiency, composition and writing skills, knowledge of economics, and an understanding of the natural world. The ACTA chastised the notion that creative alternatives to traditional courses represent sound liberal arts pedagogy. For example, they rejected the ideas that a course on popular television shows could take the place of a course on U.S. history from the Colonial Era through Reconstruction; and, they rejected the idea that a course on interior design could take the place of a course on world literature. The ACTA used actual course offerings to make their case.

When viewed through the liberal arts' lens, the purpose of the history course is not to force the memorization of a chronology of events. The purpose of history is to help students comprehend the wonder and fragility of civilization, grasp cause-effect relationships, and investigate what the great controversies and conflicts of the past teach us about being human; it is to help us understand the relationship between people and their institutions; it is to help us understand how history is created through the interpretation of available sources that meet standards of credibility, and to see that how we remember the past influences the way we regard others. Through the liberal arts' lens, the study of literature takes students far beyond the novel's characters and plot; it draws readers into existential dilemmas, crises of faith, clashes of conscience, and what is to be gained

---

24. American Council of Trustees and Alumni, "What Will They Learn."

from hatred, selfishness, revenge, love, forgiveness, courage, sacrifice, and hope. When viewed through the liberal arts lens, the integration of ethics and open discussion of spirituality in the business curriculum is to improve students' awareness of how economic, financial, and business paradigms and practices affect the well-being of others, as to arouse empathy for the vulnerable and disadvantaged, and provoke respect for the human being's rights to basic material resources.

Many parents do not like liberal arts and steer their children away from majoring in them.[25] Parents fear that they will waste tens of thousands of dollars on a college degree if their child ends up being a high school history teacher or an artist. Some complain that studying the humanities will make them soft and unable to compete in the real world. Parent's behavior often punctuates the notion that higher education's greatest value lies in its job training, and not in formation of character and civility. This notion is tough on democracy. As Professor of Law, Martha Nussbaum observed, liberal arts in the U.S. was never about reinforcing class distinctions or abandoning all scientific inquiry, but it was always about producing "informed, independent, and sympathetic citizens."[26] Democracy retains its resilience against tyranny and extreme partisanship by questioning authority, openly debating prevailing business practices, social norms, and popular beliefs, and exploring what it means to live with dignity and compassion.

MEAT AND POTATOES

For some, the integration of spirituality into the workplace may begin with formal education that challenges the individual to defend his or her moral position with a response that goes deeper than, "because there is really no right and wrong," or, "that's how I feel." The classroom might be a gateway to an intellectual life that routinely factors empathy, fairness, human suffering, and justice into decision-making. Curriculum that is capable of such feats does not require sophisticated technology, foundational grants, or Bibles. It does require clear objectives, observable outcomes, a means of distinguishing mature and sophisticated thinking from shallow and flabby thinking, the ability to facilitate meaningful analysis, personal reflection, and critiques of theory and practice, and the will to do it. It is helped along by a sound understanding of justice, ethics, critical pedagogy, and

25. Pearlstein, "Meet the Parents," para. 1–10.
26. Nussbaum, *Not for Profit*, p. 18.

epistemological development. These topics are the meat and potatoes of faculty development that aims to improve instructors' ability to integrate personal reflection and moral development across the curriculum.

Professors Johannes Brinkman and Ronald R. Sims posited that instructors could help students become more sensitive to all stakeholders impacted by business decisions by administering instruction that targeted the following outcomes:[27]

- Students will improve their knowledge of self, clarify their values, and identify the thresholds and limitations of their morality
- Students will demonstrate their ability to see moral issues and moral aspects of situations and respond effectively to them
- Students will articulate their moral outlooks and the factors that legitimize their views
- Students will define moral courage and apply it to their conflict resolutions and judgment
- Students will demonstrate a critical attitude towards the business school curriculum and disciplines

Brinkman and Sims grasp that individuals need awareness of self, awareness of others, and awareness of the moral element in order to act ethically. Such awareness aligns with many spiritual traditions. To augment the spiritual elements of these outcomes, some might supplement their list by adding:

- Students will demonstrate empathy for all and special concern for the weak and vulnerable
- Students will demonstrate their knowledge of how to access special resources, such as spiritual advisors or therapists, when faced with a particularly difficult moral dilemma
- Students will clarify their own beliefs about whether public and private enterprise have a sacred function, or ministerial role to fulfill in society
- Students will identify and discuss what various sacred teachings about ethics and virtue offer to their own development and spiritual maturation

---

27. Brinkman and Sims, "Stakeholder-Sensitive."

This approach to teaching ethics is not explicitly concerned with the salvation of the soul, life after death, or whether human beings can achieve a state of enlightenment. This approach transcends religious doctrines and creeds. This approach embodies spiritual elements inasmuch as it is immediately concerned with the right treatment of others—behavior that draws us away from the tenacious grip of ego into a realm of deep concern for others, where everyone is naturally endowed with dignity.

The pedagogical strategies to draw individuals away from ego and into a psychological space where they can imagine others' experiences and perspectives, and project potential outcomes of their decisions, are strategies that immerse students in action. Role playing, simulation, journaling, sharing experiences, debates, case studies, community service, interviewing, and critiques of literature, theories, reports, and speeches prompt students to engage in gathering, processing, and evaluating ideas. Reflections on and discussions about movies, stories, documentaries, and biographies are often especially provocative. This is true because it is often the story of our lives— and not the theories of our lives— that move us.

REFLECTIONS

1. What is your understanding of a liberal arts education and its purpose? What do you believe is the place of spirituality in higher education? Why?

2. In your experiences, has formal education explicitly or passively encouraged social Darwinism, or the Protestant work ethic and should it do either? Why?

3. How might you improve your understanding of how knowledge is created and truth is established, and what implications might this have for your empathy and caring for others?

4. Students and Instructors: Rate your own authenticity and integrity as learners and instructors and discuss the implications.

5. Instructors: Which spiritual or ethical teachings have inspired or influenced you the most? How might sharing your thoughts on these teachings help your students?

6. Instructors: to what extent have you mastered pedagogy that uses role playing, case studies, interviews, reflections, journaling, community

service, simulation, documentary film, and story analysis to foster students' development of ethical thinking and behavior? In what ways could you improve?

7. Instructors: As a result of your institution's instruction, to what extent do you believe graduates understand how economics, taxes, federal budgets, banking, investment banking, government subsidies, social welfare programs, trade, lobbying, and corporate regulations work in the U.S., and understand how to find facts on these issues?

12

The Great Crossing

JOB FROM HELL

MANY OF US BELIEVE we have jobs from hell because the relationships we have in the workplace are dysfunctional and abusive. In the job from hell, even people who believe in God often do not act like they are in God's presence, and are sometimes so traumatized by hurtful dynamics that they forget their spiritual moorings and shift their gears into survival mode. In jobs from hell, sometimes the faithful equivocate that although we are in the presence of God, what we do on the job "doesn't count." Some might rationalize that transgressions and failure to love our neighbors as ourselves were unavoidable because we were "just doing what we were told to do," or had to "go with the flow or lose my job." Many who feel like they have a job from hell believe that they are victims and become accustomed to seeing themselves as victims, even when they are not victims.

Here is a little secret about jobs from hell: *We help create the hell and we need not be victims of our own making.* Our sense of self, our boundaries, and our productivity need not be collateral damage endured for the sake employment. We make choices about how we respond to difficulties, conflict, and abuse. We are endowed with reason and will.

Some people suffer because they have irrational or unrealistic expectations that work will fill a void in self-esteem, or live up to romanticized notions of a particular career. Others suffer because they lack the courage or the skills to speak up when adversity or incompetence interferes with their productivity or well-being. Some suffer because they are unable to free themselves from toxic ambition, and they live in a state of compulsive anxiety, aggressiveness, and envy. Some suffer because they are addicted to owning, buying, and collecting, and need the big incomes that come with their wretched workplaces. Becoming aware of our roles in creating the job from hell, and distinguishing them from the role of others is a cardinal step in moving away from fire and brimstone on the job.

SOMETIMES THE DEVIL IS THE DEVIL

Sometimes, it is not our behavior or our attitudes that are problematic. Sometimes our bosses and co-workers are truly sadistic and psychologically broken people that will forever deny that they need help and healing. Having the capacity to make adjustments in our attitudes and expectations *does not* mean that the organizations and leaders for whom we work are innocent of all transgressions. It *does not* mean that bad behavior and dysfunction in the workplace should never be confronted. It *does not* mean that the company is always right.

Given human nature, there will always be bullies, poor leaders, sexists, racists, elitists, narcissists, immature, and incompetent people in the workplace. There will always be managers who punish employees who dissent from the prevailing company culture, and there will always be sycophants cooing and wooing people in high places. There will always be organizations that pursue profit at the expense of the public's well-being. There will always be companies that say one thing, do another, and then lie about it under oath. Whether we work for these types of organizations is up to us.

Bringing spirituality to bear in our workplace is about living in the material world as though we truly believe that people are more important than things. It is about making a commitment to wrestle with the paradox that while we are spirits who are mysteriously part of an eternity that is equally mysterious, we are flesh and blood who must make our way on Earth. It is about sustaining the belief in the notion that we all have a sacred purpose that calls us to love of neighbor, despite the reality that we work in places where there is frequently no regard for a sacred purpose, and no interest in the ethos that the sacred purpose evokes. There may be moments in our lives where the preservation of these beliefs can be best sustained and nurtured only by walking away from dark and dysfunctional places.

Bringing spirituality to bear in the workplace does not guarantee that workplace dynamics will improve or that companies will change their agendas and policies. Bringing spirituality to bear in the workplace is first and foremost about changing ourselves. It means that we will be more mindful on the job and be better judges of how to respond to conflict and adversity. It means that we improve our capacity to empathize with everyone, not just our pals, and will set proper boundaries for the way others treat us and the way we treat others. Leveraging spiritual capital on the job means that if we going to challenge authority, petition for change, or blow the whistle on nefarious conduct, we will do so only when we have taken a thorough inventory of matters and our own motives, are ready to proceed without malice, and are psychologically prepared to face the consequences.

CROSSING OVER

In a conversation about attitudes towards and approaches to work, a co-worker told me that me that he had "crossed over." I looked rather puzzled and quizzed, "What do you mean—do you feel like you're gonna die?" He laughed and said "no." Then he said, "What I mean is that I see things differently than I did when I was younger . . . I don't have the same expectations or take things as personally as I once did." I squinted and pressed, "So, you are at a point where you don't care about your work as much?" He indicated that he cared very deeply about his work, but for reasons that differed from the reasons he had 20 years ago. He said, "I have let go of the idea that my job defines who I am and what I am worth." He added, "I know that not everybody in my profession share my ideals; I know that not everything is fair, and that people are always jockeying for a better seat on the gravy train. I take pride in doing my best and I choose my battles more carefully than I did 20 years ago . . . I can be very productive and still get a paycheck even if I don't agree with how things are managed."

I am not sure if I would have understood my co-worker's remarks about crossing over when I was a novice in my profession. When I think about my career trajectory, certain things come into focus that were invisible to me in the past. Two things stare at me with an unyielding gaze. The first is that I allowed my ego to take the driver's seat too often. That, all by itself, compromised the quality of my discernment and my empathy for others. The second thing I see is the wish that I had more mentors in my life who had the courage, patience, and wisdom to engage me in serious reflection and self-assessment, so that I could have moved beyond my own ego and activated my spirituality a lot earlier and a lot more effectively than

I did. These things would not have made me perfect, but they would have made me better.

Crossing over is about a shift in perspective and attitudes concerning the workplace. It is a passage to serenity wherein the boss' favor, promotions, salary, popularity, public praise for work, corner offices, and reserved parking do not matter. In this place, where what matters most is one's integrity. In this place, it is easier not to personalize conflicts of opinion and work with others under imperfect conditions. Crossing over brings into view a sharper contrast between what is possible in a given organization and what is not possible. It heightens sensitivity to organizational culture, which may lead to insights about how to establish proper boundaries of trust, self-disclosure, expectations, and taking initiatives.

Crossing over is the transition from a person who allows herself or himself to be psychologically wounded, anxious, self-doubting, and self-destructive because of what others say and do, to a person who does not self-destruct in the face of criticism or mistakes. This state of serenity is not the same as indifference to the workplace, and it is not fatalistic. It is a way of being more objective in our assessments of the workplace, so that we can appreciate the fact that, like ourselves, others in the workplace are probably on their own developmental curve, and are concerned about the security of their own incomes. It is a way of being in the company of people who may be abusive and not allowing their sense of reality and truth to control us or hook us emotionally. It is drawing strength from the idea that not even the boss is allowed to occupy the place inside us that is reserved for God and conscience.

In crossing over, the things that bothered us in the past may still bother us in the present, but our reaction to them has changed. For some, the most significant aspect of the shift is a reordering of one's priorities. In some instances, people have adjusted their expectations about income and modified their consumption so that they no longer live with anxiety about raises and promotions. In other cases, people have politely excused themselves from committees that are not collaborative or productive. In other situations, people have learned how to set boundaries and not to be devastated when co-workers do not like them.

Spirituality does not ask the faithful to be indifferent to vice, illegal activity, or the suffering that these things cause. It does, however, ask the faithful to put matters into perspective. The dastardly and their defenders will always be with us. The spiritual struggle against the ills of our business organizations and legal institutions, however, is not that of a vigilante. It is the steady gait of individuals seeking in each moment to be the example of God's love, knowing that nothing will come to perfection despite their faithfulness. In spirituality's steady gait, individuals may never know which of their words or actions will one day inspire others to change what ought to be changed in themselves or in the organization.

Serenity is not the same as fatalism. The fatalistic view holds that institutions are too entrenched in their ways to change, and that managers and administrators are too powerful to confront. Serenity is the solace of conscience we experience when we do the right thing, even if others do not. It is the ability to be at peace with people while contesting their behavior. Serenity is confidence that even though we are not in control of everything, goodness may prevail. It is also the calm we feel in knowing that, while we must extend reconciliation to our adversaries, we do not ultimately answer to them as we answer to God.

Serenity is often the last thing we associate with the workplace. American culture teaches us to be impatient, and to expect immediate gratification and instant solutions to our most vexing problems. Serenity creates a space for God or sacred grace to show up on the job. Individuals who abstain from rushed judgements, furious ultimatums, and hasty decisions give the spirit a little time to work. Many of the worst experiences people have had in the workplace have happened because people imposed artificial deadlines on activities, and accelerated the speed at which people had to perform things correctly.

Serenity holds us to humility. In being humble, the boss may patiently listen to grievances, and be willing to contemplate matters for a few days before reacting. In being humble, the new kid in the office with all the great ideas may be patient in her or his observations about the merits of company culture, and be more understanding when her or his ideas are rejected. We do not know exactly how the spirit will move people when they are given time to think, question, review, and pray. We do know, however, what happens when we metaphorically put a gun to somebody's head and force undeliberated decisions, or make erroneous assumptions about people's needs and motivations.

OVERCOMING SPIRITUAL RESISTANCE

The effort we exert to cross over is often met with resistance. Under the spell of our egos, we sometimes rationalize resistance, even when we have the sense that we are making rather juvenile excuses. Objections to being charitable, forgiving, patient, and respectful is sometimes unconscious because being entitlement and impatience have been normed so deeply in our society. Americans are proud to be religious folks, but we are typically not a very spiritually mature people. We are adolescent in temperament and wants, and while spirituality calls us to rise above the self, the adolescent insists the universe must revolve around the self.

Perhaps the best way to understand this is to be still for a while—perhaps for a couple of weeks or a few months—and listen without response to what being said. We will begin to understand the power of norms when we attentively listen to what is said explicitly and between the lines of our office banter, television shows, social media, advertising, social events, and casual exchanges in our commercial activity. Listen to what gets the most attention, what arouses the most emotion; pay attention to how people steer the direction and intensity of conversations, and to the extent they exhibit genuine curiosity and regard for facts and competing opinions.

We are alerted to resistance to the spirit in many ways. It might be the steady growl in our guts when we meet with a draconian supervisor, or the voice inside our heads that mocks the need to give somebody special accommodations, or the rush of adrenaline when we feel jealous. Resistance might take the form of condescending thoughts about a colleague who in good faith suggests that we seek professional help with a specific problem.

Prayer and reflection are strategies to identify and overcome spiritual resistance. The Gospel instructs the faithful to pray for one's enemies, bless those who curse us, and to remember that both the good and the bad are under the hand of God (Matt. 5:43–45). Many spiritual people find this directive a very difficult one, and either ignore it or slide over it with a quick footnote to our prayers, wedged between clenched teeth: "God bless my boss." Meditative prayer has the potential to bring life's lessons to the surface of our awareness. It can surprise us with insights about how others might experience us, and give us new resolve to daily activate spirituality rather than offer solemn prayers only when we get in trouble. In prayer, we sometimes see the conditions we impose on empathy. Sometimes in prayer and meditation we see that our behavior is the same as those who have offended us. Prayer and meditation help us remain humble, as we remind ourselves that we are part of something bigger than ourselves.

Prayer and meditation do not cause our adversaries to stop being adversarial. They do not cause personalities to change overnight, or cause sudden reversals in corporate practices. Prayer and meditations do not keep others "in line," they help to keep us in line.

Ideally, prayers for adversaries are the same as those for everyone and ourselves: *God grant us humility and patience enough to learn what we need to learn, and ignite in us a passion for love of neighbor; grant us the awareness of how our actions have impacted our work and grant us the will and the means to restore our integrity and heal our wounds.* Rather than enter into prayer with certainty in our own righteousness, it is more important to pray to be on the right side of the fight than to pray for victory.

On occasion, it is difficult to pray because the words do not leap to mind, or because our minds are buzzing emotion. Turning to prayers others have written is sometimes a way to see, hear, and say what we need to see, hear, and say. Among my favorite prayer books is *Are You Running with Me, Jesus,* penned by the late Malcolm Boyd, former Episcopal priest. The book was written in 1965 and uses ordinary street language to bring the angst of the modern world into sacred light. One of Boyd's prayers seems to speak for those deeply wounded by co-workers:

> I can't stand anybody being around me at this moment. The sound of another voice seems to cut into my flesh. I want to be alone. I crave silence, even a vacuum, and endless echo chamber of silence upon silence upon silence. Cold. Alone. Silence.
>
> But this silence is filled with demons, Lord, so that I am not alone at all. I am with demons. And I'd rather be with other people, Jesus, and with you. I've thought it out, and this is what I want. Will you help me cut loose from these demons so I can be with you and other people?[1]

When things do not go so well in the workplace, many retreat to isolation. There, alone, we might lick our wounds and steady ourselves, but we might also wallow in vengeance, anger, and fear. In isolation, it is easy to feel superior, and easy to disparage the notion that we are all brothers and sisters. Boyd's prayer speaks to the need to be with God and others, especially when we are in pain. It is a prayer to keep deceptive and proud demons out of our cubicles.

---

1. Boyd, *Are You Running with Me, Jesus?* p. 26.

God Bless Our Cubicles
LAUGHING AT THE SHERIFF

A colleague's story makes clear that sustaining spirituality in the workplace is not all about being pensive around the water cooler or turning the office into a monastery. Morgan sustains spirituality with humor, and believes laughter is vital to faith.

> I used to make myself miserable by taking the organization too seriously. I was super-productive and brought ideas to the table, and I always got squashed. Then, I was in a meeting one day with my boss, Blair, and she said something that was so bizarrely false and offensive, it just fried my circuits. I couldn't hear anything after that comment. The only thing I could think about was how to remain polite for the rest of the meeting. My mind started to wonder, and these images just started popping into my head—all these parodies, like Charlie Chaplin doing his spin on Hitler, or the characters played by Cloris Leachman in Mel Brooks movies—like Frau Blucher and Nurse Diesel—and I literally had to push my cheeks into my jaws to stop myself from laughing. It was off-to-the-circus from there . . . whenever I had to work with her on something, all I could see was Blair dressed as Darth Vader, or something outrageous. The costumes were not threatening, they were funny—they were always the wrong size, and accessorized with goofy things. I suppose this sounds really disrespectful, but this is how I handled it . . . .Maybe I didn't act like a saint—and who knows, maybe saints laughed all the time—but I was never mean to Blair, I just gave myself permission to see things for what they are. In this case, she was the child who threw tantrums when she did not get her way. She was the sheriff in town whose hat is falling over her eyes, whose boots are two sizes too big, and whose badge came out of a Cracker Jack box, pompously announcing, that 'despite the recent disappearance of four thousand head of cattle, and reports of suspicious varments encamped outside'a town, there ain't no cattle rustlin' in these here parts.'

Morgan admitted that there is a fine line between laughing to hurt and laughing to heal. She also confided that it took many years for her to be able to see the role her own ego played in her own suffering, and that she sometimes laughs at herself. Morgan chuckled:

> I'm able to laugh because I don't take what my boss says personally—I take it seriously because I take what we do seriously, *but that's different from personally*—its serious that she mess up so

much—of course—but my work speaks to how seriously I take this profession. I care a lot about this profession, and I know it inside-out, which is why I can see who the clowns are. My laughter keeps the buffoonery of this place from dominating the way I feel about life. Its funny and its tragic at the same time that this place is so dysfunctional, but I tried to fix it and I clearly don't control it—God must have given us laughter for a reason, and I'm gonna' use it to keep my sanity.

BE THE BLESSING

People who take their spirituality seriously often feel somewhat alienated from mainstream society. Thus, our families, prayer circles, and spiritual advisors, are critical to the way we sustain our spiritual perspectives, especially when they find no validation in certain social environments. Maintaining healthy interactions with others who nourish our spirituality may require us to let go of assumptions that interdependence makes us weak and inferior. Society's reverence for self-sufficiency has sometimes led to isolationism, and the belief that people who need people are not the luckiest people, but "losers" who depend "too much" on others. Being irritated and brusk with others who need help is often an indicator that we apply conditions to the help we give others. Conditions are not evil by definition, but it is important to know what they are, why they are as they are, and whether they represent love of neighbor the way we want them to represent love of neighbor.

For the sake of spiritual development, some people may have to challenge the pride they take in being a "rugged individual." Some might need to assess whether their concepts of masculinity and femininity are barriers to spiritual growth, as these concepts may influence one's sense of independence and dependency. Some may benefit from an analysis of the psychological roles that they played while growing up in their families, so that they may understand the subconscious impulses that shape behavior in the workplace.[2]

Overcoming resistance to spiritual growth also requires that individuals remain open to pain, discomfort, and conflict. These things give

---

2. Both Friel and Friel's *Adult Children* and Gibson's *Adult Children of Emotionally Immature Parents* offer a comprehensive, scientifically sound and compassionate study of psychological roles and behavior that are shaped by dysfunctional dynamics in our youth.

us insight to our values and how others experience the world. Pain and discomfort often lead us to the awareness that our own material wants are the source of our own excruciating pain, and the source of pain for others as well.

As a child, I was told that sometimes people have to suffer in order to prevent others from suffering. Working all day where back-breaking labor, repetitive motion, or constant exposure to dirty air and noise assault both mind and body, many people get through it with grace and cheerfulness because they keep reminding themselves of the good that their paychecks accomplish. Even when jobs are not ideal, they enable us to feed, shelter, and educate our children, and to send parents on fixed incomes a little extra cash so that they can afford groceries and pay their heating bills at the same time. These are things for which to be grateful.

At present, it seems as if society has lost respect for the assertion that it is noble to endure hardship for the good others. We struggle to understand the difference between destructive co-dependence and providing for the basic needs of others who cannot provide them. We struggle in part because we have consciously or unconsciously assimilated the radical individualism implicit in the Protestant work ethic and social Darwinism. We often assume that people who cannot provide for themselves simply will not provide for themselves, and we often say that the economic playing field is level for everyone, even when we know it is not. Whether we are a senator, sales clerk, or secretary, our assumptions and fantasies about the real world can keep us in a state of spiritual immaturity.

Finally, overcoming resistance to spiritual growth requires individuals to decide where spirituality and the love of God live on one's personal scale of relevance. At one end both are completely irrelevant and even scornful. At the other end spirituality and love of God are immediate in every moment, every thought, and every action. For most of us, the relevance of spirituality and God lives in between the extremes, in a world where the faithful sometimes deny their own cherished spirituality, much like the disciple Peter denied Jesus (LK 22:54–62). It is that middle ground where many of our most important battles with faith and spirituality will be fought. The middle ground is where we will determine the extent to which we subordinate our spirituality to economic paradigms and workplace norms, or subordinate economic paradigms and workplace norms to our spirituality.

Some see spirituality as a state of purity and angelic poise. It seems to me, however, that spirituality is a state of true grit— a state of sweat-soaked shoulders, dusty jeans, and bruised knees. It is a world where we mentally wrestle with demons by day and dual with doubt by night. The faithful do not possess a magic potion for every wart in the workplace. They do, however, offer reasonable and kind alternatives to dysfunctional and unkind "business as usual."

Spirituality is ours to embrace or reject. For those who embrace it, spirituality is dynamic and hopeful. It gives us the courage to trust that our own self-improvement will somehow inspire others to improve as well. It is what makes us capable of asking God to bless our troubled workplace, and then to ask ourselves to be the blessing.

REFLECTIONS

1. Think about your own resistance to spirituality. Is the source of this resistance fear of being ridiculed? Is the resistance sourced in theological convictions or doubts? Is the resistance a defense mechanism against losing your sense of control over situations? What do you think might be gained by overcoming resistance to spiritual growth?

2. Make an inventory of an organization in which you worked and identify the ways the organization acted as though it was a ministry, and the ways in which it might have worked as a ministry but did not. What you think would have been the consequences of changes that brought its operations closer to being a ministry?

3. What do you believe are your most important social responsibilities, and how do these responsibilities relate to responsibilities to yourself?

4. Is it possible to take something seriously, but not take it personally? How might that look in the workplace? What are the merits of this approach to conflict?

5. How do you conceptualize social justice? What personal steps might you take that would enhance your understanding of it and your commitment to it?

6. How has formal education affected your personal faith and spirituality? What were its strengths and limitations? What do you see as

the benefits and challenges of integrating spirituality into life-long learning?

7. What personal habits might you adopt for improving your understanding of the world, how economic and political decisions are made, and what impact these decisions have on the quality of life for people, globally, along all the whole spectrum of income?

8. What personal habits might you adopt for being a more critical and discerning consumer of media and what it asserts about our needs and values?

Bibliography

Addady, Michael. "Study: Being Happy at Work Really Makes You More Productive." *Fortune*, October 29, 2015. http://fortune.com/2015/10/29/happy-productivity-work/.

Alford, C. Fred. *Whistleblowers: Broken Lives and Organizational Power*. Ithaca, NY: Cornell University Press, 2001.

Alterman, Eric. *When Presidents Lie: A history of Official Deception and its Consequences*. New York: Viking. 2004.

American Council of Trustees and Alumni. *What Will They Learn? A Survey of Core Requirements at Our Nation's Colleges and Universities*. Washington, D. C.: American Council of Trustees, 2010. https://www.goacta.org/initiatives/what_will_they_learn.

American Psychiatric Association. *Diagnostic and Statistical Manual of Mental Disorders*, 4th edition. DSM-IV-TRTM. Washington, D. C., 2000.

Applebaum, Herbert A. *The American Work Ethic and the Changing Work Force: an Historical Perspective*. Westport: Greenwood, 1998.

Aquinas, Thomas. *Thomas Aquinas on Faith and Reason*, Edited by Stephen F. Brown. Indianapolis: Hackett, 1999.

Austin, Cindy. L., Robert Saylor, and Phillip J. Finley. "Moral Distress in Physicians and Nurses: Impact on Professional Quality of Life and Turnover." *Psychological Trauma: Theory, Research, Practice and Policy* 9, (2017): 399.

Avila, Charles. *Ownership: Early Christian Teaching*. Eugene: Wipf & Stock, 2004.

Azagba, Sunday and Mesba M. Sharaf. "Psychosocial Working Conditions and the Utilization of Health Care Services." *BMC Public Health*, 11 (2011): 642.

Bagdikian, Ben H. *The New Media Monopoly: A Completely Revised and Updated Edition with Seven New Chapters*. Boston: Beacon, 2014.

Bakan, Joel. *The Corporation. The Pathological Pursuit of Profit and Power*. London: Constable & Robinson, 2004.

Ballman, Donna. "Eleven Sneaky Ways Companies Get Rid of Older Workers: Forbes. *Huffington Post*, November 5, 2013. https://www.huffingtonpost.com/2013/11/04/older-workers-get-rid-of-them_n_4213955.html.

Bannister, Robert C. *Social Darwinism: Since and myth in Anglo-American social thought*. Philadelphia: Temple University Press, 1979.

Bannon, Shele, Kelly Ford, and Linda Meltzer. "Understanding Millennials in the Workplace." *CPA Journal* 81, (2011): 61.

Bernhard, Virginia. "Cotton Mather and the Doing of Good: A Puritan Gospel of Wealth." *New England Quarterly*, 49, (1976): 225.

BIBLIOGRAPHY

Beard, Charles A. *An Economic Interpretation of the Constitution of the United States*, New York: Macmillan, 1921.
Beatty, Jack. *Age of Betrayal: The Triumph of Money in America: 1865–1900*. New York: Vintage, 2008.
Beggs, Jeri Mullins, and Kathy Lund Dean. "Legislated Ethics or Ethics Education? Faculty Views in the Post-Enron Era." *Journal of Business Ethics* 71, (2007): 15.
Bells of St. Mary, directed by Leo McCarey (1945, Los Angeles, CA: RKO Pictures, 2003), DVD.
Belman, Dale and Paul J. Wolfson. *What Does the Minimum Wage Do?* Kalamazoo: W. E. Upjohn Institute for Employment Research, 2014.
Benner, David. G. "Toward a Psychology of Spirituality: Implications for Personality and Psychotherapy." *Journal of Psychology and Christianity*, 8, (1989): 19.
Bennett, James R. "Trading Cards, Heroes, and Whistleblowers." *The Humanist* 57, (1997): 23.
Bennis, Warren. *On Becoming a Leader*. New York: Basic Books, 2009.
———. *Why Leaders Can't Lead: The Unconscious Conspiracy Continues*. San Francisco: Jossey-Bass, 1989.
Bennis, Warren G. and Burt Nanus. *Leaders: Strategies for Taking Charge*. New York: Harper Collins, 1985.
Bergman, Yoav S. "Ageism in Childhood, in *Ageism: Stereotyping and prejudice against older persons*, edited by Todd, D. Nelson, pp. 3–36. Cambridge, MA: MIT Press, 2017.
Bernardi, Richard A., and David F. Bean. "Ethics in Accounting Education: The Forgotten Stakeholders." *CPA Journal* 76, (2006): 56.
Bernays, Edward. *Propaganda*. New York: Ig, 1928.
———. *Public Relations*. Norman: University of Oklahoma Press, 1952.
Bickle, Peter. *The Revolution of 1525: The German Peasants' War from a New Perspective*. Baltimore: Johns Hopkins University Press, 1982.
Birkinshaw, Julian. *Becoming a Better Boss: Why Good Management is so Difficult*. San Francisco: John Wiley & Sons, 2013.
Black, Edwin. *War Against the Weak: Eugenics and America's Campaign to Create a Master Race*. Washington, D.C.: Dialogue, 2003.
Blakeley, Ruth. "Still Training to Torture? US Training of Military Forces from Latin America." *Third World Quarterly* 27, (2006): 1439.
Blistein, David and Ken Burns. *The Mayo Clinic: Faith, Hope and Science*. New York: Rosetta,. 2018.
Bloodgood, James M., William H. Turnley, and Peter E. Mudrack. "Ethics Instruction and the Perceived Acceptability of Cheating." *Journal of Business Ethics* 95, (2010): 23
Bok, Derek. "Can Higher Education Foster Higher Morals?" *Business and Society Review*, 66, (1998): 4.
———. *Our Underachieving Colleges: A Candid Look at How Much Students Learn and Why They Should be Learning More*. Princeton: Princeton University Press, 2006.
———. *The Struggle to Reform Our Colleges*. Princeton: Princeton University Press, 2017.
Bolman, Lee. G. and Terrence E. Deal. *Leading with Soul*. San Francisco: Jossey-Bass, 1995.
Bonner, Raymond, "The Diplomat and the Killer." *The Atlantic*, Feb. 11, 2016. https://www.theatlantic.com/international/archive/2016/02/el-salvador-churchwomen-murders/460320/.

Bibliography

Booth, John A., Christine J. Wade, and Thomas W. Walker. *Understanding Central America: Global Forces, Rebellion and Change*, 6th Ed. New York: Routledge, 2018.

Bork, Robert. *Slouching towards Gomorrah*. New York: Reagan, 1996.

Born, Brooksley. "Forward: Deregulation: A Major Cause of the Financial Crisis." *Harvard Law & Policy Review*, 2, (2011): 231.

Bowler, Kate. *Blessed: A History of the American Prosperity Gospel*. New York: Oxford University Press, 2013.

Boyd, Malcolm. *Are You Running with Me, Jesus?* Cambridge, MA: Cowley. 1965/2006.

Boyer, Richard O. and Herbert M. Morais. *Labor's Untold Story: The Adventure Story of the Battles, Betrayals, and Victories of American Working Men and Women*. Pittsburgh: United Electrical and Machine Workers of America, 1956.

Boys Town, directed by Norman Taurog (1938, Beverly Hills, CA: MGM, 2011), DVD.

Brack, Jessica, and Kip Kelly. "Maximizing Millennials in the Workplace." *UNC Executive Development* 22, (2012): 2.

Brinklow, Adam. SF Rents Close 2016 on a Downward Trend. *Curbed*, December 1, 2016. https://sf.curbed.com/2016/12/1/13810764/san-francisco-rent-prices-2016.

Brinkman, Johannes and Ronald R. Sims. "Stakeholder-Sensitive Business Ethics Teaching." *Teaching Business Ethics*, 5, (2001): 191.

Brogden, Mike. *Geronticide: Killing the Elderly*. London: Jessica Kingsley, 2001.

Brown, Jennifer Erin. *Millennials and Retirement: Already Falling Short*. Washington, D. C. National Institute for Retirement Security, 2018.

Brubacher, John S. and Rudy Willis. "Beginning," in Higher Education in Transition. History of American Colleges and Universities, edited by John S. Brubacher, pp. 1–26. New York: Routledge.

Buell, Samuel. *Capital Offenses: Business Crime and punishment in America's Corporate Age*. New York: W. W. Norton, 2016.

Buergenthal, Thomas. "The United Nations Truth Commission for El Salvador." *Vanderbilt. Journal of Transnational Law*. 27, (1994): 497.

Burack, Elmer. H. "Spirituality in the Workplace." *Journal of Organizational Change Management*, 12, (1999): 280.

———. "Turnaround and Renewal: Adaptive Change and Crafting New Employment Relationships," in *Corporate Resurgence and the New Employment Relationships*, edited by Elmer H. Burack, pp. 37–57. Westport: Quorum, 1993.

Burnes, David, Karl Pillemer, Paul L. Caccamise, Art Mason, Charles R. Henderson Jr, Jacquelin Berman, Ann Marie Cook et al. "Prevalence of and risk factors for elder abuse and neglect in the community: a population-based study." *Journal of the American Geriatrics Society* 63, (2015): 1906.

Buttaccio, Jennifer L. 3 Reasons why nurses are leaving the profession. *Daily Nurse*, March 22, 2017. Retrieved from: http://dailynurse.com/3-reasons-many-nurses-leaving-profession/.

Byrne, John B. "Why the MBA is Now the Most Popular Master's. *Poets & Quants*, May 26, 2014. https://poetsandquants.com/2014/05/26/why-the-mba-is-now-the-most-popular-masters/.

Caldicott, Helen. *A Desperate Passion: An Autobiography*. New York: W. W. Norton & Company,1996.

Capodagli, Bill and Lynn Jackson. *Leading at the Speed of Change: Using New Economy Rules to Invigorate Old Economy Companies*. New York: McGraw Hill, 2001.

Bibliography

Carmichael, Sarah Green. "Millennials are Actually Workaholics." *Harvard Business Review*, August 17, 2016. https://hbr.org/2016/08/millennials-are-actually-workaholics-according-to-research.

Carnegie, Andrew. "Popular Illusions about Trust" *Century Magazine*, 60. 1900.

———. "The Gospel of Wealth." *The North American Review*, 183, (1906): 526

Carver-Thomas, Desiree, & Darling-Hammond, Linda. *Teacher Turnover: Why it Matters and What We Can Do about It.* Palo-Alto: Learning Policy Institute, 2017. https://learningpolicyinstitute.org/sites/default/files/product-files/Teacher_Turnover_REPORT.pdf.

Cavanagh, Gerald F., and Mark R. Bandsuch. "Virtue as a Benchmark for Spirituality in Business." *Journal of Business Ethics* 38, (2002): 109.

Center for Responsive Politics. "Commercial Banks. Industry Profile: Summary, 2017." *Open Secrets*. https://www.opensecrets.org/lobby/indusclient.php?id=F03&year=2017.

Chait, Jonathan. "Trump isn't Inciting Violence by Mistake, but on Purpose; He Just Told Us. *Intelligencer*. New York Magazine*, November 5, 2018. http://nymag.com/intelligencer/2018/11/trump-isnt-inciting-violence-by-mistake-he-just-told-us.html.

Chappell, Thomas. *The Soul of Business: Managing for Profit and the Consumer Good.* New York: Bantam-Double Day, 1994.

Chroust, Anton Hermann. "The Philosophy of Law of Augustine." *The Philosophical Review*, 53, no. 2 (1944): 195–202.

———. and Robert J. Affeldt. "The Problem of Property According to St. Thomas Aquinas." *Marquette Law Review*, 44, (1950–51): 151.

Clapesattle, Helen. *The Doctors Mayo.* Minneapolis: University of Minnesota Press, 1941.

Clifford, Catherine. "Unhappy Workers Cost the U.S. up to $550 Billion a Year." *Entrepreneur*, May 10, 2015. https://www.entrepreneur.com/article/246036.

Cochrane, Michelle. *When AIDS Began: San Francisco and the Making of an Epidemic.* New York: Routledge, 2004.

Coffin, Bill. "Breaking the Silence on White Collar Crime." *Risk Management* 50, (2003): 8.

Cohan, William D. "How Wall Street Bankers Stayed out of Jail." *The Atlantic*, September, 2015. https://www.theatlantic.com/magazine/archive/2015/09/how-wall-streets-bankers-stayed-out-of-jail/399368/.

Cohn, Samuel K. Jr.. "After the Black Death: Labour Legislation and Attitudes towards Labour in Late-Medieval Western Europe." *The Economic History Review* 60, (2007): 457.

Cole, Gerald A. *Personnel and Resource Management.* UK: Cengage, 2002.

Collins, Mike. "The Big Bank Bailout." *Forbes*, July 14, 2015. https://www.forbes.com/sites/mikecollins/2015/07/14/the-big-bank-bailout/#637ec3a2d83f.

Conkin, Paul K. *American Originals: Homemade Varieties of Christianity.* Chapel Hill: The University of North Carolina Press, 1997.

Connaughton, Jeff. *The Payoff: Why Wall Street always Wins.* Westport: Prospecta, 2012.

Conwell, Russell Herman and Robert Shackleton. *Acres of diamonds.* New York: Harper Brothers, 1915.

Cooney, John. *The American Pope: The Life and Times of Francis Cardinal Spellman.* New York: Crown, 1984.

Cooper, David. *God is a Verb: Kabbalah and the Practice of Jewish Mysticism.* New York: Riverhead, 1997.

Cordeiro, William P. "The Only Solution to the Decline in Business Ethics: Ethical Managers." *Teaching Business Ethics*, 7, (2003): 265.

BIBLIOGRAPHY

Corn, David. *The Lies of George W. Bush.* New York: Three Rivers, 2003.

Corsellis, J. A. N., C. J. Burton, and Dorothy Freeman-Browne. "The Aftermath of Boxing." *Psychological Medicine* 3, (1973): 270.

Covey, Stephen, *Principle-Centered Leadership.* New York: Fireside, 1992.

Cowie, Jefferson. *Stayin' Alive: The 1970s and the Last Days of the Working Class.* New York: The New Press, 2010.

Cowley, Stacy and Jennifer A. Kingson. "Wells Fargo to Claw Back $75 Million from Former Executives." *New York Times,* April 10, 2017. https://www.nytimes.com/2017/04/10/business/wells-fargo-pay-executives-accounts-scandal.html.

Crimmins, Carmel & Karen Freifeld. "'Best Banker in America" Blamed for Wells Fargo Scandal." *Reuters,* April 10, 2017. https://www.reuters.com/article/us-wells-fargo-accounts/best-banker-in-america-blamed-for-wells-fargo-sales-scandal-idUSKBN17C18P.

Crowley, Katherine and Katie Elster. *Working with You is Killing Me: Freeing Yourself from Emotional Traps at Work.* New York: Warner Business, 2006.

Cuordileone, Kyle A. *Manhood and American Political Culture in the Cold War.* New York: Routledge, 2005.

———. "Politics in an Age of Anxiety": Cold War Political Culture and the Crisis in American Masculinity, 1949–1960." *The Journal of American History* 87, no. 2 (2000): 515–545.

Currarino, Roseanne. "Introduction: The Labor Question in the Nineteenth Century," in *The Labor Question in America: Economic Democracy in the Gilded Age,* edited by Roseanne Currarino, pp. 1–10. Chicago: University of Illinois Press, 2011.

Curry, T., and Shibut, L. The Cost of the Savings and Loan Crisis. *FDIC Banking Review,* 13, (2000): 26.

Daily Chart. "Latin American Homicide Epidemic." *The Economist,* April 11, 2018. https://www.economist.com/graphic-detail/2018/04/11/latin-americas-homicide-epidemic

Dalleck, Robert. *Flawed Giant: Lyndon Johnson and His Times, 1961–1973.* New York: Oxford University Press, 1998.

Davenport, David and Gordon Lloyd. *Rugged Individualism: Dead or Alive?* Stanford: Hoover Institution, 2016.

Davis, James. *Medieval Market Morality: Life, Law and Ethics in the English Marketplace, 1200–1500.* New York: Cambridge University Press, 2012.

Day, Kathleen. *S & L Hell: The People and the Politics Behind the $1 Trillion Saving and Loan Scandal.* New York: W. W. Norton, 1993.

Dayen, David. "Why the Goldman Sachs Settlement is a $5 Billion Sham." *The New Republic,* April 13, 2016. https://newrepublic.com/article/132628/goldman-sachs-settlement-5-billion-sham.

Deal, Jennifer J., David G. Altman, and Steven G. Rogelberg. "Millennials at Work: What We Know and What We Need to Do (If Anything)." *Journal of Business and Psychology* 25, (2010): 191.

DeBenedetti, Charles. *An American Ordeal: The Antiwar Movement of the Vietnam Era.* Syracuse: Syracuse University Press, 1990.

De Costa, Pedro Nicolaci. "More and More Older Americans are Slipping into Poverty. *Business Insider,* September 15, 2017. https://www.businessinsider.com/americans-65-and-up-slipping-into-poverty-2017-9.

Bibliography

Deloitte. The 2016 Deloitte Millennial Survey." Deloitte. UK, 2016. https://www2.deloitte.com/content/dam/Deloitte/global/Documents/About-Deloitte/gx-millenial-survey-2016-exec-summary.pdf.

De Mello, Anthony. *Awareness*. New York: Image Books, 1990.

———. *The Way to Love: The Last Meditations of Anthony De Mello*. New York: Image, 1995.

Department of Numbers. Topeka Kansas Residential Rent and Rental Statistics, 2015. https://www.deptofnumbers.com/rent/kansas/topeka/.

DePillis, Lydia, "The U.S. Economy Needs Seniors to Work Longer. Here's How to Make That Happen." CNN, June 28, 2018. https://www.businessinsider.com/americans-65-and-up-slipping-into-poverty-2017-9.

Derber, Charles. *Corporation Nation: How Corporations are Taking Over Our Lives and What We Can Do about It*. New York: St. Martin's, 1998.

Desilver, Drew. "U.S. Trails Most Developed Countries in Voter Turnout." Pew Research Center. May 21, 2018. http://www.pewresearch.org/fact-tank/2018/05/21/u-s-voter-turnout-trails-most-developed-countries/.

Desplaces, David E., David E. Melchar, Laura L. Beauvais, and Susan M. Bosco. "The Impact of Business Education on Moral Judgment Competence: An Empirical Study." *Journal of Business Ethics* 74, (2007): 73.

De St. Jorre, John. *The Nigerian Civil War*. London: Hodder and Stoughton, 1972.

De Tocqueville, Alexis. *Democracy in America: In Two Volumes*, edited by Eduardo Nolla and translated by James T. Schleifer. Indianapolis, IN: Liberty Fund, 2012.

Dienstag, Joshua Foa. "Serving God and Mammon: The Lockean Sympathy in Early American Political Thought. *Political Science Review*, 90, (1996): 497.

Dolan, Jay P. *The American Catholic Experience: A History from Colonial Times to the Present*. New York: Double Day, 1985.

Dorn, Jacob H. "Comrade Father Thomas McGrady: A Priest's Quest for Equality through Socialism." *Fides et Historia* 46, (2014): 1.

Drutman, Lee. *The Business of America is Lobbying: How Corporations Became Politicized and Politics Became More Corporate*. New York: Oxford University Press, 2015.

Dubisch, Jill and Raymond Michalowski. "Blessed are the Rich: The New Gospel of Wealth in contemporary evangelism." In *The God Pumpers: Religion in the Electronic Age*, edited by Marshal William Fishwick and Ray B. Brown, pp. 33–45. Bowling Green, OH: Bowling Green University Popular Press, 1987.

Dudani, Salil. "Stanford Panel Debates: Does Teaching Ethics Do Any Good? Stanford News, May 13, 2014. https://news.stanford.edu/news/2014/may/ethics-in-society-051314.html.

Ebert, John David. *The New Media Invasion: Digital Technologies and the World They Unmake*. Jefferson: McFarland & Company, 2011.

Egel, Benjy, Anita Chabria, and Ellen Garrison. "Hands Removed, Findings Changed: Pathologists say San Joaquin Sheriff 'Does Whatever He Feels Like Doing.'" *Sacramento Bee*, December 5, 2017. http://www.sacbee.com/news/local/article188145129.html.

Egan, Matt. "Wells Fargo Uncovers Up to 1.4 Million More Fake Accounts. CNN Money, August 31, 2017. https://money.cnn.com/2017/08/31/investing/wells-fargo-fake-accounts/index.html.

———. "Workers Tell Wells Fargo Horror Stories." CNN, Money, September 9, 2016. https://money.cnn.com/2016/09/09/investing/wells-fargo-phony-accounts-culture/index.html?iid=EL.

BIBLIOGRAPHY

Emerson, Ralph Waldo. *On self-Reliance and Other Essays*. New York: Dover, 1993.

Equal Employment Opportunity Commission. *EEOC Compliance Manual*. 2008. https://www.eeoc.gov/policy/docs/religion.pdf.

Evens, Christopher H. *The Social Gospel in American Religion: A History*. New York: New York University Press, 2017.

Evans, Fred J., and Leah E. Marcal. "Educating for Ethics: Business Deans' Perspectives." *Business and Society Review* 110, (2005): 233.

Fainaru-Wada, Mark and Steve Fainaru. *League of Denial*. New York: Crown, 2013.

Feldman, Egal. "The Social Gospel and the Jews." *American Jewish Historical Quarterly* 58, (1969): 308.

Ferguson, Robert A. *The American Enlightenment, 1750–1820*. Cambridge, MA: Harvard University Press, 1904.

Fischer, Derek. "Dodd-Frank's Failure to Address CFTC Oversight of Self-Regulatory Organization Rulemaking." *Columbia Law Review*, 115, no 1 (2015) 69–126.

Fisher, Stacy B. Gordon. *Strategic Influence in Legislative Lobbying: Context, Targets, and Tactics*. New York: Palgrave Macmillan, 2015.

FitzGerald, Frances. *The Evangelicals: The Struggle to Shape America*. New York: Simon & Schuster, 2017.

Fleck, Carole. "Forced Out, Older Workers are Fighting Back." AARP, March, 2014. https://www.aarp.org/work/on-the-job/info-2014/workplace-age-discrimination-infographic.html.

Folsom, Burton W. *The Myth of the Robber Barons: A New Look at the Rise of Big Business in America*, 6th ed. Herdon: Young America's Foundation, 1991.

Forbes. "America's Worst Corporate Air Polluters." *Forbes*, 2011. https://www.forbes.com/pictures/mef45kmfg/no-10-xcel-energy-inc/#7934c6a24c89.

Freud, Sigmund. *Civilization and its Discontents*, translated by James Strachey, originally published in 1939. New York: W. W. Norton, 2010.

———. *The Ego and the Id*, translated by Joan Riviere and James Strachey, originally published 1927 by Hogarth Press, London). New York: W. W. Norton, 1962.

Frey, Donald E. "Individualist Economic Values and Self-Interest: The Problem in the Puritan Ethic." *Journal of Business Ethics* 17, (1998): 1573.

Friedman Milton, "The Social Responsibility of Business is to Increase it Profits", *New York Times Magazine*, 13 September 1970, reprinted in Donaldson T and Werhane P, *Ethical Issues in Business: A Philosophical Approach*, 2nd Edition, Englewood Cliffs,: Prentice Hall, 1983.

Friel, John C. and Linda D. Friel. *Adult Children: The Secrets of Dysfunctional Families*. Deerfield Beach: Health Communications, 1988.

Frontline Interviews. "Dr. Bennet Omalu," *League of Denial: The NFL's Concussion Crisis*. PBS. 2016. https://www.pbs.org/wgbh/pages/frontline/sports/league-of-denial/the-frontline-interview-dr-bennet-omalu/.

Fulbright, J. William. *The Arrogance of Power*. New York: Random House. 1966.

Gabor, Thomas. "The Suppression of Crime Statistics on Race and Ethnicity: The Price of Political Correctness." *Canadian J. Criminology* 36 (1994): 153.

Gardner, John W. *On Leadership*. New York: Free Press, 1990.

Gerwarth, Robert. *The Vanquished: Why the First World War Failed to End*. New York: Farrar, Straus and Giroux, 2017.

Bibliography

Ghilarducci, Teresa. "The Real Reason People don't Save Enough for Retirement." *The Atlantic*, October 1, 2015. https://www.theatlantic.com/business/archive/2015/10/retirement-savings-dont-blame-people/408283/.

Gibson, Lindsey. *Adult Children of Immature Parents: How to Heal from Distant, Rejecting, or Self-Involved Parents*. Oakland: New Harbinger, 2015.

Gill, Stephen. "Leaders and Led in an Era of Global Crisis." In *Global Crisis and the Crisis of Global Leadership*, edited by Stephen Gill, pp. 23–37. New York: Cambridge University Press, 2012.

Giogi, Liana and Catherin Marsh. "The Protestant Work Ethic as a Cultural Phenomenon." *European Journal of Social Psychology*, 20, (1990): 499.

Godwin, Kenneth, Scott H. Ainsworth, and Eric Godwin. *Lobbyists and Policymakers: The Public Pursuit of Private Interests*. Thousand Oaks: Sage, 2013.

Goldin, Claudia, and Lawrence F. Katz. "The Shaping of Higher Education: The Formative Years in the United States, 1890 to 1940." *Journal of Economic Perspectives* 13, (1999): 37.

Goleman, Daniel. *Emotional Intelligence. Why it Matters More than I.Q.* New York: Bantam, 1995.

Goodman, Amy. *Democracy Now! Twenty Years Covering the Movements Changing America*. New York: Simon & Schuster, 2016.

Gorzycki, Meg. *Caesar Ate My Jesus: A Baby Boomer's Reflection on Spirituality in the American Empire*. Eugene: Resource Books, 2017.

Graf, Nikki. "Sexual Harassment at Work in the Era of #Me Too." Pew Research, April 4, 2018. http://www.pewsocialtrends.org/2018/04/04/sexual-harassment-at-work-in-the-era-of-metoo/.

Grant, Colin. "Whistle Blowers: Saints of Secular Culture." *Journal of Business Ethics* 39, (2002): 391.

Greene, Robert. *The 48 Laws of Power*. New York: Penguin,. 2000.

Grossman, Miriam. *Unprotected: A Campus Psychiatrist Reveals How Political Correctness in Her Profession Endangers Every Student*. New York: Sentinel, 2006.

Guinn, Jeff. *The Road to Jonestown: Jim Jones and the People's Temple*. New York: Simon & Schuster, 2017.

Gutierrez, Gustavo. *A Theology of Liberation*, translated by Sister Cardidad Inda and John Eagleson. Maryknoll: Orbis, 1988.

Gutman, Herbert G. "Protestantism and the American Labor Movement: The Christian Spirit in the Gilded Age." *The American Historical Review* 72, (1966): 74.

Hackard, Michael. *The Wolf at the Door: Undue Influence and Elder Financial Abuse*. Hackard: Global Media, 2017.

Hacker, Lewis and Claudia Dreifus. *Higher Education? How Colleges are Wasting Our Money, Failing Our Kids, and What We Can do about It*. New York: St, Martin's, 2010.

Harrington, Matthew. Survey: People's Trust has Declined in Business, Media, Government, and NGOs. *Harvard Business Review*, January 16, 2017. https://hbr.org/2017/01/survey-peoples-trust-has-declined-in-business-media-government-and-ngos.

Haveman, Robert, and Timothy Smeeding. "The Role of Higher Education in Social Mobility." *The Future of Children* 16, (2006): 125.

Hawkins, Mike. *Social Darwinism in European and American Thought, 1860–1945*. New York: Cambridge University Press, 1997.

Bibliography

Hedges, Kristi. "8 Common Causes for Workplace Demotivation." *Forbes*, January 20, 2014. https://www.forbes.com/sites/work-in-progress/2014/01/20/8-common-causes-of-workplace-demotivation/2/#43065f6158eb.

Hellinger, Daniel C. *Comparative Politics of Latin America: Democracy at Last?* 2nd Ed. New York: Routledge, 2015.

Herszenhorn, David M. "Congress Approves $700 Billion Wall Street Bailout. *New York Times*, October, 3, 2008. https://www.nytimes.com/2008/10/03/business/world business/03iht-bailout.4.16679355.html.

Hess, Abigale. "The 6 Most Popular College Majors." CNBC, December 5, 2017. https://www.cnbc.com/2017/12/15/the-6-most-popular-college-majors.html.

Higham, John. "Social Discrimination against Jews in America, 1830–1930." *Publications of the American Jewish Historical Society* 47, (1957): 1.

Hill, Peter C., Kenneth II Pargament, Ralph W. Hood, Jr, Michael E. McCullough, James P. Sawyers, David B. Larson, and Brian J. Zinnbauer. "Conceptualizing Religion and Spirituality: Points of Commonality, Points of Departure." *Journal for the Theory of Social Behaviour* 30, (2000): 51

Hirsh, Michael. *Capital Offense: How Washington's Wise Men Turned America's Future Over to Wall Street*. Hoboken: John Wiley & Sons, 2010.

Hodge, James, and Cooper, Linda. *Disturbing the Peace: The Story of Father Roy Bourgeois and the Movement to Close the School of the Americas*. Maryknoll: Orbis, 2004.

Hoffman, Kevin. "Feds Close Bank Where Jesus Closed Deals. *City Pages*, October 24, 2009. http://www.citypages.com/news/feds-close-bank-where-jesus-closed-deals-6531417.

Hofstadter, Richard. *Social Darwinism in American Thought*. Boston: Beacon, 1992.

Holden, Robert H. and Eric Zolov. *Latin America and the United States: A Documentary History*. New York: Oxford University Press, 2011.

Howe, Neil and William Strauss. *Millennials Rising: The Next Generation*. New York: Vintage, 2000.

Hulliung, Mark. *The Social Contract in America from the Revolution to the Present Age*. Lawrence: University of Kansas Press, 2007.

Human Rights Office of the Archdiocese of Guatemala. *Guatemala, Never Again*, translated by Gretta Tovar Siebentritt. Maryknoll, NY: Orbis, 1999.

Irwin, Neil. "This is a Complete List of Wall Street CEOs Prosecuted for Their Role in the Financial Crisis. *Washington Post*, September 12, 2013. https://www.washingtonpost.com/news/wonk/wp/2013/09/12/this-is-a-complete-list-of-wall-street-ceos-prosecuted-for-their-role-in-the-financial-crisis/?utm_term=.bfbffd072a3d.

Isaacson, Walter. *Kissinger: A Biography*. New York: Simon & Schuster, 1992.

Jackson, John L. Jr.. *Racial Paranoia: The Unintended Consequences of Political Correctness*. New York: Civitas, 2008.

Jameton, Andrew. *Nursing Practice: The Ethical Issue*. Englewood Cliffs: Prentice Hall, 1984.

Janoski, Thomas, David Luke, and Christopher Oliver. *The Causes of Structural Unemployment: Four Factors That Keep People from Jobs They Deserve*. Cambridge, UK: Polity, 2014.

Jeffries, Vincent. "Foundational Ideas for an Integral Social Science Private in the Thought of St. Thomas Aquinas." *Catholic Social Science Review* 6, (2001): 25.

John Paul II. *Laborem Exercens (On Work)*. New York: Pauline, 1981.

Bibliography

Johnson, Meagan and Larry Johnson. *Generations, Inc.: From Boomers to Linksters Managing the Friction between Generations at Work*. New York: American Management Association, 2010.
Jones Cheryl. B. "Revisiting Nurse Turnover Costs: Adjusting for Inflation." *Journal of Nursing Administration* 38, (2008): 11.
Josephson, Matthew. *The Robber Barons: The Great American Capitalists, 1861–1901*, (originally published 1934). Orlando: Harcourt, 1962.
Kamel, Jonathan D. Dying to Work: Death and injury in the American workplace. Ithaca, NY: Cornell University Press. 2017.
Kellerman, Barbara. *The End of Leadership*. New York: HarperCollins, 2012.
Kimball, Bruce. *Orators and Philosophers: A History of the Idea of Liberal Education*. New York: Columbia University Teacher's College, 1986.
King, Martin Luther Jr. "Speech at Western Michigan University," December 18, 1963. http://wmich.edu/sites/default/files/attachments/MLK.pdf.
King, Robert H. *Thomas Merton and Thich Nhat Hanh: Engaged Spirituality in an Age of Globalization*. New York: Continuum Books, 2001.
Kohn, Howard. "Malignant Giant: The Nuclear Industry's Terrible Power and how it Silenced Karen Silkwood. *Rolling Stone*, March 27, 1975. https://www.rollingstone.com/culture/features/malignant-giant-the-nuclear-industrys-terrible-power-and-how-it-silenced-karen-silkwood-19750327.
Konczal, M. "Robert Reich on Why Capitalism Needs Saving." Rolling Stone, Oct. 7, 2015. https://wwweollingstone.com/politics/politics_news/Robert-reich-on-why-capitalism-needs-saving-59443/.
Krause, Paul. *The Battle for Homestead, 1880–1892: Politics, Culture, and Steel*. Pittsburgh: University of Pittsburgh Press, 1992.
Kurtz, Annalyn. "Here's the Biggest Reason Tech Workers Quit Their Jobs." *Fortune*, April 28, 2017. http://fortune.com/2017/04/28/tech-workers-quit-jobs/.
Landrum, Sarah. "Millennials aren't Afraid to Change Jobs, and Here's Why." *Forbes*, November, 10, 2017. https://www.forbes.com/sites/sarahlandrum/2017/11/10/millennials-arent-afraid-to-change-jobs-and-heres-why/#2fa87ace19a5.
Lapidus, André. "Norm, Virtue and Information: the Just Price and Individual Behaviour in Thomas Aquinas' Summa Theologiae." *The European Journal of the History of Economic Thought* 1, (1994): 435.
Laskas, Jeanne Marie. *Concussion*. New York: Random House, 2015.
Lawson, Raef A. "Is Classroom Cheating Related to Business Students' Propensity to Cheat in the 'Real World'?" *Journal of Business Ethics* 49, (2004): 189.
Lee, Chana Kai. *For Freedom's Sake: The life of Fanny Lou Hamer*. Urbana-Champagne: University of Illinois, 2000.
Lehmann, Chris. *The Money Cult: Capitalism, Christianity, and the Unmaking of the American Dream*. Brooklyn: Melville House Publishing, 2016.
Leo XIII. *Rerum Novarum*, 1891. Papal Encyclicals Online. http://www.papalencyclicals.net/leo13/l13rerum.htm.
Lewy, Guenter. *America in Vietnam*. New York: Oxford University Press, 1978.
Li Yi., and Cheryl B. Jones. "A Literature Review of Nursing Turnover Costs." *Journal of Nursing Management* 21, (2013): 405.
Light, Paul C. *Baby Boomers*. Markham, Ontario: Penguin, 1988.
Lim, Elvin T. *The Anti-Intellectual Presidency: The Decline of Presidential Rhetoric from George Washington to George Bush*. New York: Oxford University Press, 2008.

BIBLIOGRAPHY

Link, Taylor. "The Wall Street White House: Trump Hires Fifth Goldman Sachs Staffer to the Administration." *Salon*, March 16, 2017. https://www.salon.com/2017/03/16/the-wall-street-white-house-trump-hires-fifth-goldman-sachs-staffer-to-the-administration/.

Lippmann, Walter. *Public Opinion*. (Originally published 1922), 2004. The Project Gutenberg EBook. http://pages.uoregon.edu/koopman/courses_readings/dewey/lippmann_etext_public-opinion.pdf.

———. *The Phantom Public*. (Originally published 1927 by Macmillan Company). New Brunswick: Transaction, 1993.

Lipset, Seymour Martin. "Work Ethic Then and Now." *Journal of Labor Research*, 13, (1992): 45.

Livingstone, Grace. *America's Backyard: The United States and Latin America from the Monroe Doctrine to the War on Terror*. United Kingdom: Zed, 2009.

Lloyd, Henry Demarest. *Wealth Against Commonwealth*. Elibron Classics. (Originally published 1894 by Harper & Row). New York: Adament Media Corporation, 2005.

Locke, Jill. *Democracy and the Death of Shame: Political Equality and Social Disturbance*. New York: Oxford University Press, 2016.

Lybeck, Johan A. *A Global History of the Financial Crash of 2007–2010*. Cambridge, UK: Cambridge University Press, 2011.

Lynch, Joseph H. and Phillip C. Adamo. *The Medieval Church: A Brief History*, 2nd Ed. New York: Routledge, 2014.

Macrotrends. "Johnson & Johnson-48 Year Stock Price History/JNJ. https://www.macrotrends.net/stocks/charts/JNJ/johnson-johnson/stock-price-history.

Mann, Annamarie and Jim Harter. "The Worldwide Employee Engagement Crisis." *Gallup Business Journal*, January 7, 2016. http://news.gallup.com/businessjournal/188033/worldwide-employee-engagement-crisis.aspx.

Marcic, Dorothy. *Managing with the Wisdom of Love*. San Francisco: Jossey-Bass, 1997.

Mark, Barbara, Jeanne Salyer, and Thomas T. Wan. "Impact on Organizational and Patient outcomes: Professional Nursing Practice." *Journal of Nursing Administration*, 33, (2003): 224.

Mark, Michelle. "Video Shows Brett Kavanaugh Turning Away as a Parkland Shooting's Victim's Father Tries to Shake His Hand." Insider, September 4, 2018. https://www.thisisinsider.com/kavanaugh-rebuffs-parkland-shooting-victims-father-for-handshake-2018-9.

Markey, Eileen. *A Radical Faith: The Assassination of Sister Maura*. New York: Nation, 2016.

Marks, Gene. "Study: 71 Percent of Employees are looking for new jobs." *The Washington Post*, October 19, 2017. Retrieved from: https://www.washingtonpost.com/news/on-small-business/wp/2017/10/19/study-71-percent-of-employees-are-looking-for-new-jobs/?utm_term=.23afddd14df5.

Markus, R. A. *Saeculum: History and Society in the Theology of St. Augustine*. New York: Cambridge University Press, 1970.

Marshall, Joanne M. "Nothing New under the Sun: A Historical Overview of Religion in US Public Schools." *Equity & Excellence in Education* 39, (2006): 181.

Marx, Karl and Friedrich Engels. *The Communist Manifesto: A Modern Edition*. (Originally published in 1848). Brooklyn: Verso Books, 2012.

Masse, Mark H. *Inspired to Service: Today's Faith Activists*. Bloomington: University of Indiana Press, 2004.

Bibliography

Masters, Robert Augustus. *Spiritual Bypassing: When Spirituality Disconnects Us from What Really Matters.* Berkeley: North Atlantic Books, 2010.

Matusow, Alan J. *Nixon's Economy: Booms, Busts, Dollars, and Votes.* Lawrence: University of Kansas Press, 1998.

McCabe, Donald L., Kenneth D. Butterfield, and Linda Klebe Trevino. "Academic Dishonesty in Graduate Business Programs: Prevalence, Causes, and Proposed Action." *Academy of Management Learning & Education* 5, (2006): 294.

McDonald, Gael M., and Gabriel D. Donleavy. "Objections to the Teaching of Business Ethics." *Journal of Business Ethics* 14, (1995): 839.

McDonald, M., M. Parizeau, and D. Pulman. *Toward a Canadian Research Strategy for Applied Ethics. A Report by the Canadian Federation for the Humanities.* Ottawa: The Social Sciences and Humanities Research Council, 1989.

McKinney, Cara E. "Twelve Years a Terror: U.S. Impact on the Twelve Year War in El Salvador. *International ResearchScape Journal, An Undergraduate Student Journal*, 2 https://scholarworks.bgsu.edu/cgi/viewcontent.cgi?article=1020&context=irj.

McMahon, Jeff. "And the Biggest Power Polluter is: American Electric Power Company. *Forbes*, May 28, 2014. https://www.forbes.com/sites/jeffmcmahon/2014/05/28/and-the-biggest-power-polluter-is-aep/#2aed89b434cd.

McMasters, H. R. *Dereliction of Duty: Johnson, McNamara, the Joint Chiefs of Staff, and the Lies That Led to Vietnam.* New York: HarperCollins, 1997.

Melé, Domènec. "Integrating ethics into management." *Journal of Business Ethics* 78, (2008): 291.

Melin, Anders and Shahien Nasiripour. "Wells Fargo boosts CEO Tim Sloan's Pay 36% to $17.4 million. *Bloomberg*, March 14, 2018. https://www.bloomberg.com/news/articles/2018-03-14/wells-fargo-boosts-ceo-sloan-s-pay-36-to-17-4-million-for-2017.

Miller, David, W. *God at Work: The History and the Promise of the Faith at Work Movement.* New York: Oxford University Press, 2007.

Mitroff, Ian I., and Elizabeth A. Denton. "A Study of Spirituality in the Workplace." *MIT Sloan Management Review* 40, (1999): 83.

Moore, R. Laurence. "Religion, Secularization, and the Shaping of the Culture Industry in Antebellum America." *American Quarterly* 41, (1989): 216.

Moore, Thomas. "The Fight to Save Tylenol." *Fortune*, October 7, 2012. http://fortune.com/2012/10/07/the-fight-to-save-tylenol-fortune-1982/.

Morse, C. M. *The Church and the Working-Man.* Catasauqua: Anti-Usury Society, 1889.

National Center for Educational Statistics. "Fast Facts." U.S. Department of Education. 2018. https://nces.ed.gov/fastfacts/display.asp?id=372.

Neff, Thomas J. and James M. Citron. *Lessons from the Top: The Search for America's Best Business Leaders.* New York: Doubleday, 2001.

Newfield, Christopher and Robert Strickland (Eds.). *After Political Correctness: The Humanities and Society in the 1990s.* New York: Routledge, 2018.

Newhauser, Richard. *The Early History of Greed: The Sin of Avarice in Early Medieval Thought and Literature.* New York: Cambridge University Press, 2004.

Nixon, Richard M. *No More Vietnams.* New York: Arbor House, 1985.

Nussbaum, Martha. *Not for Profit: Why Democracy Needs the Humanities.* Princeton: Princeton University Press, 2010.

O'Hara, S. Paul. *Inventing the Pinkertons or Spies, Sleuths Mercenaries and Thugs.* Baltimore: Johns Hopkins University Press, 2016.

Bibliography

Okeowo, Alisha. "Hate on the Rise after Trump's Election. *The New Yorker*, November 17, 2016. https://www.newyorker.com/news/news-desk/hate-on-the-rise-after-trumps-election.

Oliver, Myrna. "Firm to Settle Silkwood Case: Kerr-McGee will Pay $1.38 Million to Estate. *Los Angeles Times*, August 23, 1986. http://articles.latimes.com/1986-08-23/news/mn-15774_1_karen-silkwood.

Omalu, Bennet. *Truth Doesn't Have a Side: My Alarming Discovery about the Danger of Contact Sports*. Grand Rapids: Zondervan, 2017.

———. Steven T. DeKosky, Ryan L. Minster, M. Ilyas Kamboh, Ronald L. Hamilton, and Cyril H. Wecht. "Chronic Traumatic Encephalopathy in a National Football League Player." *Neurosurgery* 57, (2005): 128.

Oman, Charles. *The Great Revolt of 1381*. San Diego: Didactic, 2015.

Orey, Michael. *Assuming the Risk: The Mavericks, the Lawyers, and the Whistle-Blowers Who Beat Big Tobacco*. Boston: Little, Brown, and Company, 1999.

Ornstein, Allen C. *Class Counts: Education, Inequality, and the Shrinking Middle Class*. Lanham: Rowman & Littlefield, 2007.

Parry, J. H. *The Age of Reconnaissance: Discovery, Exploration and Settlement, 1450–1650*. Berkeley: University of California Press, 1982.

Pasquale, Theresa. *Sacred Wounds: A Path to Healing from Spiritual Trauma*. St. Louis: Chalice, 2015.

Patterson, Robert W. "What's Good for America…" *National Review*, July 1, 2013. https://www.nationalreview.com/2013/07/whats-good-america-robert-w-patterson/.

Pearlstein, Steven. Meet the Parents Who Won't Let Their Children Study Literature. *Washington Post*, September 2, 2016. https://www.washingtonpost.com/posteverything/wp/2016/09/02/meet-the-parents-who-wont-let-their-children-study-literature/?utm_term=.e3c6863e24c2.

Peltz, James F. "Wells Fargo Agrees to Pay $480 Million to Settle Securities-Fraud Lawsuit Over Fake Accounts." *Los Angeles Times*, May 4, 2018. http://www.latimes.com/business/la-fi-wells-fargo-settlement-20180504-story.html.

Pew Research Center. "Generational Replacement Helping Drive Growth of Unaffiliated, Decline of Mainline Protestantism and Catholicism." May 7, 2015. http://www.pewforum.org/2015/05/12/americas-changing-religious-landscape/pr_15-05-12_rls-01/.

———. "Younger Millennials." February 17, 2010. Religious Composition of Younger Millennials." 2018. http://www.pewforum.org/religious-landscape-study/generational-cohort/younger-millennial/.

Pfau, Bruce M. "What Do Millennials Really Want at Work? The Same Things as the Rest of Us Do." *Harvard Business Review*, April 7, 2016. https://hbr.org/2016/04/what-do-millennials-really-want-at-work.

Pfeffer, Jeffrey, *Dying for a Paycheck*. New York: HarperCollins, 2018.

Physicians Foundation. *2014 Survey of America's Physicians*, September 16, 2014. http://www.physiciansfoundation.org/uploads/default/2014_Physicians_Foundation_Biennial_Physician_Survey_Report.pdf.

Picchi, Aimee. "The New Low Wage Reality for Older Americans." CBS News, November 8, 2016. https://www.cbsnews.com/news/the-new-low-wage-reality-for-older-americans/.

Piketty, Thomas. "About Capital in the Twenty-First Century." *American Economic Review* 105, (2015): 48.

Bibliography

Pogash, Carol. *As Real as it Gets: The Life of a Hospital at the Center of the AIDS Epidemic.* Birch Lane eBooks, 1992.

Popken, Ben, "Wells Fargo Hit with Another Lawsuit—For Closing Fraud Victims' Accounts to Avoid Costs." NBC News. March 1, 2018. https://www.nbcnews.com/business/consumer/wells-fargo-accused-closing-fraud-victims-accounts-instead-investigating-n852346.

Priess, David. *The President's Book of Secrets. The Untold Story of Intelligence Briefings of America's Presidents from Kennedy to Obama.* New York: Public Affairs, 2016.

Quade, Matthew, Rebecca Greenbaum, and Oleg V. Petrenko. "'I Don't Want to be Near You Unless…' The Interactive Effect of Unethical Behavior onto Performance onto Relationship Conflict and Workplace Ostracism." *Personal Psychology*, 70, (2017): 675.

Quade, Quentin, L. *The Pope and Revolution: John Paul II Confronts Liberation Theology.* Washington, D.C.: Ethics and Public Policy Center, 1982.

Ransby, Barbara. *Ella Baker and the Black Freedom Movement: A Radical Democratic Vision.* Chapel Hill: University of North Carolina Press, 2003.

Rapoza, Kenneth. "Despite Crisis, Most Americans Believe They Will Be Rich One Day." Forbes, July 16, 2012. https://www.forbes.com/sites/kenrapoza/2012/07/16/the-impossible-dream-being-rich/#582327364491.

Rashke, Richard L. *The Killing of Karen Silkwood: The Story Behind the Kerr-McGee Plutonium Case.* New York: Houghton Mifflin, 1981.

Rauschenbusch, Walter. *A Theology for the Social Gospel* (first published in 1917 by Macmillan). Louisville: Westminster John Knox, 1945.

———. *The Social Principles of Jesus.* New York: Grosset & Dunlap, 1916.

Redell, Bob and Kiki Intarasuan. "Verizon Admits it Throttled Firefighters' Internet Connection during Mendocino Complex Fire." NBC News, August 22, 2018. https://www.nbcbayarea.com/news/local/Verizon-Reportedly-Throttled-Santa-Clara-Co-Firefighters-Internet-Connection-491435551.html.

Reed, Stephen B. "One Hundred Years of Price Change: The consumer Price Index and the American Inflation Experience." Bureau of Labor Statistics, April 2014. https://www.bls.gov/opub/mlr/2014/article/one-hundred-years-of-price-change-the-consumer-price-index-and-the-american-inflation-experience.htm.

Rees, Lawrence. *Hitler's Charisma: Leading Millions into the Abyss.* New York: Vintage, 2012.

Reich, Robert. *Beyond Outrage: What has Gone Wrong with Our Economy and Our Democracy and How to Fix It.* New York: Vintage, 2012.

Reilly, Nora P. M. Joseph Sirgy, and C. Allen Gorman. *Work and Quality of Life: Ethical Practices in Organizations.* Netherlands: Springer, 2012.

Ripka, Chuck. *God out of the Box.* Lake Mary: Charisma House, 2009.

Ritter, Barbara A. "Can Business Ethics be Trained? A Study of the Ethical Decision-Making Process in Business Students." *Journal of Business Ethics* 68, (2006): 153.

Roberts, Tom. "Roy Bourgeois: They Finally got Him." *National Catholic Reporter.* Nov. 20, 2012. https://www.ncronline.org/blogs/ncr-today/roy-bourgeois-they-finally-got-him.

Roche, James M. "The Competitive System, to Work, to Preserve, and to Protect." *Vital Speeches of the Day* 445 (1971): 141.

Rodgers, D. T. *The work ethic in industrial America, 1850–1920.* Chicago: University of Chicago Press, 1978.

BIBLIOGRAPHY

Roig-Franzia, Manuel. "Brooksley Born, the Cassandra of the Derivatives Crisis." *The Washington Post*, May 26, 2009. http://www.washingtonpost.com/wp-dyn/content/article/2009/05/25/AR2009052502108.html?sid=ST2009052502127.

Rosenblatt, Kalhan. "Parkland Victims' Father and Kavanaugh: The Handshake That Wasn't." NBC News, September 4, 2018. https://www.nbcnews.com/politics/supreme-court/parkland-victim-s-father-kavanaugh-handshake-wasn-t-n906331.

Ruiz, Don Miguel. *The Four Agreements: A Practical Guide to Personal Freedom*. San Rafael: Amber-Allen, 1997.

Ryan, Liz. "The Truth about Minimum Wage." *Forbes*, October 8, 2014. https://www.forbes.com/sites/lizryan/2014/10/08/the-truth-about-the-minimum-wage/#2f932a7e3ba3.

Salovey, Peter, and John D. Mayer. "Emotional Intelligence." *Imagination, Cognition and Personality* 9, (1990): 185.

San Francisco AIDS Foundation. "The View from Here: Dr. Michael Gottlieb and Dr. Paul Volberding." 2018. http://www.sfaf.org/hiv-info/hot-topics/from-the-experts/the-view-from-here-michael-gottlieb-paul-volberding.html.

Satel, Sally. *P. C. M. D, How Political Correctness is Corrupting Medicine*. New York: Basic, 2002.

Scharnhorst, Gary. *The Lost Life of Horatio Alger*. Bloomington: Indiana University Press, 1985.

Schneider, Mark Robert. *Joe Moakley's Journey: From South Boston to El Salvador*. Lebanon: Northeastern University Press, 2013.

Schreiner, Samuel A. *Henry Clay Frick: The Gospel of Greed*. New York: St. Martin's, 1995.

Schultz, Ellen E. and Theo Francis. "Companies Profit from Workers' Deaths through 'Dead Peasants' Insurance. *Wall Street Journal*, April 2002. http://online.wsj.com/public/resources/documents/april_19.htm.

Scott, Luis R., Sr. *Healing the Broken Spirit*. Austin: Firm Foundation Publishing, 2014.

Seifert, Tricia A., Kathleen M. Goodman, Nathan Lindsay, James D. Jorgensen, Gregory C. Wolniak, Ernest T. Pascarella, and Charles Blaich. "The Effects of Liberal Arts Experiences on Liberal Arts Outcomes." *Research in Higher Education* 49, (2008): 107.

Semuels, Alana. "How Common is Child Labor in the U.S.?" *The Atlantic*, March 15, 2014. https://www.theatlantic.com/business/archive/2014/12/how-common-is-chid-labor-in-the-us/383687/.

Senthiligam, Meer. "The Pros and Cons of Working into Your 90s." CNN, May 4, 2017. https://www.cnn.com/2017/05/04/health/working-after-retirement-age-health-benefits/index.html.

Serres, Chris. "Regulators Close Otsego Bank that Espoused Workplace Prayer." *Minneapolis Star-Tribune*, October 24, 2009. http://www.startribune.com/regulators-close-otsego-bank-that-espoused-workplace-prayer/65874567/.

Sgroi, Daniel. *Happiness and Productivity: Understanding the Happy-Productive Worker*. SMF-Cage Global perspective, October 2015. https://warwick.ac.uk/fac/soc/economics/staff/dsgroi/impact/hp_briefing.pdf.

Shanaberger, Manuel S. J. "Edward McGlynn: A Missionary Priest and His Social Gospel." *US Catholic Historian* 13, (1995): 23.

Shawn, Meekhof, Mangliers Kim, and Mishra Jitendra. "Elderly Workers in the Workforce." *Advances in Management* 7, (2014): 1.

Sheehan, Colleen A. "Madison v. Hamilton: The Battle over Republicanism and the Role of Public Opinion." *American Political Science Review* 98, (2004): 405.

Bibliography

Shen, Lucinda. "Goldman Sachs Admits it Defrauded Investors during the Financial Crisis." *Fortune*, April 11,2016. http://fortune.com/2016/04/11/goldman-sachs-doj-settlement/.

Shurden, Susan, Juan Santandreu, and Mike Shurden. "How Student Perceptions of Ethics can Lead to Future Business Behavior." *Journal of Legal, Ethical and Regulatory Issues* 13, (2010): 117.

Skeel, David. *The New Financial Deal: Understanding the Dodd-Frank Act and its (Unintended) Consequences*. Hoboken: John Wiley & Sons, 2010.

Smith, Greg. *Why I Left Leaving Goldman Sachs: A Wall Street Story*. New York: Grand Central, 2012.

Smith, Patrick. "What Happens When Suburban Police Departments don't have Enough Money?" National Public Radio, January 22, 2018. https://www.npr.org/2018/01/22/579778555/what-happens-when-suburban-police-departments-dont-have-enough-money.

Sondhaus, Lawrence. *World War One the Global Revolution*. New York: Cambridge University Press, 2011.

Spurgin, Earl W. "The Problem with 'Dead Peasants' Insurance." *Business and Professional Ethics Journal*, 22, (2003): 19.

Standiford, Les. *Meet You in Hell: Andrew Carnegie, Henry Clay Frick, and the Bitter Partnership that Transformed America*. New York: Three Rivers, 2005.

Statistia. "Number of Bachelor Degree recipients in United States from 1869 to 1870 to 2027/2028 in Thousands." https://www.statista.com/statistics/238164/bachelors-degree-recipients-in-the-us/.

Steel, Ronald. *Walter Lippmann and the American Century*, (originally published in 1980 by Littlefield). New Brunswick: Transaction, 2008.

Steenland, Sally. "Working Full Time and Still Poor. Center for American Progress, February 20, 2013. https://www.americanprogress.org/issues/religion/news/2013/02/20/53929/working-full-time-and-still-poor/.

Steinhorn, Leonard. *The Greater Generation: In Defense of the Baby Boomer Legacy*. New York: St. Martin's, 2006.

Stewart, James B. *Den of Thieves*. New York: Simon & Schuster, 1991.

Story, Louise and Eric Dash. "Bankers Reaped Lavish Bonuses during Bailouts." *New York Times*, July 30, 2009. https://www.nytimes.com/2009/07/31/business/31pay.html.

Sumner, William Graham. *What Social Classes Owe to Each Other*. New York: Harper & Brothers, 1883.

Talbot, David. *Season of the Witch*. New York: Free Press, 2012.

Tawney, R. H. "Forward" *The Protestant Ethic and the Spirit of Capitalism* by Max Weber, translated by Talcott Parsons, pp. 1–11. New York: Charles Scribner's Sons, 1952.

Teer, Faye P., and S. E. Kruck. "Students' Responses to Ethical Dilemmas in an Academic Setting and in the Work Place." *Information Systems Education Journal*, 10, (2012): 4.

The Mayo Clinic: Faith Hope and Science, directed by Erik Ewers, Christopher Loren Ewers, and Ken Burns. (2018; PBS Distribution), DVD.

"The S & L's Scandal's Cruel Truth." *New York Times*, November 21, 1989. https://www.nytimes.com/1989/11/21/opinion/the-s-l-scandal-s-cruel-truths.html.

The Warning. Directed by Michael Kirk. 2009. *Frontline* TV Series, PBS, 2010 DVD.

Thompson, Derek. "80 Percent of Americans don't Trust the Government. Here is Why." *Pew Research*, April 19, 2010. https://www.theatlantic.com/business/archive/2010/04/80-percent-of-americans-dont-trust-the-government-heres-why/39148/.

Bibliography

———. "Presidential Speeches were once College-Level Rhetoric—Now They're for Sixth-Graders." *The Atlantic*, October 14, 2014. https://www.theatlantic.com/politics/archive/2014/10/have-presidential-speeches-gotten-less-sophisticated-over-time/381410/.

Thompson, Mark. *Enough Said: What's Gone Wrong with the Language of Politics*. New York: St. Martin's, 2016.

Tise, Larry E. *Proslavery: A History of the Defense of Slavery in America, 1701–1840*. Athens: University of Georgia, 1987.

Tobin, Daniel R. and Margaret S. Pettingell. *AMA guide to Management Development*. New York: American Management Association, 2008.

Tollefsen, Christopher. "Freedom and Equality in Market Exchange: Some Natural Law Reflections." *Harvard Journal of Law & Public Policy. Policy* 33, (2010): 487.

Tompor, Susan. "Wells Fargo CEO Slams Criticism." *Detroit Free Press*, March 15, 2018. https://www.freep.com/story/money/personal-finance/susan-tompor/2018/03/15/wells-fargo-ceo-timothy-sloan/411813002/.

Toobin, Jeffry. *A Vast Conspiracy: The Real Story of the Sex Scandal That Nearly Brought Down a President*. New York: Touchstone, 2000.

Tracy, Brian. *Leadership*. New York: American Management Association, 2014.

Twenge, Jean M. "Millennials: The Greatest Generation or the Most Narcissistic?" *The Atlantic*, May 2, 2012. https://www.theatlantic.com/national/archive/2012/05/millennials-the-greatest-generation-or-the-most-narcissistic/256638/.

———. W. Keith Campbell, and Elise C. Freeman. "Generational Differences in Young Adults' Life Goals, Concern for Others, and Civic Orientation, 1966–2009." *Journal of Personality and Social Psychology* 102, (2012): 1045.

———. Stacy M. Campbell, Brian J. Hoffman, and Charles E. Lance. "Generational Differences in Work Values: Leisure and Extrinsic Values Increasing, Social and Intrinsic Values Decreasing." *Journal of management* 36, (2010): 1117

Tye, Larry. *The Father of Spin: Edward Bernays and the Birth of Public Relations*. New York: Henry Holt and Company, 1998.

United Nations. *The Global Financial Crisis: Report on the World Social Situation 2011*. United Nations Department of Economic and Social Affairs. New York: United Nations, 2011. Retrieved from: http://www.un.org/esa/socdev/rwss/docs/2011/rwss2011.pdf.

United States Catholic Bishops. *Economic Justice for All: Pastoral Letter on Catholic Social Teaching and the U.S. Economy*. Washington, D. C.: United States Conference of Catholic Bishops, 1986. http://www.usccb.org/upload/economic_justice_for_all.pdf.

United States Department of Health and Human Services. *Computation for the 2016 Poverty Guidelines. Office of the Assistant Secretary for Planning and Evaluation*, 2016. https://aspe.hhs.gov/computations-2016-poverty-guidelines.

United States Department of Labor. "Characteristics of Minimum Wage Workers, 2016." Bureau of labor Statistics, 2017. https://www.bls.gov/opub/reports/minimum-wage/2016/home.htm.

U. S. Equal Employment Opportunity Commission, "EEOC Releases Fiscal year 2016 Enforcement and Litigation Data" (January 18, 2018). Retrieved from: https://www.eeoc.gov/eeoc/newroom/release/1-18-17a.cfm.

U.S. Equal Employment Opportunity Commission. *Select Task Force Committee on the Study of Harassment in the Workplace*. Executive Report. June 2016. https://www.eeoc.gov/eeoc/task_force/harassment/report.cfm#_Toc453686298.

BIBLIOGRAPHY

Uzokwe, Alfred Obiora. *Surviving in Biafra: The story of the Nigerian Civil War.* New York: Writers' Advantage, 2003.

Vakis, Renos, Jamele Rigolini, and Leonardo Lucchetti. *Left Behind: Chronic Poverty in Latin America and the Caribbean.* World Bank. © World Bank. 2016. https://openknowledge.worldbank.org/handle/10986/21552.

Venn, Fiona. *The Oil Crisis.* New York: Routledge, 2002.

Verizon. "Mission Statement." August 22, 2018. https://www.verizon.com/about/our-company.

Viner, Jacob. *The Role of Providence in the Social Order: an Essay in Intellectual History.* Philadelphia: American Philosophical Society, 1972.

Voigtländer, Nico, and Hans-Joachim Voth. "The Three Horsemen of Riches: Plague, War, and Urbanization in Early Modern Europe." *Review of Economic Studies* 80, (2012): 774

Walsh, Lawrence E. *Firewall: The Iran-Contra Conspiracy and Cover-Up.* New York: W.W. Norton, 1997.

Wang, Long, Deepak Malhotra, and J. Keith Murnighan. "Economics Education and Greed." *Academy of Management Learning & Education* 10, (2011): 643.

Waples, Ethan P., Alison L. Antes, Stephen T. Murphy, Shane Connelly, and Michael D. Mumford. "A Meta-Analytic Investigation of Business Ethics Instruction." *Journal of Business Ethics* 87, (2009): 133.

Wareham, Jennifer, Brad W. Smith, and Eric G. Lambert. "Rates and patterns of law enforcement turnover: A research note." *Criminal Justice Policy Review* 26, (2015): 345.

Warshawsky Nora, Mary Kay Rayens, Karen Stefaniak, and Rana Rahman. "The Effect of Nurse Manager Turnover on Patient Fall and Pressure Ulcer Rates." *Journal of Nursing Management* 21, (2013): 725.

Watson, Bruce. *Freedom Summer: The Savage Season of 1964 that made Mississippi Burn and America a Democracy.* New York, Viking, 2010.

Wauzzinski, Robert A. *Between God and Gold: Protestant Evangelism and the Industrial Revolution, 1820–1914.* Cranberry: Associate University Press, 1993.

Weaver, Freerick S. *The United States and the Global economy: From Bretton Woods to the Current Crisis.* Lanham: Rowman & Littlefield, 2011

Weber, Max. *The Protestant Ethic and the Spirit of Capitalism*, translated by Talcott Parsons. New York: Charles Scribner's Sons, 1952.

Weiner, Tim. *One Man against the World: The Tragedy of Richard Nixon.* New York: Henry Holt, 2015.

Wells Fargo. "Our Vision, Values, and Goals." Well Fargo, 2018. https://www.wellsfargo.com/about/corporate/vision-and-values/.

Wenzel, Siegfried. *The Sin of Sloth: Acedia in Medieval Thought and Literature.* Chapel Hill: The University of North Carolina, 2012.

Westerhoff, John H. *McGuffey and His Readers: Piety, Morality, and Education in Nineteenth-Century America.* Nashville: Abington, 1978.

White, Gillian B. "One Year After Its Fake Accounts Scandal, Wells Fargo Isn't a Better Bank. *The Atlantic*, October 3, 2017. https://www.theatlantic.com/business/archive/2017/10/wells-fargo-fake-accounts-sloan/541875/.

Wilde, Melissa J. *Vatican II: A Sociological Analysis of Religious Change.* Princeton: Princeton University Press, 2007.

Wolf, Joseph and David J. Fritzsche. "Teaching Business Ethics with Management and Marketing Games. *Situation Gaming*, 29, (1988): 44.

Wood, Diana. *Medieval Economic Thought.* New York: Cambridge University Press, 2004.

Bibliography

Wood, Gordon S. *The Radicalism of the American Revolution*. New York: Vintage Books, 1991.

World Bank. *Poverty and Shared Prosperity: Taking on Inequality*. Washington, D. C.: World Bank, 2016. https://openknowledge.worldbank.org/bitstream/handle/10986/25078/9781464809583.pdf.

Wyllie, Irvin G. "Social Darwinism and the Businessman." *Proceedings of the American Philosophical Society*, 103, (1959): 629.

York, Helene. "Do Children Harvest Your Food?" *The Atlantic*, March 26, 2012. https://www.theatlantic.com/health/archive/2012/03/do-children-harvest-your-food/254853/.

Zaleski, Philip and Carol Zaleski. *Prayer: A History*. New York: Houghton Mifflin, 2005.

Zauzmer, Julie. "Christians are more than twice as Likely to Blame a Person's Poverty on Lack of Effort." *Washington Post*, August 3, 2017. https://www.washingtonpost.com/news/acts-of-faith/wp/2017/08/03/christians-are-more-than-twice-as-likely-to-blame-a-persons-poverty-on-lack-of-effort/?utm_term=.829b934653cb.

Zemke, Ron, Claire Raines, and Bob Filipczak. *Generations at Work: Managing the Clash of Boomers, Gen Xers, and Gen Yers in the Workplace*. New York, NY: AMACOM, 2013.

Ziegler, Phillip. *Black Death*. New York: Harper Perennial, 2009.

Zimmer, Louis B. *The Vietnam War Debate*. Lanham: Lexington Books, 2011.

Zombetti, Joseph. *Divisive Discourse: The Extreme Rhetoric of Contemporary Politics*. San Diego: Cognella Academic, 2017.

Zunz, Oliver. *Philanthropy in America: A history*. Princeton: Princeton University Press, 2012.

Zvesper, John. "The Problem of Liberal Rhetoric." *Review of Politics*, 44, (1982): 546.

www.ingramcontent.com/pod-product-compliance
Lightning Source LLC
Chambersburg PA
CBHW071445150426
43191CB00008B/1250